Volume 22 / Number 1 / March 2025

# LABOR
## STUDIES IN WORKING-CLASS HISTORY

### Workers and the "Golden Age" of Social Democracy?
Stefan Berger, Leon Fink, Jan de Graaf, and Patrick Dixon, Guest Editors

## BOOK REVIEWS

# Workers and the "Golden Age" of Social Democracy? An Introduction

Stefan Berger, Leon Fink, Jan de Graaf, and Patrick Dixon

N otions of a "golden age of social democracy" have dominated the historical perspective on the immediate postwar decades, most often envisaged as a period stretching from 1945 to the oil crisis of 1973. To take a prime example, Eric Hobsbawm's influential *Age of Extremes* endorsed this interpretation, linking it tightly to the history of the Cold War.[1] According to him, the taming of capitalism in the years after World War II had much to do with the presence of a global enemy: communism. Especially under the conditions of the postwar boom years (i.e., strong economic growth and full employment),[2] capitalism could show a friendly face and allow workers to have a share in the immense wealth produced by it. Others have emphasized how an emerging Keynesian consensus among economists further contributed to the emergence of a capitalist West that was not only politically democratic but also allowed for various forms of workplace democracy and the creation of welfare states.[3]

It was a social democratic age not so much because social democratic parties were necessarily in power when major welfare and democracy reforms were implemented.[4] Other political parties, including Christian democratic and conservative parties, shared, at least to a degree, the belief in a welfare capitalism benefiting not only the few, but the great many. Undoubtedly, these postwar reforms went furthest where they were pushed by powerful social democratic parties, as in Britain, Sweden

[1]. Hobsbawm, *Age of Extremes*.
[2]. Fourastié, *Les trente glorieuses*.
[3]. Eatwell and Milgate, *Fall and Rise of Keynesian Economics*; Berger, Pries, and Wannöffel, *Palgrave Handbook of Workers' Participation*; Hwang, "Development, Welfare Policy."
[4]. De Graaf, *Socialism Across the Iron Curtain*, has emphasized the weakness of social democratic parties in the post–World War II years.

*Labor Studies in Working-Class History*  Volume 22 • Issue 1
DOI 10.1215/15476715-11521350   © 2025 by Labor and Working-Class History Association

(where these tendencies had already started in the 1930s), or Norway.[5] There was, however, a social democratic consensus or moment within mainstream politics in virtually all Western democracies from the second half of the 1940s to the 1970s. Their representatives could argue that workers never had it so good and therefore had no need to listen to the siren songs of international communism, especially as it was not difficult to see that communism struggled to achieve similar levels of both mass consumption and democracy than the capitalist West.

The building blocks of a golden age of social democracy were thus always part of the ideological construction project of a liberal capitalist West. They were legitimating capitalism's economic, social, and political order vis-à-vis the alternative in the Cold War, communism. They were ignoring or sidelining remaining cases of social injustice and pockets of poverty as well as huge social inequalities that persisted, to varying degrees, in all democratic welfare capitalist societies. How rich you were and how educated you were, and where you ended up on the social ladder, continued to depend to a very large extent on how rich and educated your parents had been. In the 1960s and 1970s the educational systems in Western Europe and North America became more porous for a brief period, and the phenomenon of social advancement became a prominent one, but in all Western societies at the end of this period we can also observe a renewed closing of these windows of opportunities for children of the working classes to advance socially and step out of their class.[6]

With the end of the long economic boom and the emergence of repeated economic crises after 1973, capitalism's face became less humane, and its new ideology, neoliberalism, justified cuts to the welfare state and to all forms of public spending on behalf of those not privileged in society.[7] Social engineering, state intervention on behalf of the disadvantaged, a solidaristic society, planning, and public ownership all became dirty words in the neoliberal dictionary. Individual agency and merit, the family, free enterprise, technology, and the market were among the values espoused by the new ideology. After the fall of communism, when liberal capitalism stood at its most triumphant, an increasingly global capitalism under the hegemony of neoliberalism put profit before people, shareholder value before the interest of workers, and egotistical individual or group interest before notions of community and solidarity. This development of capitalism had serious repercussions also on the state of democracy in the liberal West, eroding the very foundations of democratic governance.[8]

Recurring crises of capitalism since then (e.g., the banking crisis of 2007–8) have put a question mark behind this triumph,[9] but it has not significantly destabilized the economic system that now rules the world. Capitalist crises have, however,

---

5. Moschonas, *In the Name of Social Democracy*. See also Sassoon, *One Hundred Years of Socialism*; and Eley, *Forging Democracy*.

6. Breen and Müller, *Education and Intergenerational Social Mobility*.

7. Harvey, *Brief History of Neoliberalism*.

8. Crouch, *Post-Democracy*; Streeck, *Buying Time*.

9. O'Halloran and Groll, *After the Crash*.

brought renewed calls for reining in or re-embedding capitalism. The memory of a golden age of social democracy, some on the left argued, had to be rediscovered. Anti-globalization movements have joined forces with trade union movements and political parties to bring about "movement parties" that are united in their desire to "re-embed" capitalism or transform it.[10] The popularity of left-wing populism in various parts of the world, from Bernie Sanders's campaigns in the US primary elections for the Democratic nomination for president in 2016 and 2020 to new left-wing parties in Europe (e.g., Syriza in Greece, Podemos in Spain, and Die Linke in Germany) underline this rediscovery of an alleged golden age of social democracy on the left of the political spectrum.[11] Here it has become a positive "realm of memory,"[12] used widely as a resource for attracting voters. However, it has also been adapted by right-wing populist parties and movements, even though their political orientation is often neoliberal. Yet, largely for propagandistic reasons, they attempted to appeal to the memory of a social democratic golden age, arguing that now it is no longer the left, but instead right-wing populism, that is looking after the interests of the ordinary people.[13] Hence, the legacy of the postwar social democratic moment is a contested one.

Both its historiographical construction and its contemporary topicality make it interesting to reexamine that trope of a golden age of social democracy. Any such reexamination should, however, start with conceding the Western-centric origins of the idea itself. The social democratic moment was one that happened, above all, in the industrially advanced capitalist economies of the Global North (including Australia and New Zealand), beginning in Sweden as early as the first half of the twentieth century.[14] Much of the Global South identifies the period after the end of World War II with decolonization, when powerful anticolonial movements, rooted in the first half of the twentieth century, achieved independence, either peacefully or through a series of often extremely brutal anticolonial wars.[15] Many, if by no means all, anticolonial movements were supported by the communist world that incorporated anti-imperialism into its arsenal of weapons with which to charge, combat, and hopefully defeat the capitalist world. The rhetorical and, above all, practical support it lent to anticolonial movements made it popular in the Global South,[16] where the Cold War was characterized by a series of substitute wars between an alliance of liberal capitalist states led by the United States and an alliance of communist states led by the USSR.

Hence, many of the countries that won independence in the post–World War II years sided with the Soviet Union and developed variants of authoritarian commu-

---

10. Della Porta, Fernandez, and Kouki, *Movement Parties Against Austerity*; Gautney, *Protest and Organization in the Alternative Globalization Era.*

11. Mouffe, *For a Left Populism.*

12. Nora, *Realms of Memory.*

13. Mudde, *Populist Radical Right Parties*; Mudde, *Far Right Today.*

14. On Australia and New Zealand as laboratories of the welfare state, see Castles, *Working Class and Welfare.*

15. The literature on anticolonialism is endless. For an introduction see Kennedy, *Decolonization.*

16. Drachewych, *Communist International, Anti-Imperialism and Racial Equality in British Dominions.*

nism. Those who did not allied with the Global West, receiving generous development aid but struggling with corruption and authoritarian elites more interested in enriching themselves than in serving their people. Everywhere in the Global South, communist or capitalist, independence regimes followed the logic of development thinking that becoming like the countries of the Global North would be the way toward enjoying the wealth of the nations of the Global North.[17] However, the idea of "catching up" with the Global North was hampered by continuing dependence on multinational companies from the Global North and by an ongoing colonial-style exploitation of the countries in the Global South, where large profits were ending up in the pockets of multinationals rather than in the pockets of the people of these countries.[18] Liberal capitalism, in its global struggle against communism, aligned itself with a range of dictatorial regimes that violently repressed left-wing activists in Latin America, Africa, and Asia.[19] Liberal capitalism was thus perfectly able to show, during the Cold War, two very different faces: a humane one in the Global North and an inhumane one in the Global South. Once again, we can observe how inadequate Western terms and concepts are when we speak about the non-Western world—something that global labor history has long pointed out.[20] To what extent notions of a golden age are at all relevant for the Global South is a question that remains largely under-researched, as the trope has been used very largely only in connection with the Global North.

This lacuna, alongside the above-mentioned historiographical construction and its current topicality, brought Leon Fink and Stefan Berger to think about organizing a major international conference on the theme of the golden age of social democracy. They were successful in finding the support of their co-organizers of the conference, Patrick Dixon and Jan de Graaf. And they won the support of two prominent organizations of US and German labor history: the Labor and Working-Class History Association, with its journal *Labor: Studies in Working-Class History*, of which Fink was the senior editor at the time; and the German Labour History Association, of which Berger is the chair. Financial support for the conference was won from the Thyssen Foundation, the Friedrich Ebert Foundation, the journal *Labor*, and the Institute for Social Movements (ISB) at the Ruhr-Universität Bochum, of which Berger is the director. The conference was held at the ISB in Bochum in April 2023. Subsequently, the four organizers of the conference decided to assemble some of the papers that were held there into three related special issues of labor journals: one for *Labor* (22, no. 1 [2025]), edited now by Julie Greene; and two in *Moving the Social: Journal for Social History and the History of Social Movements* (76 [2025] and 77

17. Ziai, *Development Discourse.*

18. Eley, "Corporatism and the Social Democratic Moment."

19. On US support of dictatorships in the Global South, see Gill, "Contradictions of US Supremacy"; Gardener and Young, *New American Empire.*

20. Van der Linden, *Workers of the World.*

[2016]), the journal of the ISB, coedited by Berger and Sean Scalmer from the University of Melbourne.

Several concerns related to the theme of a golden age of social democracy are covered in the three interrelated journal issues. First, there is the immediate impact of World War II on labor unions and workers' living standards across the United States, both Western and Eastern Europe, Australia / New Zealand, Japan, and Brazil. Equal to the focus on worker power, questions of democracy and worker voice—or the theme of working-class agency and its limits—receive prime attention. Even as workplace "industrial democracy" and "liberal" (in New Deal terms) or self-consciously secular "labor" or "social democratic" political strategies are recognized as Western political norms in this era, the scholarship represented here also emphasizes the influence of forms of arbitration, social Catholicism, and "corporatism" in shaping state policies. Another important development in the postwar world was the increasing feminization of the labor force across the industrially advanced countries of the Global North. How women themselves—both within and outside official labor movements—reckoned with structural and cultural barriers to full social participation is the subject of several inquiries. Finally, the Cold War itself—and the perceived threat of communism—continues to draw scrutiny both as a central feature of postwar international labor relations and as a source of conflict within national labor movements.

From the twenty-five presentations offered at the conference, *Labor* is proud to offer a forum for six original and innovative essays touching on the "golden age" conference theme. Two labor historians first address certain peculiarities of the US postwar political economy. Nelson Lichtenstein argues that both American and German labor leaders self-consciously drew on each other's experience of depression and wartime conditions to fashion distinctive systems of labor-management relations. Indeed, he suggests, the United States might well have veered toward a more German-like corporatist system of state-employer-worker trade-offs had not US management proved so recalcitrant. Aside from laying a scaffolding for worker rights to representation, American postwar liberals, as Andrew Elrod documents, were preoccupied with the problem of the wage-price spiral. Yet from Truman to Kennedy to Johnson to Carter—as indeed to this very day—inflationary pressures, and especially price rises undermining workers' standard of living, have proven largely impervious to liberal economic policy redress. Against the grain of "whiggish" treatments celebrating themes of contemporary opportunity and liberation for postwar workers, Jan de Graaf cautions that the very power of working-class movements exercised a conservative and a restraining disciplinary influence within both East and West European societies. Eloisa Betti offers a similarly sober perspective on gendered labor relations in postwar Italy. In the 1950s, as she documents, the spread of highly feminized and unstable forms of work such as industrial home-based work as well as precarious jobs highlighted the dark side of an era of Fordist mass production and spreading democracy. By contrast, Stefan Müller looks in depth at what we might consider the ideological apex of social democracy's golden age—a particular West German program, implemented in the 1970s and aimed at both modernizing and humanizing the industrial workplace. Finally, in a wide-ranging and synthetic essay covering both Western Europe and the Americas, Gerd-Rainer Horn offers an appreciative, revisionist account of the contributions of social Catholicism to the most progressive political moments of the postwar period.

Overall, the three special issues that are derived from the conference give us a rich and evocative panoply of ideas surrounding the notion of a golden age of social democracy in the three decades after the end of World War II. They also raise the intriguing question of a connection between the social democratic age and neoliberalism. The contributions assembled here seem to confirm that the trope of a golden age of social democracy was always more fitting to the Global North than the Global South and that even within the Global North it was very uneven. They also confirm the importance of the Cold War in constructions of a golden age, making it a powerful resource for liberal capitalism at times of crisis. Yet many of the articles leave us with an impression that the construction of a social democratic golden age, based on ideas of solidarity and social justice, has also been something that democrats of different persuasions have been striving for continuously. These attempts have indeed produced some significant results, at least within the industrially advanced nations of the Global North, and especially in the postwar decades that are the focus of examination here. Such real advances in the erosion of social inequalities would also explain why it has become such a powerful "realm of memory" in contemporary politics. ■

## References

Berger, Stefan, Ludger Pries, and Manfred Wannöffel, eds. *The Palgrave Handbook of Workers' Participation at Plant Level*. New York: Palgrave Macmillan, 2019.

Breen, Richard, and Walter Müller, eds. *Education and Intergenerational Social Mobility in Europe and the United States*. Stanford, CA: Stanford University Press, 2020.

Castles, Francis Geoffrey. *The Working Class and Welfare: Reflections on the Political Development of the Welfare State in Australia and New Zealand, 1890–1980*. Wellington, NZ: Allen & Unwin, 1985.

Crouch, Colin. *Post-Democracy*. Cambridge, UK: Polity, 2004.

de Graaf, Jan-Arend. *Socialism Across the Iron Curtain: Socialist Parties in East and West and the Reconstruction of Europe After 1945*. New York: Cambridge University Press, 2019.

della Porta, Donatella, Joseba Fernandez, and Hara Kouki, eds. *Movement Parties Against Austerity*. Cambridge, UK: Polity, 2017.

Drachewych, Oleksa. *The Communist International, Anti-Imperialism and Racial Equality in British Dominions*. Abingdon, UK: Routledge, 2019.

Eatwell, John, and Murray Milgate. *The Fall and Rise of Keynesian Economics*. New York: Oxford University Press, 2011.

Eley, Geoff. "Corporatism and the Social Democratic Moment: The Post-War Settlement, 1945–1973." In *The Oxford Handbook of Postwar European History*, edited by Dan Stone, 37–59. Oxford: Oxford University Press, 2012.

Eley, Geoff. *Forging Democracy: The History of the Left in Europe, 1850–2000*. Oxford: Oxford University Press, 2002.

Fourastié, Jean. *Les trente glorieuses: Ou la Révolution invisible de 1946 à 1975*. Paris: Hachette-Pluriel, 1979.

Gardener, L. C., and M. B. Young, eds. *The New American Empire*. New York: New Press, 2005.

Gautney, Heather. *Protest and Organization in the Alternative Globalization Era: NGOs, Social Movements, and Political Parties*. New York: Palgrave Macmillan, 2010.

Gill, Stephen. "The Contradictions of US Supremacy." In "2005: The Empire Reloaded," edited by Leo Panich and Colin Leys, special issue of *Socialist Register*, 23–45. London: Merlin Press, 2004.

Harvey, David. *A Brief History of Neoliberalism*. Oxford: Oxford University Press, 2005.

Hobsbawm, Eric. *Age of Extremes: The Short Twentieth Century, 1914–1989*. London: Michael Joseph, 1998.

Hwang, Gyu-Jin. "Development, Welfare Policy and the Welfare State." In *Oxford Research Encyclopedia of International Studies*, November 30, 2017. https://oxfordre.com /internationalstudies/display/10.1093/acrefore/9780190846626.001.0001/acrefore -9780190846626-e-145.

Kennedy, Dane. *Decolonization: A Very Short Introduction*. New York: Oxford University Press, 2016.

Moschonas, Gerassimos. *In the Name of Social Democracy: The Great Transformation, 1945 to the Present*. London: Verso, 2002.

Mouffe, Chantal. *For a Left Populism*. London: Verso, 2018.

Mudde, Cas. *The Far Right Today*. Cambridge, UK: Polity, 2019.

Mudde, Cas. *Populist Radical Right Parties in Europe*. Cambridge: Cambridge University Press, 2007.

Nora, Pierre. *Realms of Memory*. 2 vols. New York: Columbia University Press, 1996.

O'Halloran, Sharyn, and Thomas Groll, eds. *After the Crash*. New York: Columbia University Press, 2019.

Sassoon, Donald. *One Hundred Years of Socialism: The West European Left in the Twentieth Century*. New York: New Press, 1996.

Streeck, Wolfgang. *Buying Time: The Delayed Crisis of Democratic Capitalism*. London: Verso, 2014.

van der Linden, Marcel. *Workers of the World: Essays Toward a Global Labor History*. Leiden: Brill, 2008.

Ziai, Aram. *Development Discourse and Global History: From Colonialism to the Sustainable Development Goals*. Abingdon, UK: Routledge, 2015.

# Slaughterhouse Music

## Thomas McGrath (1916–1990)

1.

First, we feel the train
Slowing.
Then we see the pens as the train stops.
The doors open.
We leave the excrement-covered floors
Of the cattle cars and the stench of our journey.

A joy to stand in the ankle-deep dust and dried dung of the yards!
Sun?
      And a high blue sky!
We blink in the glare of light and our cries go up:
Bellowings, snorts, grunts, whines, farts and whinnys –
A bedlam of many languages lifts toward heaven.
Then we stampede to the watering troughs and the sparse food.

As evening grows out of the earth,
Uneasy in the failing light
We push at the fences ...
Moaning and bleating,
Sending our separate cries
Into the openrange beyond the wire ...
A kind of singing in all our languages
Out ...
Into the desolation –
The emptiness that we once thought was home.

A kind of singing ...
Barbaric discords before we lie down to sleep
In the feathery dust and dung.

*Labor: Studies in Working-Class History*   Volume 22 • Issue 1
DOI 10.1215/15476715-11521310   © 2025 by Labor and Working-Class History Association

2.

Morning comes in with the first train.
Others arrive and our lives are repeated.
But the afternoon brings rain
And a new thing:
A ramp at the end of our pen, leading
Up to what we had never noticed:
A vast black iron door.

They want us to ascend: to rise,
To fly up the ramp toward the black iron.
So we are lead, bullied, cajoled, prodded, bulldozed
And we resume our ascensions until – suddenly –
Turning in complaining concert, we look back
And lifting our eyes to the hills – we see:
Everywhere – ! mountain, valley, seacoast, and plain:
Wooden dog-legs, cactus-hedges, thorn-and-wattle, and barbed-wire fences:
Pens!
Everywhere!
The whole world a pen …
What we had thought unique … universal.

3.

The black gate opens on its shuddering hinge.
Our first contingent is cut out and enters.
The door swings …
But not before we hear a dull thudding
As of mauls
On wood stumps muffled by animal skins …
And we see the flash of axes, rising and falling,
Like puny lightning in the heavy gloom …
The door swings shut before we might race in and stop it –
If we could or if we would.
But we still hear and see – as if in dream.
And so we begin to sing.

Not as complaint – but loud!
Despair and defiance
To shout down all the pens and all the stars!
And it seems proper
To sing in solidarity a little while still together –
Before we go under the axe.

THOMAS MCGRATH (1916–1990) began his work-life as a young boy on the family farm in North Dakota near the Minnesota border. His poetry is known for its breadth of language and diction, range of form, and mastery of the long line, exemplified in *Letters to an Imaginary Friend*, an epic book-length poem in four parts, written over thirty years. A lifetime activist, organizer, Rhodes Scholar, and World War II veteran, he was blacklisted following his appearance before the House Un-American Activities Committee (HUAC). In addition to poetry, he wrote novels and documentary screenplays. "Slaughterhouse Music" appears in McGrath's final book, *Death Song*—edited by Sam Hamill—completed before his death and published posthumously.

—Susan Eisenberg

# Philip Tipperman:
# Forgotten Labor Painter of the 1930s

Kathy M. Newman, Joseph Entin, and Patricia Hills

*P*hilip Tipperman was a largely unknown but fascinating painter, born and educated
in Brooklyn, and later based in Silver Spring, Maryland. We are excited to present
five of his paintings from 1939, all of which have strong labor themes. We first learned of
these paintings in 2023, when Milt Tipperman, Philip Tipperman's son, approached one
of our editors to see if we might be interested in writing about the artist and/or the artworks. Kathy M. Newman, our Arts and Media editor, after extensive research, could find
little in the historical record to indicate that Tipperman was much recognized or celebrated
when he was alive. As a result, Newman assembled Joseph Entin, professor of English and
American studies at Brooklyn College, with Patricia Hills, professor emerita of American
and African American art at Boston University, and the three of them recorded, tran-
scribed, and edited their conversation about these fascinating works. The conversation
follows Tipperman's bio. To see images of these paintings in color, please visit Labor
Online at www.lawcha.org/2025/03/01/tipperman.

Philip Tipperman, born in 1916, was the son of Jewish immigrants from Poland
who ran a candy store in Brooklyn. Tipperman attended Samuel Tilden High School
and graduated from Brooklyn College, receiving his BA in fine arts in 1938. After grad-
uation, Tipperman worked briefly at the Metropolitan Museum of Art, illustrating
a book on the history of military armor. After that he moved to Washington, DC,
where he served as a firefighter for several years before starting a sign business in Silver Spring, Maryland.

Tipperman painted throughout his adult life; he donated paintings to fund-
raisers, gave paintings to his siblings, and displayed his art in his home. In 1947, he
had a one-person show of twenty-two watercolors at the Central Public Library in
northwest Washington, DC, that was featured in several local newspapers. In the
1960s he painted watercolors and produced pen-and-ink drawings depicting people, buildings, and landscapes in Maryland and in Maine and Mexico, where he had
vacationed. Tipperman suffered from undiagnosed mental illness and took his own
life in April 1969.

*Labor: Studies in Working-Class History* Volume 22 • Issue 1
DOI 10.1215/15476715-11521302 © 2025 by Labor and Working-Class History Association

Tipperman's 1939 paintings reflect both the Depression decade in which they were made and the artist's singular style and perspective. The 1930s was an era of great hardship in the United States, especially for working people, many of whom lost their jobs and their homes and struggled to put food on the table. It was also a period of intense labor activism: The Committee (later Congress) of Industrial Organizations, or CIO, was founded, and millions of workers went on strike across industries and around the country. In addition, the period saw immense creativity in the arts, which took a social turn as many writers, photographers, and painters grappled with the economic and political struggles roiling the decade.

Tipperman's paintings, which focus squarely on labor organizing, pickets, and violence directed at workers, address vital concerns that many other artists, especially those who moved to the left during the 1930s, were also engaging. In these paintings Tipperman centers everyday working people, using bold, angular shapes. Tipperman's style fuses social realism and modernist experimentation. In this way, his work seems to be in dialogue with better-known painters from the period, including Thomas Hart Benton, Philip Evergood, and Jacob Lawrence. Tipperman's lively, colorful, hard-hitting images stand out—even against this turbulent decade's rich cultural landscape.

In January 2024, *Labor* Arts and Media Associate Editor Kathy M. Newman, Joseph Entin, and Patricia (Pat) Hills had a conversation about these paintings. Newman, Entin, and Hills worked to contextualize the paintings using their knowledge of the period, combined with close readings. They talked about the paintings in this order: *Labor Strike* (fig. 1), *Labor Unity* (fig. 2), *Picketed, Beaten, and Jailed* (fig. 3), *Murdered By the Company* (fig. 4), and *After Work and Before Supper* (fig. 5).

**Kathy M. Newman**: The first thing I notice when I look at *Labor Strike* is the color palette: the soft, almost pastel colors, the turquoises, lavenders, and blues. There is a singular use of a vibrant red color above the picketers, shading what almost looks like a marquee, or the backside of a stage set, and above that is an architectural detail that looks like knives or spikes, pointing upward.

**Patricia Hills:** Well, this might surprise you, but in some ways this painting reminds me of Jacob Lawrence. It's interesting that the style is not really a realist style. In Tipperman it seems that we learn a lot from the ways in which the bodies are posed rather than from the facial expressions. It reminds me of Jacob Lawrence because Tipperman is interested in form, and so was Lawrence. There's no real chiaroscuro, that painterly contrast between light and dark, to give you the sense of three-dimensionality. The figures are almost flat, two-dimensional.

**Joseph Entin:** I agree. There's a level of abstraction here. Maybe it's the influence of cubism, because what I'm noticing is the angularity, the flatness, and the sharpness of some of the lines. At the same time, the painting picks up some of the themes of what we might consider social realism—the strike, the mass action—but then uses a modernist aesthetic to do it. We think of the thirties as the decade of realism, the decade of social realism. And certainly it is. But of course, individual artists are always working

**FIGURE 1.** Philip Tipperman, *Labor Strike*, 1939. Courtesy of Brooklyn College.

in a fluid way, drawing on multiple sources. This is an experimental work of art as well as a realist work of art. It's a work of modernism as well as realism.

**Patricia Hills:** Jacob Lawrence didn't like the term *social realism*! Lawrence preferred the term *social expressionism*. According to David Shapiro in his book *Social Realism: Art as a Weapon,* the term *social realism* wasn't even used in the 1930s! And there are so many artists who did a kind of social expressionism. There are well-known ones like Thomas Hart Benton, who specialized in twisted forms. And I think Joseph is absolutely correct about the modernism coming in via these twisted forms and exaggerations of the body that you see in German expressionism.

**Joseph Entin:** I'm interested in the way Tipperman represents the body. In thirties art the body becomes such a critical metaphor—especially for artworks that represent working people and also nonworking people, the unemployed. For these artworks the body becomes an important motif because it's a way to render the kind of material effects of hardship, things like hunger, starvation, displacement, violence, and injury. And I'm noticing this tendency in Tipperman's work. Tipperman's bodies—and they all appear to be male bodies, it should be noted—are large and angular, blocky, twisted, in some cases almost tortured.

Tipperman's work reminds me a little bit of the artist Hugo Gellert, who was producing a lot of covers for the *New Masses*. Gellert has these massive, muscular, brawny figures. However, as the critic Walter B. Kalaidjian has argued in *Revisionary Modernism and Postmodern Critique* (1993), such massive, overabundant figures are uncanny references to the absence of working-class power in the face of widespread unemployment and privation. Certainly at the beginning of the Depression, these massive figures might be overcompensating, but they might also have been a way to render the harm and also the kind of hope and power that working people come to have in this decade, as labor militancy, strikes, and organizing rise.

The last thing I want to mention is the contrast between the lone figure in the foreground and the crowd in the background. The background figures are really in the background. We can't see them very well as individuals. So there's a tension between the individual figure out front and the mass in the background. This lone figure in the foreground is one of them, wearing one of their buttons, and he's carrying a sign. He's one of their number, but very much individualized—perhaps a union leader. Does this lone figure also represent the artist? Is this a reflection of how Tipperman saw himself, as part of, but also apart from, the masses?

**Patricia Hills:** Speaking of individuality versus the crowd, we also see that going on in the works of Louis Lozowick, the Russian American artist who worked in art deco machinist style. He started painting human figures in the 1930s. He was very much on the left, as one of the editors of the *New Masses*. When he begins to paint people, we see something of what we're looking at here, which is that distinction between individuality versus the crowd. Lozowick painted working people, and, gradually, as his work progressed, they took on more and more individuality.

I'd also like to point out that this man's face seems disconnected from the rest of his body. It's almost like his body can't hold him up. His left leg looks like it's going to collapse. By contrast, when you look at his face, his face is one of determination. I think Joseph's idea of the collective versus the individual—that was a big issue for Tipperman. A lot of people who did not join the Communist Party, or who were not in that orbit, were focusing on individualism, and that's what they didn't like about communism—the pressure they might have felt to give up some of their

**FIGURE 2.** Philip Tipperman, *Labor Unity*, 1939. Courtesy of Brooklyn College.

individuality. But other people embraced the collective, because they believed that struggling together might produce a better world. *Struggle*, actually, might be a word for us to consider. It's a word that Jacob Lawrence used over and over again. If there's no struggle, there's no humanity; if there's no struggle, there's no art. *Struggle* is the operative term. Struggle is what it means to be human.

**Kathy M. Newman:** I love that, and I think we see it in this next painting, *Labor Unity*. Some of the things I notice is that the angular planes of the face look like miniature landscapes. Another visual detail that really strikes me is the kerchief that the front figure is wearing, which looks like it is covered with spiderwebs. He appears to be African American. He is wearing a button that says "CIO," and the man behind him, who is white, is wearing a button that says "AFL."

**Joseph Entin:** We've got a scene of collectivity, right? The title is *Labor Unity*. So it's suggesting that these two figures have come together, one representing the CIO and the other representing the AFL. But there are also important differences. It's a scene of tension. This is when the CIO is breaking away from the AFL, emerging out of it and distinguishing itself from it, organizing mass production workers as opposed to craft workers. And then there's the question of race, of Black and white, and the history of racial tension that's been mobilized by employers and corporations and capitalists over the years to create tension within labor's ranks. So in this painting I see an interplay of unity and division, individuality and collectivity.

In terms of the forms, the faces, the angles, the deep shadows and lines—they are all so striking, and they echo the buildings as well as the clouds. It's almost like the sky is on fire, or is being lit up with lightning, which could be a reference to the potential power of work and workers.

**Patricia Hills:** One thing I'm noticing is that the Black man is so much larger than the white man behind him. It seems appropriate that the Black worker is the one who is aligned with the CIO, since the CIO had more communist members and organizers, and the Communist Party was fighting for racial equality. The Black worker is looking West, perhaps toward hope? The white worker is looking at us. The white man is inviting us in, and the Black man is showing us the way. One last thing I noticed: The clouds are ominous. They're not nice, soft, fluffy, bouncy clouds. And there is a kind of a regimentation of the smokestacks in the background.

**Kathy M. Newman:** Like the picketer in the last painting we looked at, here the buildings can't quite hold themselves up. They seem to be waving or collapsing or undulating.

**Joseph Entin:** It is interesting that the human figures here dominate the painting and the landscape. And I think it's significant that the African American figure is foregrounded. At this particular moment, the late 1930s, to really put a Black man forward seems significant.

**Patricia Hills:** Certainly, the Black man seems to have the leadership position, which is interesting, because so often white artists will have white people in the front, and Black people behind.

**Joseph Entin:** There's a tension here between a realist impulse, a desire to tackle social issues, to confront them, but then, also, there's something allegorical, I think. This is not a specific strike that's being represented. *Labor Unity* is trying to raise in abstract form a larger set of issues about race, about labor, about unity, about the potential trouble brewing in the clouds. It's a fusing of two dimensions—a realist one and a symbolic one.

**FIGURE 3.** Philip Tipperman, *Picketed Beaten*, 1939. Courtesy of Brooklyn College.

**Kathy M. Newman:** We'll go to *Picketed Beaten* next. In contrast to the last two paintings, there are four figures who are on the same plane and are in proportion with each other. It looks like they are in jail—we see the steel bars of a jail cell behind them. The picket sign has words on it now, "On Strike," and there's another picket sign tucked underneath someone's arm. The figure at the far left looks almost like he's wearing a turban; of course it's the bandages, they've all been beaten and their heads have been bandaged. These men are bleeding, torn and bruised. There's one odd little detail that jumps out at me. There is a rip in the arm of the clothing on the man who is second from the left. The rip exposes his skin, which is purplish in color. But the rip looks like the head of a paintbrush to me. The painter's brush is the rip, the tear.

**Patricia:** We've been talking about the collective versus the individual. There's something quite nice about this picture. And that is, that the clothes all seem to kind of create their individual personality. Their clothes are quite beautiful, the way they flow down, and how the figures are dressed differently. One has a necktie on. The men's faces are differently colored, but also nonracial. Tipperman has brought these people together, these "people of color." In his use of color he seems to be gesturing toward categories of race and ethnicity. Alternatively, maybe he is complicating rigid or binary notions of whiteness and Blackness. And then I'm wondering about the figure on the left, is he smoking a cigarette? In fact, the cloud from his cigarette is also the cloud that is in the background, sort of the landscape. It's almost cheeky or, or humorous.

**Joseph Entin:** I like your observation, about the rip as a reference to painting. I'm also struck by the range of colors represented in the faces, which again I find really provocative and interesting, as establishing a play on these issues of individuality and collectivity. The faces convey some despair. They've suffered some kind of defeat, but they're also standing shoulder to shoulder, and so there's some resolve, too, even in this moment of setback. They are in jail! This work is so loaded with tension.

As in the other paintings we have discussed, here there is tension between abstraction and realism, between hope and despair, between individuality and collectivity. I don't want to overload it with a word like *dialectic*, but I do feel like these paintings are tension-filled in a way that is really productive, in a way that is really trying to grapple with the place of art in this tremulous social world. How do you represent the contradictions, the challenges, that working people in particular are facing in this decade?

**Patricia Hills:** I agree, though when you said "tension" I was looking at the one hand we can see, and here instead of it being a clenched fist, the fingers are awkwardly positioned—they look broken. There's no tension in that hand.

But there's more tension in their faces, in terms of directionality. Three of them seem to be looking at the same thing, and the last man on the right is looking just below our line of sight. There's some object offscreen that is captivating them. I am thinking now that the title is a bit odd. We would say a factory is being picketed, and people are being beaten. So what can be both picketed and beaten? Did the strike work? But then again, we know from their gashes and bandages that the men in the painting are the ones who were beaten. So there's a question about what the title means. Suddenly, as I reflect on the titles of these paintings, they seem increasingly important.

**Kathy M. Newman:** So I'm going to share the next one, titled *Murdered By*.

**Patricia Hills:** This painting is very unusual. In a lot of 1930s art we see policemen beating people. But to have somebody actually murdered, we don't see that very often as the subject of paintings from this period. Here again we have Tipperman's interesting use of color in order to indicate race. The murdered man has a purplish-colored face, and I read him as being African American. The Black man is the man that's been murdered. Also, he's wearing a necktie. We see that repeatedly in these paintings, that working men have a range of attire, from typical factory wear to something that looks more white collar. What are the other men doing? Are they rescuing him? Where is the rest of his body? We can see one of his legs coming out on the left side of the painting. There is the cuff of his pant leg, and a shoe. Here again we have these interesting rhythms in the human figures too. We have this watery, undulating rhythm that seems to travel up through the figures, through their legs and into their torsos. Tipperman is using light and shade and watery hues to create these flowy, but also substantial, human figures.

**Joseph Entin:** I love your comment, Pat, about the liquid flow of the human figures, and again there's some tension for me, between the stasis, the monumentality of the

**FIGURE 4.** Philip Tipperman, *Murdered By*, 1939. Courtesy of Brooklyn College.

figures—there's been a murder, the men are bearing the dead body of one of their comrades—and then also that fluidity, and motion. This is a labor scene—we have the factory buildings in the background at the right of the image, and picket signs—but there's also a reference to the history of lynching. A Black man has been killed, and on the left side of the background there are three large trees with substantial branches, looking like iconic lynching trees. Is this painting bringing together the history of labor struggle with racial terror, with racial violence?

**Patricia Hills:** That's a good reading. I'm also noticing that the trees on the left mimic and repeat the smokestacks on the right. I'm wondering if there is a country/industry story because the trees look like they're engulfed in, or equivalent to, smoke that is billowing from below. There is a field between the trees in the back and the men in the foreground, and it's being plowed by something we can't see that is giving off plumes of smoke. Those plumes rise up and blend with or obscure the leaves on the trees.

**Kathy M. Newman:** For some reason I'm thinking about the style of Grant Wood. Is his work anything like this? He has a lot of fields and furrows, planted rows, fields lined with stately rows of plants and shrubs.

**Patricia Hills:** Grant Wood does paint rolling hills and fields. But with Grant Wood his painting style is much more sharp, precise, with clean, clear lines. What we're seeing here in Tipperman is a very unique style, and it's very compelling.

**Kathy M. Newman:** This is the third painting we've looked at that has picket signs, I think Tipperman understands something about picket signs. Look at how awkwardly the man on the far right is holding a picket sign under one arm, sort of pinning it under his armpit, while also holding his dead comrade with both hands. Picket signs are very awkward. If you are holding a picket sign you can't properly use your hands for much else.

**Joseph Entin:** Here's another thought about the situational dynamics of this painting. It is significant that there's only one Black figure. There could have been another Black figure helping to carry the Black man who was murdered. It would've changed the dynamics. In a typical picture of a lynching we would have a lone Black figure and a large group of white men. In contrast, here there are five white men assisting the Black man. They're aiding him; he has been victimized by the forces of the factory, by the police, by the state. But there is a weird and disturbing echo between this painting and the kind of lynching scene that might have this same configuration, but in which the white figures would be the agents of murder, not recuperation. I think Tipperman is cutting against the grain in that the white men treat the Black man as a brother, a comrade, and that they are carrying him, honoring him. But in doing this, ironically, there's the potential to reconstitute the same kind of racial dynamic that might have created a lynching, which is to say a white mob descended on a Black person.

**Patricia Hills:** I see what you're saying, and I think this is a more positive image. Maybe today we would look down on this image of white men rescuing a Black man, maybe saying it's too "woke." But what you're saying, Joseph, is that this is the opposite of a lynching. It's a mob of white men, but they are rescuing, caring for, honoring their fallen Black comrade.

**Kathy M. Newman:** It's like they are pallbearers at his funeral. It's a sign of respect. And also it seems like the tension that Joseph keeps pointing us to, that tension between unity and disunity, white and Black, collectivity and individuality—we have that here again. One more thing that I'm noticing. There's a brick in the lower right corner of the painting. Was the Black man killed by that brick? Or is the brick used as a weapon by the workers in this battle? Who is throwing bricks at whom?

Another phrase that comes to mind in looking at Tipperman's work is a phrase that Michael Denning uses in his book *The Cultural Front*, which is an aesthetic category he calls the "proletarian grotesque." Denning uses this, in part, as an alternative to the concept of social realism, something we've been talking about in relation to these paintings. Tipperman's figures are grotesque, misshapen, and awkward. How do you depict working-class struggle? One answer is the "proletarian grotesque."

**Patricia Hills:** That's a good observation. You are reminding me, when I first saw the work of Philip Evergood, I thought, that's the ugliest work I have ever seen. Really

**FIGURE 5.** Philip Tipperman, *After Work*, 1939. Courtesy of Brooklyn College.

ugly. But I had an epiphany. Suddenly all those grotesque figures of Philip Evergood became beautiful to me. Since then I have actually bought a couple of Philip Evergood's paintings that were at Christie's because nobody wanted to buy them because they were so ugly. I see them now and I think they are so beautiful.

What is ugly? What is beautiful? When we think of beauty we think of Greco-Roman and Western European art, with all that symmetry and those beautiful bodies, and then here in the 1930s we have these ordinary people who have a beauty about them, but the beauty is not in their faces, or in their bodies; it is on the inside. The beauty is in their intentions, in their humanity.

**Kathy M. Newman:** This is a great segue into the last painting we're going to look at. This piece is called *After Work*.

**Joseph Entin:** So, this figure is in bed, in his clothes. His tie and collar are slightly undone, and his belt is unbuckled. The belt looks like a snake! His shoes are on the floor but he still has his socks on. He has collapsed into bed. There's a statement here about the exhaustion of work, the overwhelm, and what is required for workers to recover, and perhaps his lack of leisure time. What kind of time do working people have for themselves? Also, is this a private home? There are two beds in this room. Is this a workingman's boardinghouse, or something like the YMCA? Also, what is his class status? Like a lot of the working men in Tipperman's work he's wearing a tie. His shoes look almost like dress shoes. So he's a white-collar worker, or petit bourgeoisie. He's not a construction worker or an auto worker. Something else I'm noticing. There's a strange way in which the lamp is descending over his head. I think we're being invited to speculate that he's dreaming, and to wonder what he is dreaming about.

**Patricia Hills:** He has his eyes closed. But is his mouth open?

**Kathy M. Newman:** Yes, his mouth is open, forming a little triangle of openness. This painting reminds me of a series of photographs by elin o'Hara slavick, a contemporary artist. She has a series of photographs of workers with their eyes closed called *Workers Dreaming*. To make these photographs Slavick approaches various workers and asks them to close their eyes and dream of something, to imagine something. In this painting we're made to wonder, What is he dreaming about? What is "after work" like for him?

**Patricia Hills:** I love this painting. I love the details. Look at the little round pull on the shade behind him. We're up high in this room, we can see the top of a building across the street when we look out the window. And I love the lamp. I have a lamp just like it, and people ask, "Why do you still have that old lamp?" and, well, it's just a lamp left over the from the 1920s. It's elegant and graceful.

**Kathy M. Newman:** I too love the details of the room and the window. Out the window there is a tree barren of leaves. Next to the tree is a telephone pole with wires pulled taut around it. The sidewalks are white. There's a radiator below the window. The man's pipe is on the windowsill. The cord of the lamp meanders and twists and curls. Tipperman has put so much care into creating a three-dimensional checkered patterned blanket. But also, the angles of his body are twisted and grotesque. He's broken. He's not comfortable or relaxed. His body is tortured and misshapen.

**Patricia Hills:** Yeah, he looks exhausted. He's not even in the pose of someone sleeping. He's just sprawled. He's passed out.

**Joseph Entin:** I agree! I'm also noticing that awkwardness in the arm behind his head. It's like his arm or his hand—it's like they are broken underneath his massive head. Here again we see the aesthetics of distortion that characterizes so much of Tipperman's work. And I want to go back to something Pat was saying earlier, which is how this painting is beautiful and also ugly. Was this one of the challenges of the artist who wanted to represent working-class life in the late 1930s? There was an impulse to portray working-class people—people who have been marginalized—to make them beautiful, to put them at the center, to make them large, to make them commanding, to make them graceful. On the other hand, Tipperman might not have wanted to diminish the horror, the pain, the injuries, or the uglinesses that characterized working-class experience in this long industrial era, and still do today.

**Patricia Hills:** When writing about Philip Evergood, I called this the "poetics of ugliness."

**Joseph Entin:** Yeah, that's perfect. And again, Tipperman in his own very unique way is at once offering us images that are ugly and grotesque, misshapen and distorted, and yet also very beguiling and compelling, with fascinating color choices, really moving and flowing forms, lots that we can consider quite elegant and beautiful.

**Patricia Hills:** You know, I'm struck by these wonderful nuances and colors. I'm realizing that Tipperman's colors are colors that women wear in this period. These dark turquoises, teals, and rust colors, the light greens. And here are all of these beautiful colors undulating with the help of this watery style.

**Joseph Entin:** That's a terrific observation, given the preponderance of male figures. And even though there is this hulking male body, there is a softness to the color palette, particularly the way the clothes are rendered.

**Kathy M. Newman:** Maybe what we associate with the feminine comes through via Tipperman's muted color palette, and through the fluid movement of the clothing. We see that in all five of these paintings. There are no women that we can clearly identify, but perhaps the contrast between the male and female, perhaps that binary, that dialectic, comes through in the softness and the strangeness of Tipperman's color palette and in his watery, undulating painting style. Pat and Joseph, I thank you for agreeing to be part of this conversation. I love the specific details we have been able to highlight, and the ways we have been able to connect Tipperman to the period, both in terms of labor and politics and in terms of the cultural and artistic movements of the 1930s!

. . . . . . . .

If you want to see these paintings in person, they are currently on view at the Brooklyn College Library. For more information, visit their website. https://bclibraryart .commons.gc.cuny.edu/?s=tipperman. We are grateful to the Tipperman family for sharing these fascinating works of art! ∎

KATHY M. NEWMAN is the associate editor for Arts and Media at *Labor*. Her forthcoming book, *Labor Noir: Film, Television and the Problem of Work in the Age of the Blacklist*, will be published by Rutgers University Press in 2026.

JOSEPH ENTIN is professor of English and American Studies at Brooklyn College, City University of New York. He is the author of *Sensational Modernism: Experimental Fiction and Photography in Thirties America* (2007) and *Living Labor: Fiction, Film, and Precarious Work* (2023), and coeditor of four other books, including, most recently, with Jeanne Theoharis, *Until We're Seen: Public College Students Expose the Hidden Inequalities of the COVID-19 Pandemic* (2024).

PATRICIA HILLS is professor emerita of American and African American art at Boston University. Her most recent book is *Painting Harlem Modern: The Art of Jacob Lawrence* (2019). A Guggenheim recipient, and an experienced curator as well as scholar, Hills is an expert in nineteenth- and twentieth-century American art, genre painting, African American art, Cold War art, and art and politics.

# Relitigating the New Deal: The Stakes of Current Constitutional Challenges to the NLRB

Diana S. Reddy

Every April the staff of the National Labor Relations Board (NLRB; the board) gathers to celebrate what they call "Constitutionality Day." Here they mark the anniversary of the US Supreme Court's April 1937 decision in *NLRB v. Jones & Laughlin Steel Corp*, upholding—against all odds—the constitutionality of the National Labor Relations Act (NLRA).[1] Whether due to President Franklin Delano Roosevelt's bluster or the righteous intransigence of almost two million striking workers, the court did the unexpected in *Jones & Laughlin*:[2] It walked away from its *Lochner*-era deference to capital and toward a new constitutional paradigm, one that treated economic regulation and an administrative apparatus capable of its enforcement as consistent with both the Constitution and the public interest.

Last year, however, the NLRB's Constitutionality Day celebration was a more tempered one. That is because, in 2024, labor law's long-settled constitutionality became suddenly unsettled. Faced with escalating labor unrest, early twenty-first-century titans of industry began reviving the lost constitutional claims of their early twentieth-century counterparts. Within the first few months of 2024, SpaceX, Amazon, Starbucks, and Trader Joe's all began arguing that the NLRB was unconstitutional. The bravado of these attacks has unnerved many of labor's supporters, who know all too well that the NLRA barely scraped by the first time.

This short essay gives legal and political context to these constitutional challenges. To some extent, these attacks are a consequence of labor's recent successes. Sharp increases in new employee organizing, coupled with the board's assertiveness

---

1. NLRB v. Jones & Laughlin Steel Corp., 301 U.S. 1 (1937). According to James Gross's classic history of the NLRB, the court's decision was wildly celebrated by board staff when it was issued, and annual celebrations followed for some period thereafter. Gross, *Making of the NLRB*. The current practice of annual celebration began again in 2004, according to current board staff. This essay was written in the summer of 2024 and does not cover developments after that time.

2. Bureau of Labor Statistics, *Analysis of Strikes in 1937*.

*Labor: Studies in Working-Class History*  Volume 22 • Issue 1
DOI 10.1215/15476715-11521422   © 2025 by Labor and Working-Class History Association

under President Joe Biden, put employers on the defensive. As a result, they have hired elite corporate defense law firms to do what elite corporate defense law firms do: engage in scorched-earth litigation tactics.

But these attacks are also enabled by a much longer-term conservative campaign against administrative agencies writ large. Aggrieved employers accordingly can draw from a treasure trove of long-percolating conservative legal arguments, crafted to upend the New Deal constitutional paradigm shift and end "the administrative state" as we have known it. And they invoke these arguments at a moment when the most conservative Supreme Court since the New Deal appears ready and willing to adopt them.[3]

Exactly how worried should labor's supporters be about these challenges? As I discuss below, there is no easy answer to this question. On the one hand, this is not *Jones & Laughlin. Jones & Laughlin* was existential, about whether Congress *could* give workers collective rights at all. By contrast, the current suits challenge just the administrative specifics, questioning *how* the board goes about enforcing those rights. For the moment, the *can* and the *how* seem synonymous. The NLRA is the statute that we have; it was passed at a politically extraordinary moment, perhaps the only moment in American history when it could have been passed. If the Supreme Court were to enjoin the board from operating until Congress "fixed" any constitutional deficiencies, there is a strong possibility that nothing would make it back. Still, it is important to keep in mind that the two key elements of the New Deal, economic regulation in the public interest and the administrative state as we know it, are linked as much by historical conjuncture as by logical necessity. Other *hows* remain possible.[4]

On the other hand, this is a pivotal time in labor politics, a rare, unsettled moment when profound change seems possible. And these lawsuits are perfectly timed to arrest labor's momentum, in part by undermining the accomplishments of the most audaciously effective NLRB in recent memory. It is already working. In July 2024, a Texas federal court ruled that the board must stop prosecuting SpaceX, notwithstanding the company's seemingly flagrant violations of federal law. In that court's view, it was inequitable to subject SpaceX to an administrative proceeding likely to be unconstitutional.[5] For now, employers who sue the NLRB within the Fifth Circuit Court of Appeals can violate the NLRA with impunity.

Whatever the ultimate outcome of these challenges, it is important for labor's supporters to remain clear-eyed about how we got here. The labor movement has long had a negativity bias when it comes to law. It would be easy to let this moment become a one-track tale of repression by law. But this is *not* only a tale of losses. Over

3 Totenberg, "Supreme Court Is the Most Conservative."

4 Scholars of administrative law and political economy have argued that in contemplating the future of the administrative state, it is imperative that we "not settle for simply restoring the status quo ante." Rahman, "After Chevron." Moreover, it is worth considering whether shuffling off questions of worker freedom, economic oppression, and industrial democracy to expert-driven administrative agencies is itself a component of "the law of apolitical economy." Reddy, "After the Law of Apolitical Economy."

5 Wiessner, "SpaceX Wins."

the past decade, workers have reclaimed significant political power, and this has made labor law more functional than it has been in decades. In response, conservatives are now marshaling their political power, their frustrating efficacy in placing like-minded people in judgeships, in order to put labor law back in its place. However, the current pushback is not the end of labor's legal story; it is just another chapter.

## De-Ossifying Labor Law and Politics

I start this essay, then, not with the constitutional challenges but with their prequel.[6] Over the past several years, workers, their supporters, and the Biden NLRB were able to breathe new life into labor law—in vision and in doctrine, albeit not always in successful real-world application.

For decades, the dominant story among labor law scholars, practitioners, and even union members has been that American labor law is fundamentally broken. To some, it was always broken; the American legal system could never and would never empower the working class.[7] To others, labor law had ossified.[8] Because of its isolation from democratic renewal, labor law had failed to keep up with massive changes in the economy and labor relations during the late twentieth century. Comprehensive statutory reform was needed to fix it, but such reform was a political impossibility. The NLRB was of little help. As two legal scholars lamented in 2009, the board was "ill-informed and without influence." The agency, they said, was notable for its "seeming inability to be proactive" in making labor law relevant in a postindustrial economy.[9]

This story is not wrong. But as the past several years have shown, it was incomplete. As it turned out, with greater political power—overwhelming public support for unions and a presidential administration responsive to that sentiment—labor law got better.[10] Led by General Counsel Jennifer Abruzzo, the Biden NLRB made labor law significantly more responsive to the contemporary needs of workers, employers, and the public, *without* legislative action. These legal innovations were built on the work of previous administrations, yet the Biden board, enabled by the moment and enabling the moment in return, consistently went bigger and bolder.

There are numerous examples. In 2023, the agency employed its underutilized rulemaking power to establish a workable joint employer standard, an integral step toward adapting labor law for the fissured economy (though, consistent with the theme of this essay, that rule has since been vacated by a Texas federal court).[11] But under the rule as envisioned, franchisors, parent companies, and more would have

---

6. Portions of this section were included in the author's brief for the Roosevelt Institute, "Labor Law Breaks Free: Reviving State Capacity to Protect Workers Under the NLRA," available here: https://rooseveltinstitute.org/publications/labor-law-breaks/.

7. Tomlins, *State and the Unions.*

8. Estlund, "Ossification of American Labor Law."

9. Fisk and Malamud, "NLRB in Administrative Law Exile."

10. Gallup, "Labor Unions."

11. National Labor Relations Board, "The Standard for Determining Joint Employer Status"; National Labor Relations Board, "NLRB's Joint-Employer Rule Vacated."

been required to collectively bargain with workers *formally employed by their business partners*, as to any terms and conditions of employment over which they had some control, directly or indirectly, in practice or in reserve. Notwithstanding the rule's immediate fate, it remains a blueprint for the future, showing that it is possible to make labor law work in an economy characterized by dispersed labor control.

In its 2023 *Cemex* decision, the board used its policymaking authority to address the massive ongoing challenge of employer coercion in union elections, consistent with the NLRA's inherent remedial limitations.[12] Since the 1980s, employers have increasingly opposed worker unionization campaigns, often through flatly illegal tactics. Again, the narrative has been that the board lacked the remedial power to meaningfully influence employer behavior. But under the *Cemex* doctrine, if an employer illegally undermines a union's majority—if it refuses to voluntarily recognize a union and then engages in unfair labor practices that destabilize the democratic process—the board can impose a remedy with teeth. It can order the employer to recognize and bargain with the union anyway. Previously, bargaining orders were treated as an extraordinary remedy, available only for the most egregious unfair labor practices. As a result, employers had won effective immunity for their garden-variety violations of law. But *Cemex* refuses to let the fact that employers regularly violate the law set the legal standard. As Seth Harris and I recently argued, unlawful employer resistance may have become "ordinary," in that it is common, but it remains extraordinarily destructive to the purposes of labor law and *Cemex* finally treats it as such.[13]

The Biden NLRB also championed the principle that the NLRA matters in *all* workplaces, union and nonunion. According to Abruzzo, the NLRA reshapes the default employment contract, limiting the kinds of conditions employers may impose on any workers. In May 2023, Abruzzo issued a legal memo indicating the Board's intention to take on employer-imposed noncompetition and nonsolicitation clauses. These, she argued, violate labor law's protection for concerted employee activity by unduly restricting worker choice, speech, and mobility.[14] In so doing, she radically expanded the potential relevance of labor law to the conditions faced by working people today.

And all along the way, the NLRB steadfastly enforced the law. Notwithstanding budget limitations and a staff much too small for even its pre-surge caseload, the board supported burgeoning worker demand for industrial democracy. With ten weeks left in fiscal year 2024, the NLRB had already received over 2,600 union election petitions—more than the 2,594 petitions received in *all* of 2023.[15] Moreover, it doggedly prosecuted unfair labor practices against the biggest and most powerful employers of the twenty-first century: According to one report, in the past few years,

12. Cemex Construction Materials Pacific, LLC, 372 NLRB No. 130 (August 25, 2023).
13. Harris and Reddy, "Tragedy to Triumph at Mercedes?"
14. General Counsel of the National Labor Relations Board, Memorandum GC 23-08, May 30, 2023.
15. Wiessner, "US Union Organizing."

the board filed over 125 complaints against Starbucks alone, alleging more than 1,000 instances of illegal behavior.[16]

With this kind of success, pushback was inevitable.

## The Unconstitutionality Bandwagon

The current spate of constitutional attacks against the NLRB began in earnest early in 2024—when, in the course of defending the rights of SpaceX employees, the board took on Elon Musk. In 2022, a group of SpaceX employees circulated a letter calling out the "culture of sexism, harassment and discrimination" which they believed "pervade[d] . . . the [SpaceX] workplace."[17] This culture, they insisted, began at the top, aided and abetted by Elon Musk and his incessant tweets. SpaceX fired these letter writers for insubordination. The workers then filed a charge with the board alleging retaliation for protected activity. On January 3, 2024, the board issued a complaint against SpaceX, finding reasonable cause to believe that the company had engaged in unlawful retaliation.[18]

The very next day, SpaceX sued the NLRB in federal district court in Texas.[19] SpaceX demanded that the court step in and legally prohibit the NLRB from fulfilling its statutory obligations. According to its complaint, SpaceX sought court relief from "an unlawful attempt by the [NLRB] to subject SpaceX to an administrative proceeding whose structure violates Article II, the Fifth Amendment, and the Seventh Amendment of the Constitution of the United States."[20] The board's structure, the complaint alluded, represented "the very definition of tyranny."[21]

Within a month, other employers joined the unconstitutionality bandwagon. None of them initially went as far as SpaceX—they did not directly sue the agency—but they defended themselves in ongoing enforcement proceedings with claims about the unconstitutionality of the board's structure. In an NLRB hearing in early 2024, for instance, a lawyer for Trader Joe's proclaimed a new affirmative defense: that "the structure and organization of [the agency] . . . is unconstitutional."[22] Amazon and Starbucks quickly raised similar defenses.[23] More recently, other affirmative lawsuits have been filed against the board. In April, SpaceX filed its *second* lawsuit against the NLRB, this time challenging the board's attempt to restrict its use of noncompete

16. Greenhouse, "Major US Corporations Threaten."

17. Maidenberg, "Eight Fired SpaceX Employees Allege Company Violated Labor Law."

18. Scheiber, "SpaceX Illegally Fired Workers."

19. Grush and Eidelson, "SpaceX Sues U.S. Labor Board over Fired Employees Case."

20. Space Exploration Techs. Corp. v. NLRB ("SpaceX"), S.D. Tex., No. 1:24-cv-00001, filed January 4, 2024 (hereafter cited as SpaceX Complaint).

21. Mueller, "Musk's SpaceX Seeks to Blow Up NLRB."

22. Jamieson, "Trader Joe's Attorney Argues NLRB Is 'Unconstitutional.'" In response to the attorney, the NLRB ALJ noted he would not be ruling on his own constitutionality; constitutional claims would need to be resolved in court. The attorney clarified that Trader Joe's sought only to preserve the issues for appeal and did not expect the ALJ to rule on them.

23. Giorno and Shapero, "Corporate Giants Aim to Hobble."

clauses.[24] In June, two energy companies (also facing board prosecution for alleged unfair labor practices) followed SpaceX's lead. They, too, sued the NLRB in Texas federal court.[25]

Across the lawsuits, there are three primary constitutional claims currently being raised. It is worth discussing each to emphasize what is, and what is not, at stake.

The first claim concerns whether the president has sufficient control over NLRB judges. Here, SpaceX and other employers argue that both NLRB members and its administrative law judges (ALJs) have *too much* judicial independence.[26] Rooted in a legal doctrine called the "unitary executive theory," their argument is that because Article II of the US Constitution vests "all executive power" in the president, the president must be able to exercise full and complete authority over the entire executive branch.[27] According to conservatives, this must include the power to terminate lesser executive officials, including ALJs, at will. But because, historically, administrative law has been shaped by a competing concern—that the judicial functions of agencies operate independently of their prosecutorial functions—the NLRA and the Administrative Procedures Act protect NLRB members and ALJs from arbitrary removal without cause.[28] This layer of judicial independence, according to the plaintiffs, improperly insulates the agency from the "constitutionally required degree of electoral accountability."[29]

A second claim concerns the scope of the Seventh Amendment's right to trial by jury and whether it should limit the board's authority to hear claims and provide remedies. According to SpaceX and others, the Biden NLRB's decision in *Thryv, Inc.*—a ruling that permits plaintiffs to recover for "direct or foreseeable" pecuniary harms, in addition to the traditional remedies of reinstatement and back pay—runs afoul of the Seventh Amendment.[30] According to these employers, monetary dam-

24. Over vigorous objection from the company, SpaceX's first suit was transferred from Texas to California, where most of the underlying events occurred. By filing a second suit, SpaceX created another opportunity to have its claims decided by the notoriously anti-agency Fifth Circuit. The Fifth Circuit includes the federal courts of Texas, Louisiana, and Mississippi. Fry, "Tracking Attacks on the NLRB: SpaceX Tries Its Luck Again"; Space Exploration Techs. Corp. v. NLRB ("SpaceX II"), W.D. Tex., No. 6:24-cv-00203, filed April 19, 2024.

25. Thompson, "In Lawsuit, Oil and Gas Companies." Other pending federal court cases that involve claims about the board's unconstitutionality include Kerwin v. Trinity Health Grand Haven Hospital, case number 1:24-cv-00445, filed in a Michigan federal court (within the Sixth Circuit Court of Appeals), in which the defendant hospital is disputing the board's constitutionality in response to a board petition for a Section 10(j) injunction; and Cortes v. National Labor Relations Board, case number 1:23-cv-02954, filed in 2023 in a federal court in DC (within the District of Columbia Circuit Court of Appeals). Cortes is a Starbucks barista who had unsuccessfully sought to decertify her store's new union. She is represented by the National Right to Work Legal Defense Foundation.

26. SpaceX Complaint.

27. Sunstein and Vermeule, "Unitary Executive."

28. 5 U.S.C. §§ 1202(d), 7521(a); 29 U.S.C. § 153(a).

29. SpaceX Complaint.

30. Thryv, Inc., 372 NLRB No. 22 (December 13, 2022); National Labor Relations Board, "Board Rules Remedies Must Compensate."

ages require a trial before a jury. Careful readers of labor law history may note that this was one of the claims raised and summarily rejected by the Supreme Court in *Jones & Laughlin*. As the court ruled in 1937, the Seventh Amendment applies only to suits at common law; it has never been interpreted to apply to administrative enforcement of statutory causes of action.[31] However, there has been a concerted conservative attempt in recent years to limit agency power by expanding the reach of the Seventh Amendment. SpaceX and others argue that evolving constitutional standards and the board's broader interpretation of its make-whole powers mean that *Jones & Laughlin* no longer controls.

A third claim concerns separation of powers. Employers assert that the NLRB improperly mixes its legislative, executive, and judicial functions.[32] While there are broader (and more worrisome) versions of this argument, SpaceX's initial complaint specifically focuses on the board's procedures for seeking Section 10(j) injunctions. Section 10(j) of the NLRA authorizes the general counsel to seek injunctions in federal court to stop unfair labor practices when stakes are particularly high. Agency rules require that the general counsel obtain approval from the board before doing so.[33] The reason for this procedure, ironically, is to protect defendants like SpaceX from the risk of overzealous prosecution by requiring quasi-judicial approval prior to going to court. But SpaceX contends that this procedure compromises the independence of the board's judicial role. Since the board is the ultimate adjudicator of unfair labor practices, SpaceX argues that it violates core separation of powers principles to allow them this one-sided sneak peek at claims that they may later consider as a neutral adjudicator.[34]

There are various other arguments percolating out there as well. The American Civil Liberties Union briefly argued that President Biden unconstitutionally terminated General Counsel Abruzzo's predecessor before appointing her. If a court were ever to adopt this argument, it could call into question all that has been accomplished on Abruzzo's watch.[35] Meanwhile, Amazon has attempted to revive the nondelegation doctrine—which the Supreme Court has not used to curtail agency power since 1935—to argue that the NLRB is unconstitutional because its broad discretion amounts to legislative power.[36]

### A War on the Administrative State

While the lawsuits against the NLRB are largely opportunistic, the specific claims being wielded by employers are not. Rather, these arguments have been decades in development, part of a comprehensive campaign by conservatives against what they

31. NLRB v. Jones & Laughlin Steel Corp., 301 U.S. 1 (1937).

32. SpaceX Complaint.

33. 29 U.S.C. § 160(j).

34. SpaceX Complaint.

35. American Civil Liberties Union, Case Nos. 05-CA-300367, 05-CA-302762.

36. Fry, "Tracking Attacks on the NLRB: Amazon Invokes the Major Questions Doctrine."

see as the outsized role of administrative agencies in modern governance. As such, for those wondering how courts might just *now* be discovering the constitutional infirmities of a ninety-year-old agency, that is not what is happening. These arguments are newly viable. Just five to ten years ago, before President Donald Trump's judicial appointees shifted the political leanings of the federal judiciary, these claims would likely have been deemed frivolous. This is because they seek to upend long-settled questions of law, from as far back as *Jones & Laughlin* itself. Make no mistake: They are trying to relitigate the New Deal.

And if their last term is any indication, this Supreme Court has few qualms about flipping over the whole table. In June of 2024, the court issued two major decisions, each scrapping settled administrative law principles, and each with important implications for the future of the NLRB and the viability of the constitutional claims against it.

In *SEC v. Jarkesy*, the court considered a case against the Securities and Exchange Commission (SEC). Here the plaintiffs raised two of the arguments currently pending against the NLRB—that the SEC's ALJs were not sufficiently accountable to the executive branch and that the Seventh Amendment prohibited the SEC from adjudicating certain claims that required a trial by jury (they also raised a third claim about the nondelegation doctrine).[37] While the Fifth Circuit Court of Appeals ruled against the SEC on all claims, the Supreme Court focused only on the Seventh Amendment issue. It held that the SEC acted unconstitutionally when it imposed civil penalties on a defendant for securities fraud. According to the court, administrative agencies could not award monetary damages intended to deter or punish without a jury trial.

Thanks to the remedial inadequacies of the NLRA, the court's holding in *Jarkesy* may be of limited relevance to the NLRB. The board lacks the power to punish, and its new monetary remedies remain compensatory, intended to reimburse a plaintiff for actual losses. Moreover, the court's avoidance in *Jarkesy* of whether the Constitution can tolerate "good cause" protection for administrative law judges may signal that it is *not* willing to adopt a legal theory that would thrust many administrative agencies into turmoil. Or perhaps the court is just biding its time. While it bides its time, though, the Fifth Circuit's decision ruling against the SEC on the ALJ issue remains good law in that circuit, incentivizing employers to keep filing suit there.

Second, in *Loper Bright Enterprises v. Raimondo*, the court overruled the long-standing administrative law principle known as *Chevron* deference, which held that courts should defer to reasonable agency interpretations of the law when the statute at issue is ambiguous or silent.[38] Interpreting the law, the court held, is a job for Article III courts and not administrative agencies. Given the centrality of *Chevron* deference

37. SEC v. Jarkesy, 603 U.S. ___ (2024).

38. The principle was named after the 1984 Supreme Court decision Chevron USA Inc. v. Natural Resources Defense Council, Inc., 467 U.S. 837 (1984), officially adopting it. Loper Bright Enterprises v. Raimondo, 603 U.S. ___ (2024).

to modern agency practice, *Loper Bright* will mean a major change in how administrative agencies operate. It will likely also mean a major power shift from agencies to the federal courts.

Again, what this decision will mean for the NLRB is unclear. *Chevron* has never been as foundational for the board as it has been for other agencies. In part this is because the court adopted NLRB-specific deference principles long before *Chevron*, grounded in Congress's clear delegation of policymaking authority to the board at the time of enactment.[39] Yet the court's conservative members have separately indicated a reluctance to continue traditional forms of deference to the board.[40] Whatever the standard applied, though, there seems little question that courts have been given the green light to more readily substitute their judgment for that of the NLRB.

### How Worried Should We Be?

What is likely to come of all these attacks? Given the complex and contingent relationship between law, politics, and social change, there is no clear answer.

The pessimistic view is that one way or another, the board will be incapacitated. It may have already lost its ability to deploy its expertise in labor relations independent of aggressive judicial scrutiny; it could now be embroiled in legal battles for years to come. Then, when it loses some or all of the pending claims, it will have to radically restructure its operations. Union lawyers are fast at work coming up with potential solutions: at-will judges, administrative juries, abandoning new remedies, abandoning rulemaking. This work will consume the board, diverting its attention from the working people who are currently clawing tooth and nail to organize workplaces previously seen as unorganizable.

There is also the worst-case scenario alluded to earlier. Although the pending challenges focus on relatively discrete board attributes and the NLRA is clear about the severability of its provisions, it is always possible that the court would refuse to separate the putatively unconstitutional elements of the NLRB's structure from the constitutional.[41] The court might accordingly enjoin the board from operating, until and unless Congress fixes the statute. Given the state of American politics today, it is unclear if Congress would do so. At that point, we return to the law of the jungle, the streets, or the states.[42]

---

39. 29 U.S.C. § 160(e), (f); NLRB v. Hearst Publications, 322 U.S. 111, 130 (1944). In a decision by the DC Circuit shortly after *Loper Bright* was decided, that court continued to afford the board "a very high degree of deference." Kullgren and Iafolla, "D.C. Circuit Signals Labor Board Shielded."

40. Starbucks Corporation v. McKinney, 602 U.S. ___ (2024); Glacier Northwest, Inc. v. International Brotherhood of Teamsters Local 174, 598 U.S. ____ (2023). Ironically, some conservatives have argued that the NLRB is unconstitutional precisely because Congress made it clear that the agency should be afforded deference in its legal and factual decisions. Giving the board that kind of deference, the argument goes, means an unconstitutional delegation of Article III power.

41. U.S.C. §166.

42. From the view of labor voluntarists, of course, this is not necessarily a bad thing. A return to unregulated industrial unrest may be dangerous for American labor unions, but it is not without risk for American employers either.

The more legally optimistic view is that these challenges do not approximate the magnitude of what was at stake in *Jones & Laughlin*. These challenges, even if successful, should mean procedural tweaks. And the NLRB is great at tweaks. Perhaps more than any other agency, the NLRB is used to being flexible, to making things work under less than ideal circumstances. The NLRB made things work when the NLRA was first enacted, and employers were so sure it would be found unconstitutional that they completely ignored the law, along with the board's entreaties to comply with it.[43] The NLRB made things work when it was permanently barred from engaging in expert economic analysis, even as expert economic analysis became the raison d'être of the modern administrative agency.[44] Fifteen years ago, the NLRB made things work when a Republican Congress refused to confirm a third member to the board, forcing it to operate for twenty-six months with only two members; it continued making it work when the Supreme Court went on to invalidate all five-hundred-plus decisions made by those two members, for lack of a quorum.[45] In the current war on administrative agencies, the NLRB is arguably at an advantage. It is used to the fight.

## Law and the Reshaping of the American Labor Movement

Right now, things look bleak. But they looked bleak in the run-up to *Jones & Laughlin* too. One great lesson of labor history is that law has never been a self-contained system. This is *not* to say that we should expect a miraculous change of heart at the Supreme Court anytime soon, at least not without a drastic increase in strikes. It is to suggest caution, though, in how we make sense of this moment. As legal historian William Forbath tells it, the American labor movement was indelibly marked by its early legal battles; the young movement's experience of "government by injunction" was a trauma that it never fully recovered from.[46] Even though labor unions have experienced many legal victories since then, the movement remains characterized by a deep-seated, essentializing mistrust of law as an institution.

How should working people and their supporters think about the promises and perils of law, in light of all the Biden NLRB accomplished *and* all the pushback that has resulted? The legal struggle is intertwined with the political struggle, and the struggle continues. ■

DIANA S. REDDY is a law professor and the Faculty Codirector for the Center for Law and Work at the University of California, Berkeley School of Law, where she teaches courses about the regulation of work, the role of labor unions in American democracy, and the relationship between economic justice and civil rights. She is also a Fellow with the Roosevelt Institute's Worker Power and Economic Security Program. Before entering legal academia, Diana was a litigator, representing labor unions and workers at the AFL-CIO,

---

43. Gross, *Making of the NLRB*.
44. Hafiz, "Economic Analysis in Labor Regulation."
45. New Process Steel, L.P. v. NLRB, 560 U.S. 674 (2010).
46. Forbath, *Law and the Shaping of the American Labor Movement*.

Altshuler Berzon LLP, and the California Teachers Association. She has a PhD in jurisprudence and social policy from UC Berkeley and received her law degree, magna cum laude, from NYU School of Law, where she was a Root Tilden Kern Scholar.

## References

Bureau of Labor Statistics. *Analysis of Strikes in 1937*. Accessed August 1, 2024. https://www.bls.gov/wsp/publications/annual-summaries/pdf/analysis-of-strikes-in-1937.pdf.

Estlund, Cynthia L. "The Ossification of American Labor Law." *Columbia Law Review* 102, no. 6 (2002): 1527–1612. https://doi.org/10.2307/1123792.

Fisk, Catherine, and Deborah Malamud. "The NLRB in Administrative Law Exile: Problems with Its Structure and Function and Suggestions for Reform." *Duke Law Journal* 58, no. 8 (2009): 2013–85. https://scholarship.law.duke.edu/dlj/vol58/iss8/3.

Forbath, William E. *Law and the Shaping of the American Labor Movement*. Cambridge, MA: Harvard University Press, 1991.

Fry, John. "Tracking Attacks on the NLRB: Amazon Invokes the Major Questions Doctrine." *OnLabor*, accessed July 14, 2024. https://onlabor.org/tracking-attacks-on-the-nlrb-amazon-invokes-the-major-questions-doctrine.

Fry, John. "Tracking Attacks on the NLRB: SpaceX Tries Its Luck Again." *OnLabor*, accessed July 13, 2024. https://onlabor.org/tracking-attacks-on-the-nlrb-spacex-tries-its-luck-again.

Gallup Inc. "Labor Unions." *Gallup.com*, August 31, 2007. https://news.gallup.com/poll/12751/Labor-Unions.aspx.

Giorno, Taylor, and Julia Shapero. "Corporate Giants Aim to Hobble National Labor Relations Board." *The Hill* (blog), February 28, 2024. https://thehill.com/business/4491063-corporate-giants-aim-to-hobble-national-labor-relations-board/.

Greenhouse, Steven. "Major US Corporations Threaten to Return Labor to 'Law of the Jungle.'" *The Guardian*, March 10, 2024. https://www.theguardian.com/us-news/2024/mar/10/starbucks-trader-joes-spacex-challenge-labor-board.

Gross, James A. *The Making of the NLRB: A Study in Economics, Politics, and the Law*. Albany: State University of New York Press, 1974.

Grush, Loren, and Josh Eidelson. "SpaceX Sues US Labor Board over Fired Employees Case (3)." *Bloomberg Law*, January 4, 2024. https://news.bloomberglaw.com/daily-labor-report/spacex-sues-us-labor-board-over-fired-employees-case.

Hafiz, Hiba. "Economic Analysis in Labor Regulation." *Wisconsin Law Review* 2017, no. 6 (2018): 1116–88. https://wlr.law.wisc.edu/wpcontent/uploads/sites/1263/2018/01/Hafiz-Final.pdf.

Harris, Seth, and Diana Reddy. "Tragedy to Triumph at Mercedes? How the NLRB and the Biden Administration Might Still Make Things Right for Workers." *Power at Work*, June 16, 2024. https://poweratwork.us/tragedy-to-triumph-mercedes.

Jamieson, Dave. "Trader Joe's Attorney Argues National Labor Relations Board Is 'Unconstitutional.'" *HuffPost*, January 26, 2024. https://www.huffpost.com/entry/trader-joes-attorney-nlrb-unconstitutional_n_65b41e7ae4b014b873b11cc2.

Kullgren, Ian, and Robert Iafolla. "D.C. Circuit Signals Labor Board Shielded from Chevron's Shift." *Bloomberg Law*, July 5, 2024. https://news.bloomberglaw.com/daily-labor-report/dc-circuit-signals-labor-board-shielded-from-chevrons-shift.

Maidenberg, Micah. "Eight Fired SpaceX Employees Allege Company Violated Labor Law." *Wall Street Journal*, November 17, 2022. https://www.wsj.com/articles/eight-fired-spacex -employees-allege-company-violated-labor-law-11668716597.

Mueller, Eleanor. "Musk's SpaceX Seeks to Blow Up NLRB." *Politico*, January 4, 2024. https:// www.politico.com/news/2024/01/04/musks-spacex-seeks-to-blow-up-nlrb-00133919.

National Labor Relations Board. "Board Rules Remedies Must Compensate Employees for All Direct or Foreseeable Financial Harms." Accessed July 13, 2024. https://www.nlrb.gov /news-outreach/news-story/board-rules-remedies-must-compensate-employees-for-all -direct-or.

National Labor Relations Board. "NLRB's Joint-Employer Rule Vacated by U.S. District Judge." https://www.nlrb.gov/news-outreach/news-story/nlrbs-joint-employer-rule-vacated-by -us-district-judge (accessed August 1, 2024).

National Labor Relations Board. "The Standard for Determining Joint-Employer Status." https://www.nlrb.gov/about-nlrb/what-we-do/the-standard-for-determining-joint -employer-status-final-rule (accessed August 1, 2024).

Rahman, K. Sabeel. "After Chevron: Political Economy and the Future of the Administrative State." LPE Project, July 24, 2023. https://lpeproject.org/blog/after-chevron-political -economy-and-the-future-of-the-administrative-state/.

Reddy, Diana. "After the Law of Apolitical Economy: Reclaiming the Normative Stakes of Labor Unions." *Yale Law Journal* 132, no. 5 (2023): 1213–1599. https://www.yalelawjournal.org /feature/after-the-law-of-apolitical-economy.

Scheiber, Noam. "SpaceX Illegally Fired Workers Critical of Musk, Federal Agency Says." *New York Times*, January 3, 2024, Business sec. https://www.nytimes.com/2024/01/03 /business/spacex-elon-musk-nlrb-workers.html.

Sunstein, Cass R., and Adrian Vermeule. "The Unitary Executive: Past, Present, Future." *Supreme Court Review* 2020, no. 1 (2021): 83–117. https://doi.org/10.1086/714860.

Thompson, Cameron. "In Lawsuit, Oil and Gas Companies Challenge Constitutionality of NLRB Hearing." *Courthouse News Service*, June 27, 2024. https://www.courthousenews .com/in-lawsuit-oil-and-gas-companies-challenge-constitutionality-of-nlrb-hearings/.

Tomlins, Christopher. *The State and the Unions: Labor Relations, Law, and the Organized Labor Movement in America, 1880–1960.* Cambridge: Cambridge University Press, 1985.

Totenberg, Nina. "The Supreme Court Is the Most Conservative in 90 Years." NPR, July 5, 2022. https://www.npr.org/2022/07/05/1109444617/the-supreme-court-conservative.

Wiessner, Daniel. "SpaceX Wins Block on US Labor Board Case over Severance Agreements." Reuters, July 10, 2024. https://www.reuters.com/legal/spacex-wins-block-us-labor-board -case-over-severance-agreements-2024-07-10/.

Wiessner, Daniel. "US Union Organizing, and Unions' Election Win Rate, Is Surging, NLRB Says." Reuters, July 17, 2024. https://www.reuters.com/legal/litigation/us-union-organizing -unions-election-win-rate-is-surging-nlrb-says-2024-07-17/.

# Why No Corporatism in the United States? American Versus German Models of Industrial Relations in the Early Postwar Era

Nelson Lichtenstein

Today industrial relations in the United States and Germany operate along strikingly divergent patterns, but in the early postwar years they had much in common. Indeed, the United States emulated Germany, and not so much the other way around. That might seem an exceedingly strange proposition, because Germany was just emerging from utter destruction and the United States and Britain were occupying powers in the late 1940s; moreover, the American economy then seemed a productive wonder, a model for others to follow. And within that economic colossus was a powerful trade union movement whose membership had risen fivefold in just fifteen years. Nevertheless, the de facto corporatism that characterized industrial relations in some key industries during the 1940s and 1950s contained many similarities to the regime that German unionists, employers, and politicians were seeking to construct, or reconstruct, in the early postwar era.

But within two decades, German and American unionists took quite different paths. In the 1950s and 1960s when Walter Reuther's United Auto Workers (UAW) sought to persuade German unionists of the virtues inherent in American-style collective bargaining, the Germans soundly rejected the gambit because it would have subverted the sectoral bargaining model they advanced and the social market economy they sought to preserve. And given the evident dysfunctionality of firm-centered collective bargaining in the United States, that German resistance seems to have made good sense, a view that many American unionists have now come to recognize.

## Corporatism in New Deal America

The great industries of Germany and the United States were not dissimilar. Steel, automobiles, coal, electrical products, chemicals, construction, textiles, and transport constituted the economic core in both nations. Many enterprises were very large,

*Labor: Studies in Working-Class History* Volume 22 • Issue 1
DOI 10.1215/15476715-11521334 © 2025 by Labor and Working-Class History Association

and many had long been wracked by strikes and strife from the nineteenth century onward. In Germany, beginning in the Weimar era and then resuming in surprisingly rapid fashion after the fall of Nazism, corporatist structures were developed to govern industry on a basis that might achieve a degree of social peace. Germany was not as corporatist as Sweden or Austria—the state played a weaker role—but many elements of what we think of as the corporatist arrangement were there: powerful employer associations that bargained for an entire industry or region, big unions seeking a recalibration of class relations on an industry-wide or even a national basis, and a state that framed and regulated industrial conflict through law and politics. Unions in Germany were often socialist, left-wing supporters of the Social Democratic Party (SPD, Sozialdemokratische Partei Deutschlands). Codetermination was both an ideological ideal and a legal reality, the latter never quite living up to the former.[1]

One might assume that little of this existed in the United States, where a system of firm-centered collective bargaining was backstopped by employer power, judicial writ, union parochialism, and the 1935 National Labor Relations Act (NLRA). But during the New Deal era and its immediate aftermath, industrial relations in many of the key industries listed above were often corporatist in a de facto fashion. Firm-centered collective bargaining existed, of course, but it was frequently subordinated to conflict resolution structures that had a highly "European" flavor.[2]

A politicized system of interclass conflict and accommodation put not just wages and working conditions in play across the negotiating table, but the fate of the New Deal impulse itself. Elections, strikes, organizing campaigns, legislative battles, government edicts, and labor negotiations were seamlessly interwoven. By 1945 the trade unions stood near their twentieth-century apogee. About 30 percent of all US wage earners were organized, a density greater than at any time before and a level that for the first time approached the coverage of that in northern Europe. Though he wasn't very happy about it, in 1947 the sober-minded Harvard economist Sumner Slichter famously counted US trade unions "the most powerful economic organizations which the country has ever seen." A year later C. Wright Mills, the radical sociologist, would write a book about American trade union leaders and title it *The New Men of Power*.[3]

The New Deal had thoroughly politicized all relations between the union movement, the business community, and the state. In this system, organized social blocs struck periodic economic bargains through a process of political, society-wide negotiation. Corporatism of this sort placed capital-labor relations within a centralized context, where representatives of the contending "peak" organizations bargained politically for their respective constituencies. Thus, in November 1945 President Harry Truman convened a tripartite conference designed to project such arrangements into the postwar

---

1. My understanding of German politics cum industrial relations has relied on Silvia, *Holding the Shop Together*; Thelen, *Union of Parts*; and Markovits, *Politics of West German Trade Unions*.

2. An elaboration of this idea is found in Lichtenstein, "From Corporatism to Collective Bargaining," 122–52.

3. Slichter, *Challenge of Industrial Relations*, 4; Mills, *New Men of Power*.

years, establishing a new, nationwide wage policy and "union security" guideline that would more clearly and permanently demark the frontier whereby union power met the prerogatives of management. Truman's gambit failed, thereby setting the stage for a massive set of work stoppages in 1945 and 1946, which, in the absence of wartime price controls, touched off the debilitating price-wage spiral that did much to prepare the way for the conservative, anti-labor Congress that held sway after the 1946 elections.[4]

Another failure, but an instructive one in terms of any German-US comparison, came with American trade union advocacy, during the 1940s and early 1950s, of a set of "industry councils" designed to inject a governmental and union voice into the highest levels of corporate decision-making, not unlike codetermination in the German iron and steel industry (*Montanmitbestimmung*). Historians of German industrial relations have noted that the deployment of this most far-reaching example of worker-manager partnership had the endorsement of a still-influential slice of the postwar occupation authorities, especially the British, who were nationalizing outright those very same industries at home.[5] But the German reform also came with a relative paucity of resistance from the Konrad Adenauer government and the conservative parties, not only because in 1951, when the law was passed, the memory of Nazi destruction of independent unionism in those industries was still fresh, but also because German Catholics, including Adenauer himself, saw such governing arrangements as a step toward an organicist governance of the plant community. In 1949 a German Catholic Social Conference had gone on record supporting codetermination, and in the early 1950s so too did the Christian Democratic Union faction in the German Parliament.[6]

In the United States something similar was happening—if not in legislation, then certainly in aspiration. Beginning early in World War II Philip Murray, the leader of the steelworker union in the United States, and also a Catholic, put forward an industrial council plan designed to integrate labor and the state into a tripartite governance of a steel industry now increasingly subject to governmental wage and production controls. Inspired by the social reformist encyclicals of Pope Leo XIII and by NLRA wage- and price-setting experiments, a new set of corporativist councils in steel, auto, aircraft, and other war industries would bring together representatives of labor, management, and the new mobilization agencies to jointly administer those industries now so vital to the war effort.[7] The Murray proposals were hailed by liberals and progressive Catholics but were considered far too visionary until the up-and-coming Walter Reuther of the UAW captured headlines with a program to convert Detroit auto factories into "one great production unit" to fulfill Roosevelt's ambition to manufacture fifty thousand aircraft a year. The "Reuther plan" provided a detailed blueprint for speeding defense production and advancing a practical social democratic reorganization of the auto industry.[8]

4. Zieger, *CIO*, 141–252; Workman, "Manufacturing Power," 279–301.

5. Fink, *Undoing the Liberal World Order*, 48–74.

6. Markovits, *Politics of West German Trade Unions*, 79; McGaughey, "Codetermination Bargains," 35.

7. Brody, "Origins of Modern Steel Unionism," 28–29.

8. Lichtenstein, *Walter Reuther*, 160–67.

After the war, elements of such tripartite governance could be readily found in the steel and coal industries, in garment manufacture, and in trucking and among the Hollywood film studios, where industry associations bargained with strong trade unions under a regulatory regime that sought to stabilize and rationalize prices, wages, and markets in the years following World War II. In the steel industry, this American version of German codetermination never achieved the formalization envisioned by the industrial council plans, but for more than two decades at midcentury, the federal government presided over tripartite arrangements in which virtually all the key decisions affecting steel wages and working conditions were decided either in the White House itself or some other government agency. All this largely took place on an ad hoc basis, but so regular was the recourse to such corporatist arrangements that governance of the American steel industry looked rather similar to that taking place in Germany, where IG Metall, the big West German union in steel, automobiles, and electrical manufacturing, also bargained with the steel industry on a sectoral basis.[9]

In the US coal industry, corporatism was even more deeply entrenched. This was an industry where half a century of bitter conflict had generated a regime of industrial anarchy. The United Mine Workers (UMW) saw cartelization of an industry composed of hundreds of mining operations, many price and wage "chiselers," as the only solution that might generate stability. During the New Deal, mine-worker militancy was for the first time backstopped by governmental regulation of prices, wages, and markets. Thereafter, and for a third of a century, the UMW and the association of coal mine operators jointly governed the industry, with tonnage royalties the crucial stabilizing mechanism. They were structured to penalize nonunion coal production while paying for an elaborate hospital and pension scheme largely controlled by the union. In the late 1950s the demand for coal was on the decline, so poverty spread throughout Appalachia, indicative of the socioeconomic limits inherent in the corporatist governance of only a single industry.[10]

Strike action that sought a corporatist outcome may well have been best exemplified by the first big postwar automobile industry strike. Under Walter Reuther's leadership the UAW struck General Motors for 113 days in the fall and winter of 1945–46. Reuther called for a 30 percent increase in wages without a rise in the cost of cars. GM denounced his demand as un-American and socialist, but in reality Reuther was seeking to put some backbone into the Truman administration's efforts to sustain price controls and working-class living standards during the demobilization era. To forestall the widely expected postwar slump, left Keynesians like Reuther were not so much interested in a new round of government spending, the fiscal prescription favored by liberals a generation afterward. Instead, the UAW program, "Purchasing Power for Prosperity," saw the progressive redistribution of income as the key lever by which unions and the government might sustain aggregate demand. Or, as Reuther put it early in 1946, "The fight of the General Motors workers is a fight to save trulyfree enterprise from death at the hands of its self-appointed champions."[11]

9. Lichtenstein, *Labor's War at Home*, 67–81; Stebenne, *Arthur Goldberg*; Smemo, Sonti, and Winant, "Conflict and Consensus," 39–73.

10. Vittoz, *New Deal Labor Policy*, 47–69, 106–18; Dubofsky and Van Tine, *John L. Lewis*, 371–86, 415–40.

11. Lichtenstein, *Walter Reuther*, 270.

If the state was to be an organic element in the construction of a corporatist regime, de facto or formal, then the labor movement had to make its political weight felt in an aggressive fashion. The United States had no labor party, but both the old American Federation of Labor and the new Congress of Industrial Organizations built political machines that gave labor a distinctive, well-defined political profile at both the national and local levels. American unions invented the political action committee in the 1940s: During the 1944 and 1948 elections, both union federations proved essential to New Deal reelection efforts in the urban, industrial North. Labor wanted to "realign" the Democratic Party by purging the Dixiecrats, and the CIO toyed with the idea of building a new, labor-based party. Heavily unionized states like New York, Pennsylvania, Ohio, Michigan, Illinois, and California were industrial powerhouses at midcentury. Unionism boosted turnout and Democratic Party loyalty for fully a third of the electorate, so partisan politics in the early postwar era had something of a social democratic flavor. From 1948 until 1964 every Democratic candidate for president launched his campaign with a Labor Day rally in Detroit's Cadillac Square.[12]

## In the United States: Confident Capitalists

But the larger ambitions of the union movement were defeated in the immediate postwar years. A union-backed corporatism would not be the American way. Since the early years of this century, scholars and journalists have devoted much ink to explaining why the American working class is "exceptional" when compared with the ostensibly more radical and/or class-conscious workers of Europe and Latin America. But the most exceptional element in the American system of labor-capital relations has been the hostility managers have shown toward both the regulatory state and virtually all systems of worker representation.[13]

Business hostility to trade unionism and to the state structures that supported it arose, first, out of a profound ideological commitment to what most businessmen saw as their inherent managerial prerogatives; second, it reflected the relatively decentralized, hypercompetitive structure of many industries across a huge market of great regional variation. The tradition of American management was one of self-confidence and autonomy. In contrast to their counterparts in Britain or Germany, American businessmen had presided over economic institutions that were of both continental scope and vast revenue long before the rise of a powerful state or the emergence of overt class politics. Although the government famously aided railroad development in the nineteenth century, such assistance and regulation proved the exception rather than the rule when it came to the great industries of the second industrial revolution: chemicals, autos, rubber, food processing, chain stores, and film. This legacy made business leaders hugely jealous of their prerogatives when they confronted both the new unionism and the New Deal. Indeed, it was in the 1930s that American executives first began to use the term *free enterprise* to describe the American capitalist system.

---

12. Gall, *Politics of Right to Work*, 55–93; Brody, *Workers in Industrial America*, 215–21; Plotke, *Building a Democratic Political Order*, 190–226; Boyle, *UAW and the Heyday of American Liberalism*, 35–82.

13. See generally Jacoby, *Masters to Managers*, 173–200; Gordon, *New Deals*, 5–34.

Such nomenclature reflected an effort, however crudely put, to distinguish US conditions from those abroad where the state, the cartel, the unions, and most parties of the left often constrained entrepreneurial activity and regulated the labor market. Business conservatives labeled the New Deal "creeping socialism." They declared industry-wide bargaining "monopoly unionism."[14] Echoing many of these sentiments, F. A. Hayek's *The Road to Serfdom*, which the University of Chicago Press first published as an academic tome in 1944, was selling hundreds of thousands of copies each year by the end of the decade.[15]

Meanwhile, American business, large as well as small, had emerged from the war with enormous sophistication and an aura of patriotic success. Unlike their counterparts in continental Europe, or even the British Isles, who had been tarred with the brush of collaboration or appeasement, American business leaders found the wartime experience one of both commercial success and political advance. They felt little need for the kind of state-sponsored labor-management collaboration that helped legitimize a mixed capitalist economy in Germany, France, and Italy in the immediate postwar era. American employers never came to see a system of collective bargaining as a lesser evil when compared to socialist radicalism or state regulation.[16]

The contrast with Germany was stark. From the nineteenth century onward a reactionary "iron and rye" coalition had sustained Prussian militarism and a focus on the economic and political domination of Eastern Europe. Most business associations were powerful and hostile to both trade unionism and democracy, certainly of the Weimar sort. After 1933, collaboration with the Nazi regime was the norm. Thus, in the unsettled years right after the end of World War II the leaders of virtually all German enterprises and business associations were desperate to win a measure of democratic legitimacy. In the East, the Soviets were dismantling whole factories, while in the West the Allies broke up eight of the most notorious industrial combines, including I. G. Farben and the Krupp steel and armaments firm. When in 1950 German businesses created the Organization of German Employers Associations (BDA), it was both far more centralized and far more committed to collective bargaining than anything in the United States. Indeed, it was the BDA that in 1953 produced a basic program, "Reflections on the Social Order," that became an ideological and negotiating touchstone for many years. It advocated cooperative labor-management relations within an open "social market economy" as the best means to promote social stability and economic growth.[17]

When he visited West Germany in the early 1950s, Clark Kerr, director of UC Berkeley's Institute of Industrial Relations, was impressed by the self-discipline of the

---

14. Glickman, *Free Enterprise*, 79–110; Vogel, "Why Businessmen Distrust Their State," 45–78; Gordon, "Why No Corporatism in the United States," 29–46.

15. For a discussion of Hayek's impact see Brinkley, *End of Reform*, 157–61.

16. Maier, *In Search of Stability*, 153–84; Carew, *Labour Under the Marshall Plan*; Wilson, *Destructive Creation*, 241–88.

17. Silvia, *Holding the Shop Together*, 184–90; Otto Jacobi and Walter Muller-Jentsch, "West Germany: Continuity and Structural Change."

employer associations, a sharp contrast to the go-it-alone propensity of so many US firms. In an undoubted reference to the difficulties Kerr had personally encountered as a West Coast mediator during the war and afterward, he observed that "employer organization in Germany runs counter to no established tradition of an individual firm's independence—quite the contrary." He was struck by the highly un-American disinclination of individual firms to bargain directly and alone with a specific trade union. Instead, the unions had themselves lobbied the occupation authorities to allow employers to once again form industry-wide associations so that sectoral bargaining might resume on an even more stable basis than during the Weimar era. (This was a project Kerr had tried to advance in the United States, to limited effect.) In turn, the German trade union movement was less concerned with shop-level bargaining on behalf of the daily needs of its members than with "class representation at high political levels," a "mild form of class war with the employer group over broad questions of societal organization."[18]

### Firm-Centered Collective Bargaining

The 1947 Taft-Hartley law prefigured much of US labor's postwar retreat. Union failure to win some leverage over corporate pricing policy in 1946 represented a defeat for the kind of politicized economic bargaining that was so distasteful to American businessmen. When an inflationary spiral during the summer and fall of that year did much to discredit the Rooseveltian state, ten million working-class voters remained at home in the midterm elections. The result was a Republican sweep and the election of a new Congress that put the containment and the privatization of collective bargaining at the top of its agenda.[19]

Backed by a coalition of business conservatives, southern Bourbons, and anti-labor ideologues, the new Republican Congress quickly passed the Taft-Hartley Act over President Harry Truman's veto. Passage of the law proved a milestone, not only for the actual legal restrictions it imposed on the trade unions but also as a symbol of the shifting relationship between labor, state, and capital at the dawn of the postwar era. By purging radicals from their leadership, constraining interunion solidarity, and making new organizing more difficult, Taft-Hartley made certain that for the unions, the next several decades would generate an increasingly insular, firm-centered collective bargaining regime. It encouraged trade union parochialism and penalized any serious effort to project a class-wide strategy.[20]

These were the political and social constraints that C. Wright Mills labeled "the main drift," what a generation of industrial relations experts would define as "free collective bargaining," and what Walter Reuther would reluctantly endorse as the only practical road forward for American labor. Thus, in a radio debate of May 1946, when labor's corporatist aspirations still seemed realizable, Reuther told his listeners that rhetoric about a "government-controlled economy" was a big-business scare tactic. But in the

18. Kerr, "Collective Bargaining in Postwar Germany," 324, 325–26, 330.

19. Jacobs, *Pocketbook Politics*, 221–31.

20. Lichtenstein, *State of the Union*, 114–25.

wake of the massive Republican victory of November 1946, Reuther made a rhetorical about-face, now urging "free labor" and "free management" to join in solving their problems; otherwise, a "superstate will arise to do it for us." Still later, after the Taft-Hartley restrictions were in place, Reuther put the issue even more bluntly: "I'd rather bargain with General Motors than with the government.... General Motors has no army."[21]

In the United States, the de facto corporatism that structured industrial relations in coal and steel would prove the exception. Much more typical was the sort of bargaining that put the UAW, the Packinghouse Workers, or the United Rubber Workers in direct negotiations with an individual corporation: General Motors, Armour Meatpacking, or Firestone Rubber. Until the 1970s such periodic bargains between leading companies and powerful unions often generated a "pattern" that extended to other firms in the same industry sector. This pattern bargaining constituted a kind of "soft corporatism" in which critical wage and benefit bargains negotiated between a big union and a large firm would set the norm, thus generating the kind of wage advances and social welfare settlements in the United States that were characteristic of the more formally corporatist industry-labor relationships in northern Europe. To avoid unionization, managers at IBM, DuPont, TRW, Kodak, Weirton Steel, Polaroid, and other unorganized firms in the core industrial sector usually tracked the pattern established in automobiles and steelmaking.[22]

But no matter how good the wages, the firm-centered character of this bargaining system generated the kind of workplace parochialism that soon gave capital a decisive advantage. During these years, strikes and lockouts were far more frequent in the United States than in Germany. There was no "labor-management accord" in the United States. Instead, trench warfare was the norm as each union and enterprise probed enemy lines for opportunistic advantage. After the recession of 1957–58, managers were as likely to be the aggressors as organized labor. Corporations held the initiative when it came to the introduction of new technology, the redeployment of capital, and the pattern of enterprise growth or decline. Although workers might stop production for a week or a month, management always had the option to do so permanently, by shifting capital to a new facility, state, or nation. And because workers had to create a crisis, to halt service or production to make their voice heard, capital seemed the champion of social peace in the court of public opinion and in the corridors of power. Thus, working-class militancy, if confined to any given work site—or even an entire company—had a self-limiting character, because it generated both higher production costs and overt industrial disharmony, which management sought to flee. This was not always apparent during the 1940s and 1950s, when unemployment was low and production capacity in high demand, but it became disastrously clear as early as the late 1950s, when the great deindustrialization of the urban Midwest began in earnest.[23]

21. Mills, *New Men of Power*, 233–39; Lichtenstein, *Walter Reuther*, 261.

22. Stebenne, *Arthur Goldberg*, 120–53; Stieber, *U.S. Industrial Relations 1950–1980*, 1–46.

23. A discussion of why the United States had no "labor-management" accord can be found in Lichtenstein, *State of the Union*, 98–140; for good exemplifications of capital mobility see Cowie, *Capital Moves*, 41–99.

In Germany, by way of contrast, sectoral bargaining created a very different terrain of struggle. In the United States the organization of a particular workplace or company was the lifeblood of union power and influence, thus incentivizing managerial resistance. In Germany, union membership—majority or minority—mattered only indirectly, because bargaining happened at the sectoral level and agreements applied to both unionized and nonunionized workers in participating firms. Thus, in Germany the Ford Motor Company had no recognition agreement with IG Metall. Instead, Ford dealt directly with its works council on plant problems and only indirectly with IG Metall on pay matters via the employers federation of which it is a leading member. Almost all works council members are active in IG Metall, but a creative tension is nevertheless often present between the council, the national union, and the company. German unions have therefore remained relatively strong in the private sector even as union membership has diminished, whereas in the United States low union density has devastated private sector union power.[24]

In the United States even the soft corporatism embodied through pattern bargaining had a remarkably anemic life. Where unions were weak, as in electrical products and textiles, or where domestic competition was fierce, as in automotive parts and food processing, wage and benefit guidelines established in Detroit, Pittsburgh, or Chicago were reproduced only imperfectly. In 1947, for instance, retail clerks earned about two-thirds as much as autoworkers, but after the first big inflationary surge of the late 1960s and early 1970s they took home only one-third as much. Even in the unionized auto parts industry only about one-quarter of all companies, employing 40 percent of the workforce, followed the Big Three pattern during the 1950s.[25] Nor did the corporatized welfare state encompass more than a highly segmented fraction of the American working class. White male workers in stable firms were its chief beneficiaries. Women, whose work careers were often episodic, were far less likely to build up the continuous employment time necessary for a pension or a long vacation. Likewise, African American and Latino men found that the firm-centered benefit system worked against them because their disproportionately high level of employment in low-wage, marginal firms often deprived them of full access to the social benefits and regular wages characteristic of the core economy.

Because so much of the postwar social struggle took place at the level of the firm rather than within a broader political arena, the American industrial relations system reinforced the economy's tendency to construct such segmented and unequal benefit and compensation schemes. This multitiered system of social provision has served to erode solidarity within the working class and made it difficult to counter claims that welfare spending and the push for social equity were a zero-sum game, with one section of the working class advantaged over another. In turn, "big labor" was often perceived (and all too often perceived itself) as a special interest group,

24. Jager, "German Model of Industrial Relations," 7–8.
25. US Department of Labor, *Handbook of Labor Statistics*, 201–3; Levinson, "Pattern Bargaining," 299.

whose collectively bargained contracts harmed consumers and benefited only a slice of the working class.[26]

## Walter Reuther Versus the Germans

These dysfunctionalities may well have been difficult to foresee in the late 1950s when Walter Reuther sought to take abroad the UAW system of firm-centered bargaining. By then the steadily advancing wages and benefits of American automobile workers seemed to speak volumes. In trade union circles Reuther was an international celebrity, a representative of all that seemed politically progressive and organizationally sophisticated in the world's dominant economy. His chief goal was to strengthen communications and build a set of world automobile councils composed of unions representing workers laboring within a single multinational firm. General Motors and Ford were the key targets, but Volkswagen, whose cars were already pouring into the United States, was not far behind. By the late 1950s tariff barriers were coming down and US "multinationals" were investing abroad. Volkswagen (VW) and BMW were beginning to carve out a slice of the US market. "The day of the purely U.S. auto corporation is gone forever," Reuther told European unionists in 1959. "Profits know no patriotism. . . . Technologies are the same and corporate policies are uniform, yet the workers are divided by national differences in social policies and in trade union custom and development. This is a division we must bridge."[27]

Like most American trade unionists of that time, Reuther favored free trade and rejected protectionist measures both as a matter of internationalist principle and because US industry was so competitive and productive. But to safeguard the jobs and incomes of his members Reuther wanted some assurance that the huge wage differentials then in existence—in 1958 Ford workers in the United States earned four times as much as German autoworkers—would soon narrow. At a 1959 conference of the International Metalworkers' Federation (IMF), where Reuther was chair of the world automotive department, he called the German export drive "wage dumping."[28]

To solve the problem Reuther envisioned a sharp increase in wages and a rapid reduction of hours for workers in those industries—chief among them automobile manufacturing—where postwar productivity gains had outstripped improvements in wages and working conditions. "We have to find a rational way to bring to bear the maximum power of international solidarity," he told an IMF congress meeting in Rome in 1961, "or we will be isolated and divided, weak and defenseless in the face of the growing power of international capital to exploit us separately."[29] He soon proposed to "coordinate bargaining with the international corporations" through a "practical organization of corporation councils representing wage earners" throughout the world auto industry.[30]

26. Edsall, *Chain Reaction*, 116–53; Klein, *For All These Rights*, 204–57.

27. Barnard, *American Vanguard*, 376.

28. Lichtenstein, *Walter Reuther*, 338.

29. Opel, *Seventy-Five Years of the Iron International*, 172.

30. UAW, *19th Constitutional Convention*, 268.

European unionists hailed Reuther's confident internationalism,[31] but even among comradely unionists within the IMF, Reuther encountered much resistance. This was especially true of the Social Democrats who led IG Metall. IG Metall was not a German version of the UAW. As a union for the entire metalworking sector, IG Metall had no special divisions for individual firms (VW was a partial exception). Strikes were usually conducted on a regional basis by workers in a variety of companies. Because no single industry employed a majority of its membership, union leaders saw productivity bargaining of the sort prevalent in the United States as highly divisive. Higher wages for workers in high-productivity firms was a recipe for intraclass division. Equally important, IG Metall's links to the Social Democratic Party were qualitatively far closer and more decisive than those between union leaders and Democrats in the United States; collective bargaining and political action, therefore, were organically linked. In the 1950s and 1960s German trade unionists saw the reconstruction of industry as a national project predicated on the maintenance of a relatively egalitarian wage structure and a labor market regulated by the state. There was some opportunism here, in part based on the low-wage advantage then enjoyed by German carmakers in the international market, but IG Metall's rejection of the linkage between wages and company-specific productivity represented a fundamental critique of one of the key elements of the UAW's famed Treaty of Detroit.[32]

Centralized bargaining was advanced in the mid-1950s when the nation's most important labor federation, the German Trade Union Confederation (DGB), adopted a new "action program" in which the achievement of a forty-hour workweek was a high priority. In 1956 IG Metall made the crucial breakthrough when Gesamtmetall, the association of metalworking employers, signed the Bremen Accord, the first in a series of agreements on working time reductions, which in turn set the pattern for almost all of German industry. Significantly, the Bremen Accord enabled IG Metall's top leadership to wrest even more control over collective bargaining from regional officers, a centralization of union authority ardently endorsed by Gesamtmetall and other employer associations.[33]

Thus, Reuther's efforts to strengthen the world automobile councils and coordinate transnational bargaining proved controversial. He wanted the IMF to devote more of its resources to the auto campaign than to the rest of metalworking, and in the mid-1960s he repeatedly pressed for the extension of the auto council construct to cover workers at Chrysler, Fiat, Simca, Rootes, and Volkswagen. By the mid-1960s Walter Reuther and his brother Victor, then in charge of the UAW's international affairs department, were in frequent dispute with the AFL-CIO's George Meany and his

31. For example, Reuther won an enthusiastic response from over half a million Berliners at a 1959 Mayday rally next to the Brandenburg Gate. Sydney Gruson, "West Berliners Affirm Freedom in Record Rally," *New York Times*, May 2, 1959, 1.

32. Markovits, *Politics of West German Trade Unions*, 174–236 passim; Jacobi and Muller-Jentsch, "West Germany: Continuity and Structural Change"; Alexis, "Neo-Corporatism and Industrial Relations," 75–92.

33. Thelen, *Union of Parts*, 81.

CIA-connected operatives, Jay Lovestone and Irving Brown. The latter three thought European social democrats naive or worse when it came to fighting the Cold War, and they considered the Germany-centered IMF "dangerously effective." By contrast, the Reuther brothers saw progressives and socialists in the union movement, in Africa and Latin America as well as Europe, as the most effective allies and comrades in the anticommunist struggle. Not unexpectedly, German unionists found Reuther a far more sympathetic figure when it came to this ideological fight.[34] But those Cold War fireworks have obscured the degree to which Meany and Reuther were in substantial agreement when it came to how trade unions should actually advance working-class interests: Both thought the American brand of firm-centered bargaining the only road forward. It was the essence of the "free collective bargaining" that eschewed political radicalism and kept the state at arm's length.[35]

The Reutherite strategy had some support in German trade union circles. At Ford and Opel, a GM subsidiary, trade unionists in the late 1950s and early 1960s favored a decentralized bargaining regime so as to force these high-productivity companies to offer wages above those negotiated by IG Metall's large, regional bargaining units. Agitation along these lines boosted union density and shop-floor activism, creating the more militant level of unionism that all IG Metall leaders sought. Hans Matthofer, head of the IG Metall Education Department, endorsed Reuther's enterprise-oriented approach toward this end. Matthofer had spent years in the postwar United States, where he developed personal contacts with a number of key UAW figures, including Victor Reuther. Matthofer came to regard UAW bargaining strategy as a model IG Metall should emulate, favoring a set of separate negotiations with Ford in Germany and, beyond that, participation in the world auto councils that Reuther wanted the IMF and the UAW to set up. By the early 1960s, he was the de facto spokesman for the shop militants who argued that IG Metall's high degree of centralization was both undemocratic and geared toward a minimal set of wage standards that thwarted significant wage increases within the highly profitable automobile firms especially Ford, Opel, and VW.[36]

However, Reuther and Matthofer met with determined resistance from IG Metall president Otto Brenner (fig. 1) and a large majority of that union's top leadership. Brenner and Reuther had both been born in 1907, had been skilled metalworkers in their youth, and had lurched to the left in the early years of the Great Depression. Nevertheless, they were steadfast anti-Stalinists by the time they became union leaders in the 1940s. Brenner was a left-wing Social Democrat, but as leader of IG Metall in the 1960s, he made it clear that decentralization schemes needed to be treated "with great

34. Jay Lovestone, "Report on Meetings of Executive Committee of International Metal Workers Federation," San Francisco, November 27–30, 1972, 2 in file 8, box 22, IMF: Correspondence, 1971–1975, George Meany Memorial Archives, University of Maryland; for the most complete story see Carew, *American Labour's Cold War Abroad.*

35. Schuhrke, *Blue-Collar Empire.* Schuhrke makes the point that in Latin America and Africa US-style collective bargaining could not work, even when attempted by the most conservative of unionists.

36. Fetzer, "Exporting the American Model?," 182–85.

**FIGURE 1.** Otto Brenner: *Porträt Vorsitzunder IG Metall Otto Brenner,* courtesy of Archiv der sozialen Demokratie, Godesberger Allee 149, 53175 Bonn, Germany.

**FIGURE 2.** Walter Reuther: *Photograph of President Truman in the Oval Office, Conferring with Labor Leader Walter Reuther* (detail). Photograph by Abbie Rowe, Harry S. Truman Presidential Library.

caution" because they might open the door to an unconstrained syndicalism. A wholesale shift to company bargaining would mean that workers in less productive firms and sectors were likely to lose out, which would lead to tensions within IG Metall.[37]

The irony here is considerable. Walter Reuther (fig. 2) was proposing a de facto alliance with the German militants, some now evoking an early New Left sensibility, but that species of autoworker internationalism would have subverted the corporatist wage egalitarianism championed by IG Metall and the DGB. Indeed, as European economic and political integration became more of a reality in the 1970s, IG Metall took the lead in establishment of an exclusively European Metalworkers Federation designed to advance working-class interests within a new set of corporatist structures.[38] At the UAW's urging, the IMF did set up a series of world automobile councils, but Brenner and other German union leaders made sure that they merely

37. Thelen, *Union of Parts,* 89; Fetzer, "Exporting the American Model?," 180–81, 186–87. Fetzer points out that both GM and Ford management feared shop militancy and therefore favored Brenner's sectoral bargaining strategy. With the rise of global competition at the end of the twentieth century, they would reverse course and seek enterprise-level bargaining.

38. "Structure, Purpose and Objectives of the EMF," file 19, box 22, IMF: Correspondence, 1975–76.

shared information and insights as to corporate strategy; they were not collective bargaining institutions.[39]

Otto Brenner made a comradely appearance at the UAW's 1966 convention in Long Beach, but by this point IG Metall had effectively thwarted Reuther's ambitions and those of the German union's own internal oppositionists. The SPD entry into a coalition government in 1966 strengthened the commitment of top IG Metall officials to centralized bargaining, since any plant- or company-level wage advance would prove detrimental to union participation in the national-level incomes policy advocated by the Social Democratic government. That stance had its dangers, of course: The eruption of shop-floor militancy across Europe—from the May–June factory occupations in France to the Italian "hot autumn" and the German wildcat strikes in steel and auto—made clear that corporatism might contain the seeds of its own destruction. Brenner and his leadership comrades therefore channeled demands for decentralized power within the union into a struggle to extend the rights of works councils vis-à-vis management, often backing the informal "wage drift" that enhanced the real incomes of workers in high-productivity firms. But equally important, Brenner relied on Willy Brandt's Social Democratic government to enact, in 1972, a new Works Constitution Act that gave all works councils, and not just those in coal and steel, more power over plant issues not involving a general wage advance. In sharp contrast to most unionized workplaces in the United States, German managers had to consult works councils on changes in production systems, job assignments, and reclassifications.[40] Union institutional influence was further advanced in 1976 when Helmut Schmidt's Social Democratic government enacted a new Codetermination Act requiring companies with more than two thousand employees to have half of the supervisory board of directors as representatives of the workers, something virtually unheard of in the United States.[41]

In the 1960s the US government also wanted wage restraint, especially in pattern-setting industries such as steel, auto, and construction. This "jawboning" had an ad hoc character and was hardly predicated on the sort of political bargain the DGB struck with Brandt's SPD government. Labor in the United States won nothing from the Democrats comparable to the German Works Constitution Act of 1972. During the brief mid-1960s window of liberal-labor opportunity in the United States, most unions cheered passage of the civil rights laws, Medicare, and immigration reform,

39. Rebhan, *Trade Unions and the World*, 27–28. Some monetary and training assistance was also offered to auto industry unions in repressive but newly industrialized countries, especially in Spain, Brazil, and South Africa.

40. Rebhan, *Trade Unions and the World*, 90–100; Brenner's speech is found in UAW, *20th Constitutional Convention*, 112–13.

41. Although a government bailout provided the occasion for UAW President Douglas Fraser to sit briefly on the Chrysler board in the early 1980s, Herman Rebhan, a longtime UAW official then serving as IMF secretary general, was a member of the board of directors of Ford Motor Company's German subsidiary, joining nine other union representatives as well as ten from management. Rebhan, *Trade Unions and the World*, 102–4.

but even the most overwhelming Democratic Congress since the New Deal failed to muster the votes to repeal Section 14b of the Taft-Hartley Law, thereby ensuring that union strength would continue to erode in the "right-to-work" states of the South and Mountain West. (And for decades hence, Democrat-controlled Congresses would fail again and again to pass pro-union legislation: in 1978, 1994, 2009, and 2022.)[42]

In the third decade of the twenty-first century barely 6 percent of all private sector employees work under a union contract. Few of the companies that compose the economy's new commanding heights—in high tech, finance, big box retail, fast-food, and health provision—have been organized. Notable recent victories in education, both secondary and in the university, reflect in part the more favorable organizing terrain in the public sector. Conversely, the failure of a new generation of union-conscious young workers to actually secure collective bargaining contracts at Starbucks, Amazon, and Apple reflects the persistence of both a dysfunctional labor law and the militant anti-unionism incentivized by the American tradition of firm-centered unionism. Labor partisans in the United States could learn a lot from Germany. ∎

NELSON LICHTENSTEIN'S most recent book is *A Fabulous Failure: The Clinton Presidency and the Transformation of American Capitalism* (2023).

## References

Alexis, Marion. "Neo-Corporatism and Industrial Relations: The Case of German Trade Unions." *West German Politics* 6 (1983): 75–92.

Barnard, John. *American Vanguard: The United Auto Workers During the Reuther Years, 1935–1970*. Detroit: Wayne State University Press, 2004.

Boyle, Kevin. *The UAW and the Heyday of American Liberalism, 1945–1968*. Ithaca, NY: Cornell University Press, 1995.

Brinkley, Alan. *The End of Reform: New Deal Liberalism in Recession and War*. New York: Knopf, 1995.

Brody, David. "The Origins of Modern Steel Unionism: The SWOC Era." In *Forging a Union of Steel: Philip Murray, SWOC, and the United Steelworkers*, edited by Paul Clark, Peter Gottlieb, and Donald Kennedy, 13–29. Ithaca, NY: Cornell University Press, 1987.

Brody, David. *Workers in Industrial America: Essays on the Twentieth Century Struggle*. New York: Oxford University Press, 1981.

Carew, Anthony. *American Labour's Cold War Abroad: From Deep Freeze to Détente, 1945–1970*. Edmonton: AU Press, 2018.

Carew, Anthony. *Labour Under the Marshall Plan: The Politics of Productivity and the Marketing of Management Science*. Detroit: Wayne State University Press, 1987.

Cowie, Jefferson. *Capital Moves: RCA's Seventy-Year Quest for Cheap Labor*. New York: The New Press, 2001.

42. The dismal tale is told in Dark, *Unions and the Democrats*; Halpern, *Unions, Radicals, and Democratic Presidents*; and Minchin, *Labor Under Fire*.

Dark, Taylor. *The Unions and the Democrats: An Enduring Alliance*. Ithaca, NY: Cornell University Press, 1999.

Dubofsky, Melvyn, and Warren Van Tine. *John L. Lewis: A Biography*. New York: Quadrangle Books, 1977.

Edsall, Thomas Byrne, with Mary D. Edsall. *Chain Reaction: The Impact of Race, Rights, and Taxes on American Politics*. New York: W. W. Norton, 1991.

Fetzer, Thomas. "Exporting the American Model? Transatlantic Entanglements of Industrial Relations at Opel and Ford Germany (1948–1965)." *Labor History* 51, no. 2 (May 2010): 173–91.

Fink, Leon. *Undoing the Liberal World Order: Progressive Ideals and Political Realities Since World War II*. New York: Columbia University Press, 2022.

Gall, Gilbert. *The Politics of Right to Work: The Labor Federation as Special Interest, 1943–1979*. New York: Greenwood, 1988.

Glickman, Lawrence. *Free Enterprise: An American History*. New Haven, CT: Yale University Press, 2019.

Gordon, Colin. *New Deals: Business, Labor, and Politics in America, 1920–1935*. New York: Cambridge University Press, 1994.

Gordon, Colin. "Why No Corporatism in the United States: Business Disorganization and Its Consequences." *Business and Economic History* 27 (Fall 1998): 29–46.

Halpern, Martin. *Unions, Radicals, and Democratic Presidents: Seeking Social Change in the Twentieth Century*. Westport, CT: Praeger, 2003.

Jacobi, Otto, and Walter Muller-Jentsch. "West Germany: Continuity and Structural Change." In *European Industrial Relations: The Challenge of Flexibility*, edited by Guido Baglioni and Colin Crouch, 127–53. London: Sage, 1990.

Jacobs, Meg. *Pocketbook Politics: Economic Citizenship in Twentieth-Century America*. Princeton, NJ: Princeton University Press, 2005.

Jacoby, Sanford, ed. *Masters to Managers: Historical and Comparative Perspectives on American Employers*. New York: Columbia University Press, 1991.

Jager, Simon, et al. "The German Model of Industrial Relations: Balancing Flexibility and Collective Action." *IZA Institute of Labor Economics*, August 2022.

Kerr, Clark. "Collective Bargaining in Postwar Germany." *Industrial and Labor Relations Review* 5 (April 1952): 323–42.

Klein, Jennifer. *For All These Rights: Business, Labor, and the Shaping of America's Public-Private Welfare State*. Princeton, NJ: Princeton University Press, 2003.

Levinson, Harold. "Pattern Bargaining: A Case Study of the Automobile Workers." *Quarterly Journal of Economics* 74, no. 2 (Spring 1959): 296–317.

Lichtenstein, Nelson. "From Corporatism to Collective Bargaining: Organized Labor and the Eclipse of Social Democracy in the Postwar Era." In *The Rise and Fall of the New Deal Order, 1930–1980*, edited by Steve Fraser and Gary Gerstle, 122–52. Princeton, NJ: Princeton University Press, 1989.

Lichtenstein, Nelson. *Labor's War at Home: The CIO in World War II*. Philadelphia: Temple University Press, 2003.

Lichtenstein, Nelson. *State of the Union: A Century of American Labor*. Princeton, NJ: Princeton University Press, 2013.

Lichtenstein, Nelson. *Walter Reuther: The Most Dangerous Man in Detroit*. Urbana: University of Illinois Press, 1996.

Maier, Charles S. *In Search of Stability: Explorations in Historical Political Economy*. New York: Cambridge University Press, 1987.

Markovits, Andrei. *The Politics of West German Trade Unions: Strategies of Class and Interest Representation in Growth and Crisis.* Cambridge: Cambridge University Press, 1986.

McGaughey, Ewan. "The Codetermination Bargains: The History of German Corporate and Labour Law." *LSE Law, Society and Economy Working Papers,* October 2015.

Mills, C. Wright. *The New Men of Power.* Urbana: University of Illinois Press, 2001.

Minchin, Timothy. *Labor Under Fire: A History of the AFL-CIO Since 1979.* Chapel Hill: University of North Carolina Press, 2017.

Opel, Fritz. *Seventy-Five Years of the Iron International, 1893–1968.* Geneva: International Metalworkers Federation, 1968.

Plotke, David. *Building a Democratic Political Order: Reshaping American Liberalism in the 1930s and 1940s.* New York: Cambridge University Press, 1996.

Rebhan, Herman. *Trade Unions and the World.* London: Anvil Press, 1980.

Schuhrke, Jeff. *Blue-Collar Empire: The AFL-CIO and the Global Cold War.* New York: Verso, 2023.

Silvia, Stephen. *Holding the Shop Together: German Industrial Relations in the Postwar Era.* Ithaca, NY: Cornell University Press, 2013.

Slichter, Sumner. *The Challenge of Industrial Relations.* Ithaca, NY: Cornell University Press, 1947.

Smemo, Kristoffer, Samir Sonti, and Gabriel Winant. "Conflict and Consensus: The Steel Strike of 1959 and the Anatomy of the New Deal Order." *Critical Historical Studies* 4, no. 1 (Spring 2017): 39–73.

Stebenne, David. *Arthur Goldberg: New Deal Liberal.* New York: Oxford University Press, 1996.

Stieber, Jack, Robert B. McKersie, and D. Quinn Mills. *U.S. Industrial Relations 1950–1980: A Critical Assessment.* Madison, WI: Industrial Relations Research Association, 1981.

Thelen, Kathleen. *Union of Parts: Labor Politics in Postwar Germany.* Ithaca, NY: Cornell University Press, 1991.

UAW (United Automobile Workers). Proceedings of the 19th Constitutional Convention, 1964.

UAW (United Automobile Workers). Proceedings of the 20th Constitutional Convention, 1966.

US Department of Labor. *Handbook of Labor Statistics,* Bulletin 2217. Washington, DC: US Department of Labor, 1984.

Vittoz, Stanley. *New Deal Labor Policy and the American Industrial Economy.* Chapel Hill: University of North Carolina Press, 1987.

Vogel, David. "Why Businessmen Distrust Their State: The Political Consciousness of American Corporate Executives." *British Journal of Political Science* 8 (January 1978): 45–78.

Wilson, Mark. *Destructive Creation: American Business and the Winning of World War II.* Philadelphia: University of Pennsylvania Press, 2016.

Workman, Andrew. "Manufacturing Power: The Organizational Revival of the National Association of Manufacturers, 1941–1945." *Business History Review* 78 (Summer 1998): 279–301.

Zieger, Robert. *The CIO, 1935–1955.* Chapel Hill: University of North Carolina Press, 1995.

# Workers and Catholicism in Postwar Western Europe and Latin America

Gerd-Rainer Horn

Postwar Catholicism experienced a successive series of progressive currents. The first wave of left Catholicism emerged as a result of the turbulence of European and world politics in the interwar time period, and then was amplified by the experience of Nazi terror, occupation policies, and antifascist resistance movements during World War II. Strongest in the mid-1940s, this first wave came to an end with the definitive defeat of such currents after the outbreak of the Cold War, which had a negative effect within world politics and on the internal operations of the Catholic Church.

A second wave of left Catholicism arose as a result of broad changes elaborated and codified in the course of the World Council of the Catholic Church: Vatican II (1962–65). This second wave rapidly grew in importance, fueled by the belief that the church leadership as such was suddenly on the side of progressive insurgents, who quickly concentrated on helping to animate powerful social movements in Europe as well as Latin America. More influential than its 1940s predecessor, this second surge played a major role in giving concrete shape to what is often regarded as the "spirit of 1968" in both Latin American and European societies.

## The Colorful and Multilayered Nature of Catholicism

*Catholicism* is a term fraught with multiple possible meanings, allowing sometimes overlapping but also conflictual interpretations. Catholicism is, first of all, a system of belief and a theology, an ideology of sorts, which is about two thousand years old and has undergone many significant changes over time. In this article I wish to address only aspects of Catholic theology that have been relevant in Europe and Latin America between 1945 and 1975, as there have been a number of crucial discussions within Catholic theology in the first three post–World War II decades that have had a great impact on the workers of our world.

Precisely during the postwar boom, multiple schools of thought within Catholic theology were often at loggerheads with each other. Conservative Catholic thinkers

*Labor: Studies in Working-Class History* Volume 22 • Issue 1
DOI 10.1215/15476715-11521406   © 2025 by Labor and Working-Class History Association

were in full control of Catholic institutions and public life when the period opened in 1945, though frontal challenges to traditional Catholic theology from within the Catholic Church were experiencing a first coming-out, so to speak. Within a few years after the war's end, however, these challenges to received dogma experienced a devastating defeat, their concrete projects forcibly dismantled by the apex of the Catholic conservative hierarchy, with leading proponents of innovation exiled and, on occasion, even excommunicated from the Church.

Catholicism, however, is more than just theology; it is also an institution. And like any institution of some size, it is an organization of multiple levels, which mandates mastery of a succession of levels of analysis. A top-down system of organization par excellence, Catholicism cannot be understood without some knowledge of the upper ranks of the hierarchies, and I consciously choose to use the plural form here. Rome, the Vatican, and the upper echelons of the Catholic Church's administration are levels of power that cannot be underestimated in a system of government consciously modeled on the format of the Roman Empire many centuries ago. But whereas the Roman Empire crumbled five hundred years after its founding, the Catholic monarchy hardened its dictatorial features as modernity approached. The doctrine of the infallibility of the pope became dogma only with the First Vatican Council in 1869–70.

Below the Roman curia exists, to varying degrees, the second tier of the upper hierarchies of the Catholic Church, often organized into national compartments or, in the case of Latin America, the Latin American Episcopal Council, the latter in existence only since 1955. The institutional hierarchies of the Catholic Church thus constitute the second level of analysis.

Catholic political parties, first emerging in the late nineteenth century in Europe and, much later, in Latin America and elsewhere, must be regarded as the third level of analysis; these organizations were themselves internally divided between, at the very least, leadership and rank and file. Catholic Action forms the fourth level of analysis. Catholic Action movements and organizations gradually emerged from the late nineteenth century onward and were codified and streamlined in the early 1920s. Elsewhere I have termed Catholic Action a quintessential and powerful transnational social movement of the twentieth century.[1] Catholic Action organizations were created to give voice and influence within society and notably within the Church to the vast majority of Catholics not belonging to any of the various hierarchies. Catholic Action movements were Catholicism's answer to the emergence of mass democratic movements in the wake of the industrial revolution with the rise of labor movements and social democracy as the key innovations and challenges to the powers-that-be and traditional society—including the Church.

Catholic trade unions form a fifth category of analysis, separate and distinct from Catholic Action. Last but not least, grassroots social movements within the

---

1. Horn, *Western European Liberation Theology*, chap. 1: "Catholic Action: A Twentieth Century Social Movement."

Catholic milieu, which arose separate and distinct from any of the above five levels of analysis, form a sixth category of analysis, though once again they are often internally divided. Between 1945 and 1975, this level included, for instance, the movement of worker priests but also the transnational phenomenon of base communities, two manifestations of grassroots activism that exerted a significant influence on Catholic working-class communities then evolving into a distinctly progressive if not even radical direction. But so-called New Ecclesial Movements, charismatic prayer groups, and social action groups of mostly middle-class Catholic constituencies could also easily be placed in the same category of grassroots social movements forming a sixth layer in this colorful kaleidoscope that we sometimes refer to as the "Catholic Church."

All these different layers were by no means internally unified and homogeneous. Also, the history of Catholicism, 1945–75, is full of examples of how individuals and organizations belonging to any one of these levels formed alliances with elements within at least some other of the categories.

## Divisions Within the Labor Movement

Clearly, religion has often played a part in rendering labor movements less unified and powerful than they might have been. To take the case of the fifth level of analysis alluded to in the opening section of this article, the existence of confessionally based trade unions alongside other, secular trade unions will be difficult to understand as anything other than a factor complicating the tasks and prospects of labor movements. And plenty of countries in Western Europe and Latin America between 1945 and 1975 witnessed precisely such a multiplicity of trade union structures. Some countries of course developed nominally unified trade union confederations. On the other hand, a few countries, such as the Netherlands, were exceptional in having not just one but at least two separately operating trade unions based on Christian religious affiliation—one Catholic, the other Protestant.

Two observations may, however, temper this view of Catholic trade unions as factors of division. First, secular organizations within the labor movement were no more united than their religious comrades. Between 1945 and 1975 the labor movement often split into socialist or social democratic federations, on the one hand, and communist-dominated federations, on the other, and unity often remained elusive within these nonreligious federations. Moreover, some countries, such as Belgium to this day, have relatively vibrant liberal trade union federations. The second point to make here is to caution against the widespread suggestion, often based on stereotypical assessments, that Catholic federations were by nature less combative and more moderate than their mostly socialist / social democratic or communist counterparts. In fact, much of what follows in this essay is to demonstrate that such views are frequently mistaken. Particularly toward the end of the *trente glorieuses*, the thirty years of postwar economic boom, the opposite was often the case. Catholic federations often stood in the vanguard of insubordinate actions by working-class communities and associated allies in radical social movements, the latter likewise headquartered in popular neighborhoods.

## The First Wave

One such moment when the Catholic milieu by no means stood on the conservative margins of the workers' movement was the tail end of World War II and the immediate postwar period, certainly in Europe. To be sure, most of the working-class communities at that time stood considerably to the left of the median political orientation of the average European. And the "average European" in 1943–48 stood considerably to the left of the median for all of the twentieth century. In fact, the moment of liberation in Western Europe must be regarded as the point in historical time when public opinion as such stood further to the left than at any other time in the twentieth century. After the harrowing experience of war, occupation, and resistance, the latter often strongest in urban working-class communities, the proverbial average European worker was firmly anchored to the left of the political center.[2]

Catholic workers were usually second to none in this lineup of forces that shaped labor struggles and other sociopolitical conflicts in the first years after liberation. The Catholic world of workers, which in earlier decades and centuries had often indeed shown distinct sympathies for moderate political orientations, if not outright conservative sentiments, was now frequently a constituent part of the European left. Even Catholic political parties rarely belonged to the spectrum of conservative or even middle-of-the-road organizations. The German Christian Democratic Union in the immediate postwar period notably included powerful currents that belonged to the spectrum of Christian socialism. The French Mouvement Républicain Populaire (MRP), the closest thing France ever experienced that could be considered a Catholic party, from the summer of 1944 to the end of 1945 was by no means less virulently antifascist and progressive than their socialist or even communist competitors.

The MRP's founding manifesto, adopted at its first national congress on November 25–26, 1944, proudly proclaimed, "We want a Revolution that will guarantee to each and everyone the right to live in security and dignity. We want a Revolution that will make political and social democracy a full reality." And the manifesto then dotted some of its i's: "This revolution necessitates an economy directed by a state that is freed from the powers of moneyed interests, as well as the nationalization of the most important industries, private monopolies, and credit." And here is what the MRP's manifesto called for with regard to the role and function of trade unions as a result of this successful "revolution": "It likewise includes the participation of the various freely organized trade unions within the running of the economy and individual enterprises."[3]

Any glance at the significant number of local or regional daily newspapers during the moment of liberation run by editors belonging to the spectrum of Catholic politics around the MRP demonstrates that the MRP was then a phenomenon of the left. And so it was in Italy. Democrazia Cristiana (DC), which later became a

2. See Horn, *Moment of Liberation in Western Europe.*
3. A reproduction of "Le Manifeste du M.R.P." is included in Letamendia, *Le Mouvement Républicain Populaire,* 65; my translation.

mainstay of Atlanticist Catholic published opinion, in the immediate postliberation period included factions that fervently defended radical social justice, offered egalitarian solutions to the multiple challenges of the day, and ardently opposed efforts by Christian Democratic power brokers to enthusiastically embrace Italian membership in NATO, once the latter alliance was founded. These consistent critics of laissez-faire ideology, as late as the June 1949 DC party congress, garnered no less than 35 percent of the votes cast at the DC party conference in Venice.[4]

Apart from Catholic party politics, Catholic public opinion at the moment of liberation was likewise greatly influenced by the radical atmosphere of that era. The (in)famous experience of worker priests, ordained priests who exchanged their soutane and their parish for working-class blue and a slot in one of the vast factories or construction sites at the center of economic life in Belgium and France, is relatively well-known, though there never were more than one hundred of them in total. Curiously enough, far less well-known is the more astounding movement that existed within the far-flung universe of Catholic Action organizations, which had a membership of more than one hundred thousand at its high point in the mid-1940s. Most firmly implanted in francophone regions of Belgium and then France itself, the Mouvement Populaire des Familles (MPF) fulfilled the role of a radical social action group within the working class, engaging in direct action tactics vis-à-vis any and all secular or religious authorities when deemed necessary, including frequent housing squats. Strongest in those districts and regions where industrial capitalism was strongest, even in cities with a Communist Party in positions of power, the MPF for an all-too-brief moment was considered a serious competitor to the secular radical left.

The Belgian Jesuit Philippe de Soignie, the national chaplain of the Belgian MPF, had this to say about what he regarded as the tasks of true Christian organizations: "All great contemporary social movements . . . build on a mystique that puts the spotlight on the person of the worker and shows the grandeur of his mission"; "Marxism points out very well the uplifting characteristic of labor, and it manages to construct a corresponding mystique." The Jesuit chaplain then penned a ringing defense of the need for Christians to develop a similar mystique, which is of course precisely what left Catholic mass social movements such as the MPF were then in the process of doing. And, referring to the dire material and spiritual circumstances in which much of working-class Europe was living after five years of world war and corresponding deprivations, de Soignie reasoned, "Antoine de Saint-Exupéry, when contemplating the beautiful child of a couple living in dire circumstances, once wrote: 'What torments me is that within each of these human beings one can visualize, more or less, a person with the talents of a Mozart assassinated in cold blood!'" Philippe de Soignie then continued: "Would it not be more precise and Christian to say: 'What

---

4. See Horn, *Western European Liberation Theology*, chap. 3: "The Politics of Left Catholicism in the 1940s," 110–74.

torments me is that within each of these human beings, one can visualize, more or less, Christ assassinated in cold blood?'"[5]

## The Long 1950s

Of course, by no means *all* Catholics, or even all working-class Catholics, thought and acted like Philippe de Soignie, the MPF, the worker priests or the left-wing currents in Catholic political parties. When the dark clouds of the Cold War began to dominate national and international politics, preexisting ideological gaps within working-class organizations began to deepen and widen. The primary lines of division did not run along secular/religious lines but occurred within the largely secular portions of the movement. The opposition between increasingly Atlanticist movements, on the one hand, often animated by socialist or social democratic currents of opinion, and Moscow-oriented federations, currents, and opinion shapers, on the other hand, were the talk of the town from the late 1940s onward, dominating much of the long 1950s and certainly continuing to make working-class unity an elusive dream all the way into the 1960s and beyond. In this inauspicious geopolitical context, the Catholic components quickly aligned on the side of the defenders of the Free World, but the Catholic (or Christian) milieus did not play the decisive role in this realignment.

In fact, the International Federation of Christian Trade Unions (IFCTU), founded in 1920, retained its organizational autonomy throughout the second half of the twentieth century, including during 1945 to 1949, when, in the wake of the wartime alliance between the Soviet Union and the Western Powers, the communist and most noncommunist trade union federations joined up in the unitary World Federation of Trade Unions (WFTU). When the Cold War increasingly overdetermined international politics, the WFTU eventually witnessed the walkout of pro-Western forces in January 1949, which led to the foundation of a pro-Western competitor, the International Confederation of Free Trade Unions (ICFTU), in December 1949.[6] The Christian Federation was equally anticommunist compared to the newly founded ICFTU, but as a historian of Christian international trade unionism, Patrick Pasture, points out, "Because Christian trade unionism rejected American liberal capitalism [as well], from the beginning of the 1950s onwards, they appeared less anticommunist than the so-called 'free' trade unions."[7]

5. De Soignie, *Culture et milieux populaires*, 51, 21, 128; my translation. On this largely forgotten experience of the MPF, see Horn, *Western European Liberation Theology*, chap. 4: "The Mouvement Populaire des Familles," 175–224. The Groupement pour la Recherche sur les Mouvements Familiaux (GRMF) published a remarkable collection of fifteen book-length Cahiers du GRMF between 1982 and 2006, a veritable treasure trove of information on this mass social movement produced by the first wave of left Catholicism.

6. The literature on this split is vast and often rather partial. A much neglected and informative account of the history of the brief honeymoon period of international trade union unity between 1945 and 1949 is Pohrt, *Der international Gewerkschaftsbund (WGB) von der Gründungsphase bis zu seiner Spaltung (1941–1949)*.

7. Pasture, *Histoire du syndicalisme chrétien international*, 356.

At this stage, there were few differences between Catholic milieus in Western Europe and in Latin America. If there emerged some dissident voices within the Catholic world of workers, these came from an unsuspected corner of southwestern Europe. After a brutal civil war that raged from 1936 to 1939, Spain had become a vicious dictatorship, largely supported by the so-called Free World, until Francisco Franco's death in November 1975. The labor movement in Spain, solidly in the hands of socialist and anarchist federations up to the late 1930s, was completely wiped out in the aftermath of Franco's victory, leading to years of intense and unrelenting suffering for Spanish working-class communities. Never particularly beholden to Catholicism even before the civil war, the Spanish working class was reinforced in its distaste for Catholic religion and officialdom by the Spanish Catholic hierarchy's enthusiastic support for and embrace of General Franco's dictatorship. It was as an attempt to heal this gap between Spanish working-class communities and the Spanish Catholic Church that Pope Pius XII, in a communication to the Spanish ecclesial hierarchy in 1946, gave the green light to a new Catholic institution, the Hermandad Obrera de Acción Católica (HOAC), henceforth the Spanish branch of Catholic Action organizations geared toward adult Catholic workers.

The product of an explicitly conservative and orthodox measure, the HOAC evolved into the first mass-based radical Catholic social movement anywhere in Europe and, in fact, anywhere in the world. It emerged *independently from and subsequent to* the earlier ("first") wave of radical Catholic sentiment and organizations in the mid-1940s. The HOAC soon began to take seriously a key task of its organization: representing its grassroots membership. In the context of Francoist repression, the HOAC, supported by the Spanish Catholic hierarchy, quickly became the sole legal outlet for activities in support of improved conditions for the vast number of precarious workers throughout industrial Spain. Profiting from the presence of Catholic intellectuals, journalists, and activists at the leadership levels of the HOAC, devout Catholics who had been at the same time profoundly affected by the social unrest and the social gains of the Spanish Second Republic moved in directions diametrically opposed to the ideas of the hierarchy that had called the HOAC into existence in the first place.

The HOAC's flagship newspaper, *Tu!*, began to publish voices protesting the abysmal social conditions of working-class existence in Francoist Spain. Already in the second half of 1947, *Tu!* experienced censorship from the political authorities, when the newspaper was suspended for a while. In the course of 1951, *Tu!* was forced to close up shop for good, though the HOAC as such continued to operate. For the dynamic and selfless leaders of the HOAC, the loss of *Tu!* turned out to be a blessing in disguise. They now refocused their energies on training workers to become apostles of a better future among their cohort of working-class poor. During the 1950s, the HOAC evolved into the quintessential vehicle for concrete social improvements for its constituency and the most visible vehicle for radical actions by Spanish working-class communities. When, from the late 1950s onward, the first underground trade union associations, the Workers' Commissions (CCOOs), were created in the mining and industrial regions of northern Spain, particularly Asturias, the HOAC stood in the forefront of such subversive moves.

The CCOOs are today frequently regarded as organizations closely linked to the Spanish Communist Party (PCE). Doubtless, communist workers often played leading roles in the groups from the very beginning, and in the second half of the 1960s, the PCE consolidated its hold over many of these CCOO branches. Yet in the early stages of the CCOOs, the Catholic contribution (particularly HOAC's) to the conception, birth, initial growth, and development of the various groups had been crucial. The HOAC, then, was crucially at the very least coresponsible for the rise of an increasingly powerful underground anti-Francoist organizational network. At the same time, the HOAC, unsurprisingly, developed into an increasingly left-leaning progressive Catholic organization, which anticipated many of the later developments in other European and Latin American countries. The significance of the HOAC lies above all else in the fact that its activists developed such an innovative course without any support from outside sources. The subsequent radicalization of significant parts of Catholic public opinion in Latin America and Europe, by contrast, benefited tremendously from the official support for such innovations emerging in the course of Vatican II.[8]

### Changes at the Top

The story of the HOAC was a singular exception in the 1950s in the far-flung universe of the Catholic lifeworld. Elsewhere in Europe, the 1950s saw setbacks in what I have called the first wave of left Catholicism, strongest in the mid-1940s. Often enough, up to the mid-1960s, the various national branches of Catholic Action were indeed staunchly conservative.

Prior to the mid-1960s, the situation in Latin America was in many ways similar to what was then happening in Europe, as liberation theology had yet to emerge on any serious scale. Latin America in fact had not been touched significantly by the first wave of radicalization of parts of European Catholicism in the mid-1940s. And thus, into the 1960s, the intellectual impulses for what eventually became liberation theology arrived for the most part from European activists, theologians, and other protagonists, including a small army of European Catholics, many of them priests or members of religious orders, who chose to settle in Latin America. At the same time, individuals who would soon emerge as key figures in the development of a specifically Latin American liberation theology, such as Gustavo Gutiérrez, Camillo Torres, Leonardo Boff, and others, spent many of their younger years in various Western European countries, where they were influenced by European left Catholicism. They brought some of those traditions back to their native lands and creatively adapted what they had learned, quickly developing a distinctly Latin American left Catholicism. In addition, the often abysmal social conditions of Latin American societies provided the fertile soil for the eventual emergence of a uniquely radical tradition of its own.

---

8. On the HOAC, see Horn, *Spirit of Vatican II*, 230–45, but, above all, these two books by López García: *Aproximación a la historia de la HOAC (1946–1981)* and *Tomás Malagón Almodóvar*.

What allowed the emergence of a second wave of left Catholicism, which rapidly became far more influential than the first wave in the 1940s, was the accidental circumstance of the election of Angelo Roncalli to become Pope John XXIII in October 1958. Not known to be particularly radical during his prior career in the Catholic diplomatic service and episcopate, the elderly Roncalli had been chosen by the conclave precisely to guide the Church through a relatively calm transition period after the previous pontificate of Pius XII, who had been a controversial figure in his twenty-year reign. To everyone's great surprise, however, Pope John XXIII took a number of initiatives that shook up the Catholic world, notably the convocation of a Second Vatican Council, which officially opened on October 11, 1962. And already in the run-up to this World Council of the Catholic Church, Roncalli began rehabilitating the work of a number of leading first-wave theologians and activists who had been punished by his predecessor for their radical ideas. Moreover, Roncalli penned several path-breaking encyclicals in his brief pontificate, which were milestones on the road to an orientation toward the real world within the history of the Catholic Church. As papal pronouncements were of utmost importance in a worldwide institution that was extremely hierarchical, a brief summary of the key steps in the evolution of Catholic social teaching with regard to the world of labor and relations between the developed and underdeveloped worlds is in order.

## The Social Teaching of the Catholic Church

It took a long time before Catholic officialdom reacted to the social consequences of the industrial revolution. The 1891 papal encyclical *Rerum Novarum* by Pope Leo XIII is generally regarded as the Magna Carta of the world of labor from the standpoint of the Catholic Church. In *Rerum Novarum*, Leo XIII vividly portrayed the trials and tribulations industrial capitalism caused for the rapidly swelling industrial working class. Though serving as a clarion call for Catholic public opinion, *Rerum Novarum* exclusively presented a moral condemnation of the effects of industrial capitalism on blue-collar workers. There was not a hint of any structural analysis of the causes of the distress of working-class communities. It took another forty years for another pope to extend the critique of industrial capitalism into more than a moral condemnation of contemporaneous living and working conditions, which tended to echo views extolling a supposedly more golden past. It was Pope Pius XI's 1931 encyclical *Quadragesimo Anno* which, to be sure, decried the brutalities of modern-day capitalism; simultaneously, though, it took on a more all-encompassing view and began to express an understanding of capitalism not just as a cause of social dislocations and sorrow but also as a potential, if controversial, source for the forward march of humanity. Most crucially, perhaps, *Quadragesimo Anno* "not only concerned itself with the concrete situation of the laboring masses but addressed the economic and social order as a whole, whose guiding principle should be social justice."[9]

9 I cite here from the German translation of perhaps the most convincing and concise long-range view of the evolution of Catholic social theory: Chenu, *Kirchliche Soziallehre im Wandel*, 39.

Pope Pius XII never published a similarly pathbreaking social encyclical, but Pius XII should be remembered for another contribution. Increasingly anticommunist, Pius XII is perhaps best-known as "Hitler's Pope"—a pejorative characterization that is not entirely unjustified—and the 1949 decree excommunicating Catholics who openly supported communism. But it was the same Pius XII whose various pronouncements opened up another frontier in the social theory of the Catholic Church. For instance, the Belgian authority on Catholic social teaching, Roger Aubert, takes note of the absence of innovations with regard to the world of labor in Pius XII's thought, but Aubert goes further and writes that "one is struck foremost by [the] displaced perspective in which the problem of social justice is viewed: the contrast between the rich and the proletariat within industrial societies is increasingly supplanted in the pope's concern by the contrast that exists between rich countries and developing countries. This new contrast even becomes a habitual theme in the speeches and documents of the last years of the pontificate."[10] Pope Pius XII died on October 9, 1958, and Pope John XXIII succeeded him on October 28, 1958.

What had happened in the course of Pius XII's twenty-year-long pontificate to make this conservative figure become aware of the inequalities between the different parts of this world? Such a growing awareness of inequalities on a global scale must be seen in direct connection with the massive rise of anticolonial movements from the 1940s onward. The two decades from the mid-1940s to the mid-1960s experienced a tremendous wave of colonial independence struggles throughout Africa and Asia that changed the map of the world beyond recognition. The most convincing event that symbolized the arrival of a new era was the April 1955 Bandung Conference, which assembled representatives from twenty-nine newly independent nations, representing more than half of the world's population, as well as some colonial independence movements in those parts of the world where colonial powers were still in control.

Pius XII's successor, John XXIII, picked up and developed this new dimension of Catholic social theory, a concern for global inequalities, at the same time that he further sharpened papal pronouncements on inequalities concerning the world of labor. In the 1961 encyclical *Mater et Magistra*, a term hitherto studiously avoided in Catholic social theory, "socialization," made entry into the vocabulary of the Church—and this not at all in a negative sense. And although it was John XXIII's successor, Pope Paul VI, who presented the most explicit and ringing condemnation of inequalities between richer and poorer portions of this world in his 1967 *Populorum Progressio*, such developments stood in a direct line of continuity with the mission of John XXIII. After all, Paul VI had been a close cothinker of John XXIII, who headed the Church for less than five years. The signal contribution by progressive forces liberated by the bold and decisive action of John XXIII, the pastoral constitution *Gaudium et Spes*, was announced to the world on the very last day of Vatican II, October 8, 1965, more than two years after John XXIII's death, but it is rightfully considered by

10. Aubert, *Catholic Social Teaching*, 224.

admirers and detractors alike as the true heritage of Angelo Roncalli and his behind-the-scenes advisers.

## Gaudium et Spes

*Rerum Novarum* (1891) and *Quadragesimo Anno* (1931) had set benchmarks in coming to terms with the conflictual relationship between capital and labor. As in so many other things, it was "the Christian Pope," John XXIII, who finally expanded the boundaries of official church doctrine in this respect beyond what Leo XIII and Pius XI had dared to say. Both his encyclical *Mater et Magistra* (1961) and, to some extent, certain passages in *Pacem in Terris* (1963) had proclaimed the need to strengthen workers' rights as well as the need for increasing the remit of organizations set up to collectively defend the rights of labor. Nonetheless, *Gaudium et Spes* broke further new ground in this respect.

Article 67, the first specific mention of labor and of workers in the constitution, already established the atmosphere within which the ensuing articles of the subsection "Certain Principles Governing Socioeconomic Life as a Whole" must be seen. It opened with an unequivocal statement highlighting that, in the conflictual relationship between capital and labor, the council's sympathies lie on the side of the weak: "Human labor that is expended in the production and exchange of goods or in the performance of economic services is superior to the other elements of economic life, for the latter have only the nature of tools."[11] As Pius XI had already mentioned in *Quadragesimo Anno*, Article 68 of *Gaudium et Spes* noted, "Amongst the basic rights of the human person is to be numbered the right of freely founding unions for working people," adding that strikes may "remain in present-day circumstances a necessary, though ultimate, aid for the defense of the workers' own rights and the fulfilment of their just desires."[12]

Yet *Gaudium et Spes* goes beyond *Quadragesimo Anno* in explicitly enlarging the terrain of fruitful activity for unions and other workers' associations in general, recommending "the active sharing of all in the administration and profits of their enterprises in ways to be determined," a conciliar stamp of approval for various schemes of codetermination and workers' participation in the running of their enterprises.[13] Amazingly enough, *Gaudium et Spes* went one step further: "Since more often, however, decisions concerning economic and social conditions, on which the future lot of the workers and of their children depends, are made not within the business itself but by institutions on a higher level, the workers themselves should have a share also in determining these conditions—in person or through freely elected delegates."[14]

11. *Gaudium et Spes*, 67.

12. Karl Rahner and Herbert Vorgrimmler add in their astute commentary, "A right of lock-out for employers is not mentioned'; see their *Kleines Konzilskompendium: Alle Konstitutionen, Dekrete und Erklärungen des Zweiten Vatikanums in der bischöflich genehmigten Übersetzung*, 440.

13. *Gaudium et Spes*, 68.

14. *Gaudium et Spes*, 68.

If the articles on labor's rights were already clear calls for an attenuation of the prevailing social order, *Gaudium et Spes* reserved its most explicit condemnation of the status quo to class relations in the Third World:

> In many underdeveloped regions there are large or even extensive rural estates which are only slightly cultivated or lie completely idle for the sake of profit, while the majority of the people either are without land or have only very small fields, and, on the other hand, it is evidently urgent to increase the productivity of the fields. Not infrequently, those who are hired to work for the landowners or who till a portion of this land as tenants receive a wage or income unworthy of a human being, lack decent housing and are exploited by middlemen.[15]

And the council fathers then, in full logic, mandated that "reforms are necessary," notably including the socialization of landed estates: "Indeed, insufficiently culti-vated estates should be distributed to those who can make these lands fruitful,"[16] a truly revolutionary measure of enormous relevance to the majority of countries in the world of the 1960s and one of the driving forces behind the genesis of liberation theol-ogy in subsequent years. It is easy to see how such passages in *Gaudium et Spes*—and there were plenty of other topics raised in this constitution that cannot be addressed in this context—encouraged social justice campaigners around the world, including certainly the small army of such activists drawing on inspiration for their work from Catholic teachings.

### Green Light to Radical Reform Movements

From the early 1960s onward, left Catholics felt that history was on their side. Pope John XXIII and Paul VI were clearly supportive of a drastic change. Leading theolo-gians felt wind in their sails and founded an international journal, *Concilium*, which saw itself as a theological support mechanism for new departures in the Catholic life-world. One of its editors was the young Joseph Ratzinger, the future Pope Benedict XVI. Catholic Action organizations now began to openly air the need for change, and soon followed up their words with concrete actions.

One of these groups was the Associazioni Cristiane Lavoratori Italiani (ACLI). Founded in the summer of 1944 in Rome, the ACLI for a long time remained loyal to the hierarchy's vision for Catholic Action groupings, and there was no question about the ACLI's role as a transmission belt for mainstream Democrazia Cristiana policies. By 1966, however, voices critical of the guiding role of conservative DC could be heard with increasing frequency and resonance within both the ACLI leadership and its rank and file. The Hot Autumn of 1969 ensured that this radical turn toward autonomy and independence would emerge victorious. The 1970 Summer School in the Vallombrosa, the traditional summer retreat of ACLI activists, signed and sealed the ACLI's determination to break with DC and to openly proclaim the need for

15. *Gaudium et Spes*, 71.
16. *Gaudium et Spes*, 71.

a *socialist* solution to the problems confronting Italian politics and society. A mass organization of Catholic Action that in 1969 counted at least six hundred thousand members throughout Italy had broken with the traditionally conservative Catholic mainstream tradition and struck out on a path of its own.[17]

Progressive base communities began to pop up in the mid-1960s in Latin America and in Italy and Spain. Later in the decade they spread across much of the rest of Western Europe. In late October 1965, an extraordinary plenary assembly of French bishops unanimously approved the resumption of the worker priest experience, which had been ordered shut in the mid-1950s. The first wave had been strictly limited to Belgium and France, and the total number of first-wave worker priests never exceeded one hundred. The second wave spread literally to all Western European states and to other parts of the world, and to give a sense of the dramatically higher numbers of such priests in working-class blue, in France alone their numbers exceeded two thousand! And they were sometimes present at particularly prominent and conflict-laden locations (the Holy Ghost was working overtime, no doubt). Thus, perhaps the most representative and symbolic labor struggle characterizing the "long sixties" in Western Europe, the case of the watch factory LIP near Besançon in eastern France, saw the worker priest Jean Raguénès playing an absolutely crucial role behind the scenes as a key strategist and tactician in this bitterly fought contest.[18]

Even Catholic political parties were eventually to some extent affected by this sea change of opinion within Catholicism. Mathieu Dubois has retraced the exemplary evolution of an organization generally not known to be within the orbit of the left, the West German Junge Union, in the late 1960s and early 1970s, which then, for about half a dozen years, guardedly but steadily moved closer to the orbit of the left.[19] Apart from some of their youth branches, however, European Christian Democratic or Catholic parties were rarely deeply affected by the radicalization of Catholic milieus in the wake of Vatican II.[20] The decoupling of Catholic political parties from the Catholic Church as such was sufficiently far advanced to insulate—up to a point—Christian Democracy from the spirit of Vatican II, the latter soon reinforced by the spirit of '68. In Latin America, by contrast, Catholic parties sometimes embarked on a rather different course. Here the case of Chile may be instructive. The

17. On the history of the ACLI, consult Casula, *Le ACLI*, 29–52, notably the interview with Emilio Gabaglio, who was ACLI president in the hottest phase of radical action, 1969–72. The most detailed account of the period of rapid and far-reaching changes within ACLI remains Sermanni, *Le ACLI*. An astute and concise insiders perspective is also accessible in Tortora, "Le ACLI e la scelta socialista."

18. See the autobiography by Raguénès, *De Mai 68 à LIP*; but more generally see also Divo, *L'Affaire LIP et les catholiques de Franche-Comté*.

19. Dubois, *Génération politique*, 118–24, 140–43 and passim. Note the difference in comportment, hairstyles, and clothes worn by delegates to the 1967 and then the 1973 national conferences of the *Junge Union*, as depicted in three photos reproduced in Dubois, *Génération politique*, 301.

20. Standard reference works on European Christian Democracy include Buchanan and Conway, *Political Catholicism in Europe, 1918–1965*; Lamberts, *Christian Democracy in the European Union*; and Keselman and Buttigieg, *European Christian Democracy*.

Chilean Christian Democratic Party had already developed a certain penchant for radical reform measures all along its trajectory from the 1930s onward. Then, by 1969, a radical left Catholic political party as such, the Movimiento de Acción Popular Unitaria (MAPU), emerged in Chile and eventually formed part of Salvador Allende's Unidad Popular coalition, in fact a direct consequence of the radicalization of Chilean Christian Democracy's youth organization.[21]

## Ferment Within Catholic Trade Unions

Last but not least, how did all this affect Catholic trade unions, the portion of the Catholic organizational spectrum closest to its working-class audience? Here the 1950s and even the early 1960s saw no unusual developments. Catholic trade unions, where they existed as independent entities, did not stick out from their nominally nonreligious brothers and sisters. When changes began to make themselves felt within the IFCTU, they emerged from a corner of the world where, hitherto, Catholic trade unions had not made major waves if they had been in existence at all: Latin America. A regional federation, the Confederación Latinoamericana de Sindicalistas Cristianos (CLASC), was founded in December 1954. Toward the very end of the 1950s the first signs of a certain radicalization began to make themselves felt within the CLASC. It was under the leadership of the Argentinian Emilio Maspero that Christian-inspired trade unions in Latin America eventually became a "democratic and revolutionary" organization,[22] no doubt in part a reflection of the growing unrest among grassroots Catholics throughout the continent.

In the 1960s, the International Christian Trade Union Federation as a whole gradually became affected by the spirit of rebellion that eventually gave the long sixties its subversive fame. One significant anecdote may suffice. Within Europe, three of the flagship national trade union federations originating in the Catholic lifeworld— the Confédération Française Démocratique du Travail, the Confederazione Italiana Sindacati Lavoratori, and, in Belgium, the Algemeen Christelijk Vakverbond / Confédération des syndicats chrétiens—quickly evolved to become the confederations closest in orientation and action to the proverbial spirit of '68 within working-class communities in those three states.[23] As the example of the ACLI mentioned earlier exemplifies, Catholic Action organizations operating within working-class communities—adult and youth branches to an equal extent—likewise fully engaged in the various actions and debates, which created the radical image and gave rise to the reality of social movements operating in the proverbial sixties.

21. Moyano Barahona, *MAPU o la seducción del poder y la juventud*.

22. The citation is in Pasture, *Histoire du syndicalisme chrétien internationale*, 318. Patrick Pasture's pioneering study remains to date the sole transnational survey and analysis of this topic from a consistently global perspective.

23. The literature on this topic is vast. For a concise survey of the evolution of Western European Catholic trade unions in the long sixties, see Horn, *Spirit of Vatican II*, 215–30, part of a chapter titled "The Working Class Goes to Paradise."

## Conclusion

A detailed look at workers and Catholicism in postwar Western Europe and Latin America demonstrates that Catholic organizations and working-class constituencies were anything but a brake on working-class activism and unity. A first significant incursion by progressive activists hailing from the Catholic world into the discussions and life circumstances affecting Catholics took place in the years from 1943 to 1948/53. The second wave of left Catholicism (1965–75) interpreted the decisions emanating from Vatican II as a green light to fully engage in ongoing social movements to improve the present and the future of humanity. Progressive Catholics, including those who formed a constituent part of the world of labor, frontally attacked what were regarded as outdated holdovers of earlier decades and centuries, when Catholicism appeared to represent above all else the forces of tradition, defending conservative positions and attitudes in society, culture, and politics.

In fact, in the brief honeymoon phase between the end of the Vatican Council (1965) and the turbulent events of 1968, progressive Catholics in all walks of life often played a (temporary but important) vanguard role. Because secular (nonreligious) social movements in the run-up to 1968 were sometimes slow to join the frontline of contemporaneous battles, Catholic activists, inspired by Vatican II, often took the lead. That in societies as different as Belgium, France, and Italy, trade union federations hailing from the Catholic lifeworld stood closest to the increasingly restless generation of student activists also mobilizing at that time speaks volumes about the role of Catholics within the world of labor during the sixties. ∎

GERD-RAINER HORN is professor of twentieth-century political history at Sciences Po, Paris. His research interests include social movements in Western Europe, the transnational history of Western Europe, progressive (left) Catholicism, and the long sixties. His most recent monograph is *The Moment of Liberation in Western Europe: Power Struggles and Rebellions, 1943–1948.*

## References

Aubert, Roger. *Catholic Social Teaching: An Historical Perspective.* Milwaukee: Marquette University Press, 2005.

Bedeschi, Lorenzo, et al. *I cristiani nella sinistra: Dalla resistenza a oggi.* Rome: Coines, 1976.

Buchanan, Tom, and Martin Conway, eds. *Political Catholicism in Europe, 1918–1965.* Oxford: Clarendon, 1996.

Casula, Carlo Felice. *Le ACLI: Una bella storia italiana.* Rome: Anicia, 2008.

Chenu, Marie-Dominique. *Kirchliche Soziallehre im Wandel: Das Ringen der Kirche um das Verständnis der gesellschaftlichen Wirklichkeit.* Fribourg: Exodus, 1991.

De Scignie, Philippe. *Culture et milieux populaires.* Tournai: Casterman, 1944.

Divo, Jean. *L'Affaire LIP et les catholiques de Franche-Comté.* Yens-sur-Morges: Cabédita, 2003.

Dubois, Mathieu. *Génération politique: Les "années 68" dans les jeunesses des partis politiques en France et en RFA.* Paris: Presses de l'université Paris-Sorbonne, 2014.

*Gaudium et Spes: Pastoral Constitution on the Church in the Modern World, Promulgated by His Holiness, Pope Paul VI on December 7, 1965.* Accessed October 8, 2024. https://www.vatican.va/archive/hist_councils/ii_vatican_council/documents/vat-ii_const_19651207_gaudium-et-spes_en.html.

Horn, Gerd-Rainer. *The Moment of Liberation in Western Europe: Power Struggles and Rebellions, 1943–1948.* Oxford: Oxford University Press, 2020.

Horn, Gerd-Rainer. *The Spirit of Vatican II: Western European Progressive Catholicism in the Long Sixties.* Oxford: Oxford University Press, 2015.

Horn, Gerd-Rainer. *Western European Liberation Theology, 1924–1959: The First Wave.* Oxford: Oxford University Press, 2008.

Keselman, Thomas, and Joseph A. Buttigieg, eds. *European Christian Democracy: Historical Legacies and Comparative Perspectives.* Notre Dame: University of Notre Dame Press, 2003.

Lamberts, Emiel, ed. *Christian Democracy in the European Union.* Leuven: Leuven University Press, 1997.

Letamendia, Pierre. *Le Mouvement Républicain Populaire: Le MRP. Histoire d'un grand parti français.* Paris: Beauchesne, 1995.

López García, Basilisa. *Aproximación a la historia de la HOAC (1946–1981).* Madrid: Ediciones HOAC, 1995.

López García, Basilisa. *Tomás Malagón Almodóvar.* Madrid: Ediciones HOAC, 2014.

Moyano Barahona, Cristina. *MAPU o la seducción del poder y la juventud.* Santiago de Chile: Ediciones Alberto Hurtado, 2009.

Pasture, Patrick. *Histoire du syndicalisme chrétien international: La difficile recherche d'une troisième voie.* Paris: L'Harmattan, 1999.

Pohrt, Oliver. *Der international Gewerkschaftsbund (WGB) von der Gründungsphase bis zu seiner Spaltung (1941–1949).* Regensburg: S. Roderer Verlag, 2000.

Raguénès, Jean. *De Mai 68 à LIP: Un dominicain au cœur des luttes.* Paris: Karthala, 2008.

Rahner, Karl, and Herbert Vorgrimmler, eds. *Kleines Konzilskompendium: Alle Konstitutionen, Dekrete und Erklärungen des Zweiten Vatikanums in der bischöflich genehmigten Übersetzung.* Freiburg: Herder, 1966.

Sermanni, Maria Cristina. *Le ACLI: Alla prova della politica 1961–1972.* Naples: Dehoniane, 1986.

Tortora, Fausto. "Le ACLI e la scelta socialista." In *I cristiani nella sinistra: Dalla Resistenza a oggi,* edited by Lorenzo Bedeschi et al., 199–213. Rome: Coines, 1976.

# Fordism's Underside:
# Women's Work in Postwar Italy

Eloisa Betti

This article deconstructs some of the allegedly positive features of the Fordist era by analyzing postwar Italy from a gender perspective. As Marcel Van Der Linden and Jan Breman pointed out in their inspiring article, the full-employment capitalism that characterized Western Europe until the late 1960s included continuity and stability of employment; a full-time job with one employer; a decent wage that could support a nuclear family; and legal rights to representation, protection, participation, and social insurance provisions attached to employment.[1]

In the Italian case, the Fordist factory became a paradigmatic image of Italian modernity in the years of the economic miracle, obscuring the mixture of old and new that continued to characterize the industrial system and labor relations in 1950s and 1960s Italy.[2] The industrial triangle embodied the industrial modernity of Fordism as part of an idealized construction based on large northern cities such as Milan and Turin, the capitals of the Italian miracle.[3] The unifying character inherent in the concept of "Fordism" has also been applied to the analysis of labor relations and working conditions in the mass-production factory, allegedly characterized by the prevalence of (stable) full-time, permanent employment relationships.[4]

Yet job stability was never fully achieved for women in the so-called golden age of the twentieth century. Feminist historians and feminist scholars have pointed out that only the (white) male breadwinner in Western countries fully benefited from the economic growth and the improvement of labor and social rights that was achieved in the 1950s and 1960s.[5] Women workers, by contrast, often experienced unequal

---

1 Breman and Van der Linden, "Informalizing the Economy," 920–40; Neilson and Rossiter, "Precarity as a Political Concept."

2 Causarano, "La fabbrica fordista e il conflitto industriale."

3 Berta, *L'Italia delle fabbriche*. The term *industrial triangle* refers to the industrial core of Italy, the area between the industrial cities of Milan, Turin, and Genoa, where Fordist production reached its peak.

4 For a critic of Fordism, see also Settis, *Fordismi*; and Betti, *Le ombre del fordismo*.

5 The debate has been reconstructed in Betti, "Historicizing Precarious Work"; see, for instance, Fudge and Owen, *Precarious Work*; Puar, "Precarity Talk"; Boris and Dodson, *Working at Living*.

*Labor: Studies in Working-Class History* Volume 22 • Issue 1
DOI 10.1215/15476715-11521438 © 2025 by Labor and Working-Class History Association

wages, discrimination, and precarity, since their work was not considered essential and/or necessary for the development of a democratic society. Nevertheless, women workers' demands and activism in the Fordist period were crucial for achieving better labor and social rights for them and, in countries like Italy, for the working classes as a whole.

This contribution begins by analyzing the social and working conditions of women in postwar Italy as a way to address the concept and reality of Fordism. A gender perspective demonstrates that working-class stability was an exceptional condition related precisely to the golden age of social democracy, while precarity can be conceptualized as a pervasive feature of both earlier industrial and neoliberal, postindustrial capitalism. In the 1950s, however, the spread of highly feminized and unstable forms of work such as industrial home-based work as well as precarious jobs revealed to what degree the spread of Fordist mass production and the glittering golden age of social democracy also displayed a dark side that undermined the quality of work.

Second, this article addresses the agency of female trade unionists and Members of Parliament (MPs) as well as the role played by women's associations in unraveling the gender-blind political discussions on full employment.[6] Despite the important role of Italian women workers in the thirty years after World War II in quantitative terms, the discussion of economic planning and full employment in the 1960s considered neither women's employment nor women's thinking on the matter. For this reason, women trade unionists and politicians argued for the full inclusion of women workers in economic and public policies so that they would not be left behind.

Finally, the article focuses on the role played by women workers along with women's associations and trade unions in passing key laws between the 1960s and 1970s, such as one that enabled the creation of a network of nurseries across the country. Gendering social services and welfare provisions became a crucial demand for achieving full emancipation for women workers. Women's emancipation through paid work was, in fact, a shared agenda for the Italian General Confederation of Labor (CGIL), the Italian Communist Party (PCI), the Italian Socialist Party (PSI), and the Union of Italian Women (UDI). The latter was a mass organization politically close to the PCI and PSI that reached a million women in the 1950s.[7]

### Deconstructing Fordism in Postwar Italy Through Women's Work

The social conditions of women in the twenty years following the birth of the Italian Republic (1946) were quite different from those in other Western countries and deserve to be addressed in order to fully understand Italian women's role in the

6. For a recent interpretation of the multiple forms of women's activism in the world of work, see Betti et al., *Women, Work and Activism*.

7. On UDI, see Betti, *Gli archivi dell'UDI*; Gabrielli, *La pace e la mimosa*.

labor market.[8] Although socially accepted and even desired, especially by Catholics, the diffusion of the male breadwinner model remained limited in postwar Italy for several reasons. Some women had no choice but to become breadwinners themselves. Some had been widowed by the war, while others had been left behind by the mass migration of men to the capital of industrial growth, both in northern Italy and across continental Western Europe.[9]

In addition, the low level of male wages and the persistent underemployment in sectors such as agriculture required women's economic contribution to the household, whether via formalized or completely informal labor. The level of poverty in the decade following World War II, as parliamentary inquiries showed,[10] limited and delayed the development of the so-called affluent society and the golden age.[11] Only during the economic boom of 1958 to 1963, which was also the period of the greatest industrial and economic growth of the twentieth century in Italy, did the level of consumption begin to increase significantly.[12] During this period the number of women workers, especially the youngest, increased and became more visible to the public thanks to television documentaries.[13]

Women made an important contribution to the development of the industrial system in Fordist Italy, constituting the bulk of some particularly feminized sectors, such as textiles and clothing, but also working informally as home-based workers.[14] In quantitative terms, they contributed less than men to the growth of formal employment in the industrial sector: At the beginning of the 1970s, women working in the Italian factories represented 25 percent of the total industrial workforce (1.4 million out of 5.3 million).[15] If we look at industrial homework outside the factories, which was almost entirely feminized, the picture is quite different. According to one estimate, there were between 1 and 1.5 million homeworkers in the early 1970s. If we take these data seriously, which were provided during the legislative process that led to the passage of the 1973 law regulating industrial homework, about 20 percent of the total industrial workforce was working informally in Fordist Italy, and women represented more than 40 percent of the total (formal and informal) workforce.[16]

8 For a general overview see Bravo et al., *Storia sociale delle donne*; Salvatici, *Storia delle donne*; Wilson, *Women in Twentieth-Century Italy*.

9 Pescarolo, *Il lavoro delle donne*; Signorelli, "Il pragmatismo delle donne"; Badino, *Tutte a casa*.

10. See, for instance, Pesenti, "Sottoretribuzione e miseria"; Ruffolo and Parasassi, *La disoccupazione in Italia*.

11. Galbraith, *Affluent Society*; Hobsbawm, *Age of Extremes*.

12. Capuzzo, *Genere, generazioni e consumi*; Liguori, *Donne e consumi*; Scrivano, "Signs of Americanization."

13. The documentary *The Working Woman* (*La donna che lavora*) consisted of eight episodes and was released in 1959 thanks to the contributions of journalist Ugo Zatterin and director Giovanni Salvi.

14. For an overview see Loreto, "Ma j'òm a i capissu nèn!"

15. *V Censimento generale dell'Industria e commercio 25 ottobre 1971*, vol. 2, f. 38, tav. 11, 49–52; vol. 3, "Industrie," 2, tav. 15, 76–87 and tav. 29, 784–805; vol. 8, "Dati generali riassuntivi," tav. 15, 66–87; and tav. 28, 424–511.

16. See the reconstruction provided in Betti, "Industrial Homework and Fordism."

Industrial homework was widespread throughout the Italian peninsula, but it was more present and persistent in regions characterized by small and medium-sized enterprises, despite their political connotations. Homeworking was often integrated into the production chain of sectors such as clothing or stockings. The case of Emilia-Romagna is illustrative.[17] At the 1973 Regional Conference on Women's Employment, the number of home-based workers in Emilia-Romagna was estimated at between 127,000 and 180,000; more conservative estimates put the figure at 100,000. About 90 percent of the workers were women.[18]

Rereading "Fordist" industrial development by adopting a gender perspective requires considering the issue of informality and the problem of precarity.[19] To what extent the Fordist model contributed to the stabilization of the labor force remains an open question, as gender-blind economic analyses have not fully addressed the role of women's labor (formal and informal).[20] Perceiving the Fordist era as one of stability centers around a male breadwinner model that ignores the multiple forms of work performed by women and their different labor conditions.[21] As research on Canada, France, the United States, and Switzerland has shown, a secondary, precarious, and feminized labor market existed in several Western countries during the golden age, targeting housewives, migrant women, or women from the lower classes in general.[22]

In the Italian case, scholars have generally overestimated the pervasiveness of the Fordist system, without taking into account the diversification and nature of Italian capitalism, which is largely made up of small and medium enterprises in addition to truly Fordist production, such as Fiat and others in the industrial triangle.[23] It is no coincidence that women workers played a role in the development of the factory system in the regions of the so-called Third Italy (Veneto, Emilia-Romagna, Tuscany), where labor costs were lower and there was a higher rate of home-based work.[24]

The social conditions of women and the secondary role assigned to women workers both socially and in the labor market forced them to accept unequal, precarious, and exploitative working conditions in the Fordist period. Women were more

---

17. Tommasetta, *Il lavoro a domicilio nell'Emilia-Romagna*.

18. Regione Emilia-Romagna, *Una politica di riforme economiche e sociali*.

19. On Fordism see also Settis, *Fordismi*; on the gender perspective, see also Boris and Janssens, "Complicating Categories"; Boris, "Gender of Labor History."

20. For a critical approach see Hudson, "Historical Construction of Gender."

21. See, for a conceptualization of "work" from a gender and feminist perspective, Papanek, "Family Status Production"; Sarti, Bellavitis, and Martini, *What Is Work?*

22. Hatton, *Temp Economy*; Vosko, *Temporary Work*; Shaukat, "Emigrer et travailler en Valais"; Beau, *Un siècle d'emplois précaires*; Badino, *Tutte a casa*; Betti, "Gender and Precarious Labor."

23. On different perspectives on the Italian industrialization process, see Sabell and Zaitlin, *Worlds of Possibilities*; Felice, *Divari regionali e intervento pubblico*; Berta, *L'Italia delle fabbriche*; Barca, *Storia del capitalismo italiano*; Brusco, "Emilian Model"; and Beccattini, "Riflessioni sullo sviluppo socio-econoomico della Toscana."

24. For an overview of the debate in Italy on "Third Italy," see Bartolini, *La Terza Italia*. Until 1969, Italian salaries varied according to the geographical area where the worker worked. Salaries in the regions of the Third Italy were lower than in the industrial triangle (Milan, Turin, etc.).

exposed to abuse and discrimination, made possible by the lack of protection against dismissals, and they were often hired with fixed-term contracts so that employers could get rid of them if they wanted to have a family or could simply dismiss them when they decided to marry. These practices were described by official sources such as the Parliamentary Commission of Inquiry into the Conditions of Workers (1955–58), whose role in Republican Italy was crucial in promoting improved conditions for both male and female workers.[25] After studying four thousand workers in 195 companies, mainly in the industrial sector, the commission formulated recommendations that led to the passage of four different laws relating to labor precarity: home-based industrial work (1958), subcontracted work, fixed-term contracts (1962), and dismissals for marriage (1963).[26]

At the beginning of the 1960s, the socialist senator Lina Merlin produced a "white book" that collected stories of women who had been dismissed after getting married.[27] In addition to precarious contracts and discrimination, women had less access to stable positions in the industrial context, especially if they were working mothers. The lack of social services and childcare reduced their chances of finding formal employment and pushed thousands into the informal economy, usually industrial homework or domestic work.

Rosy accounts of the glorious Fordist system failed to consider the quality and stability of jobs, which can be better understood by looking at the conditions of women workers. In 1962, for example, the economist Pasquale Saraceno published *L'Italia verso la piena occupazione* (*Italy Toward Full Employment*), which was deeply influenced by Italy's economic performance during the boom years.[28] The book enthusiastically declared that Italy had finally gotten rid of unemployment and had begun to function according to the mechanisms of an advanced economy. In 1964, Saraceno's report to the minister of the budget provided estimates of economic growth and employment dynamics that completely ignored the relevance of women's employment and unemployment.[29]

The Italian case, from this point of view, has shown that women constituted a reserve army of labor, as contemporary observers dubbed it, that was particularly useful and convenient. The high level of instability experienced by women was considered something typical of women's work due to their primary roles as mothers and wives. If women lost their jobs, they were not even considered unemployed, because they could return to housewifery, a socially accepted role in golden age Italy.[30] As a direct consequence, the precarity of female work was not even perceived as such,

25. See, e.g., Commissione parlamentare, *Relazioni*, vol. 8: *Rapporti particolari di lavoro*; Commissione parlamentare, *Relazioni*, vol. 3: *Qualifiche e carriera del lavoratore*.

26. For a historical reconstruction of the laws see Betti, *Precarious Workers*.

27. Merlin, *Libro bianco sui licenziamenti*.

28. Saraceno, *L'Italia verso la piena occupazione*.

29. Saraceno, *Rapporto del Vice Presidente della Commissione Nazionale per la Programmazione Economica*.

30. For a discussion of women's employment and statistics, see Curli and Pescarolo, "Genere, Lavori, 'Etichette statistiche'"; on the contradictory figure of the housewife, see Bergonzini, "Casalinghe o lavoranti a domicilio?"

and wage equality was systematically opposed. In the late 1950s, for example, Furio Cicogna, president of the employers' association Assolombarda and subsequently of Confindustria (General Confederation of Italian Industry), declared that the female brain weighed less than a man's, clearly justifying gender wage inequality on the grounds of that assumption.[31]

## Economic Planning and Full Employment: Women's Critique and Political Mobilization

The economic crisis following the end of the economic boom (1963–64) changed the terms of the debate on women's work in Italy, a debate that saw trade unionists, Communist Party officials, and above all the leaders of the UDI among the protagonists.[32] Nora Federici, professor of statistics at the University of Rome and UDI leader, highlighted how by the end of 1963 as many as 310,000 women literally vanished from the labor market, while 50,000 new unemployed and underemployed women were registered.[33] Meanwhile, unregulated forms of employment such as homeworking increased. The need to promote the stabilization of female labor was cited by Federici as one of the primary goals of the UDI. The leaders of the association saw, in the ebbing in employment generated by the above-mentioned crisis, a threat to the new and "modern" role acquired by women in the productive and social spheres. In 1965, the issue of working stability thus became the subject of an ad hoc campaign by the UDI, demanding that the government include "full employment for women" among the objectives of economic planning, and formulating hypotheses of intervention to reduce the problem of women's precarious access to the labor market.[34]

In June 1965, the UDI promoted a national conference in Milan titled "Per il diritto delle donne al lavoro stabile e qualificato" ("For the Rights of Women to Stable and Qualified Work"), an occasion for an explicit denouncement of the "unfair and precarious conditions of female labor."[35] The conference was followed by a protest by some four thousand women, who marched along the streets of Milan chanting. Following the Milanese conference, the association launched a public petition: Over forty thousand signatures were collected and handed over to Parliament in December 1965.[36]

The UDI women demanded an amendment to the Economic Plan for 1965–68 to include estimates of the hoped-for increase in women's employment, but also a full evaluation of the work of female rural workers and adequate safeguards for

31. Bagnoli, "Cicogna contro le donne."

32. De Rosa, Lo sviluppo economico; Graziani, Lo sviluppo dell'economia italiana.

33. UDI National Archive, Thematic Section, DILA, b. 10, f. 82, sf. 3, Nora Federici, I problemi del mondo del lavoro; Relazione alla conferenza stampa d'inizio d'anno indetta dall'UDI (Roma, 12 gennaio 1965).

34. UDI National Archive, Thematic Section, DILA, b. 10, f. 82, sf. 2, letter from April 7, 1965.

35. UDI National Archive, Chronological Section, 1965, b. 112, f. 894, sf. 4, Per il diritto delle donne al lavoro stabile e qualificato. Atti della conferenza nazionale (Milano, 12–13 giugno 1965).

36. Bonucci, "Il lato forte"; UDI National Archive, Thematic Section, DILA, f. 82, sf. 1, UDI, Petizione al Parlamento. "Per il diritto delle donne al lavoro stabile e qualificato."

homeworkers. They also believed that a fair vocational training policy, a reform of the school system, and a radical change in the law on apprenticeships were essential to achieving more stable and qualified jobs.[37]

Even before the crisis of 1963–64, Agostino Novella had criticized the governments economic plan at the National Conference of Women Workers organized by the CGIL in 1962.[38] The male unionist underscored the absence in the debate on "full employment" of any gender perspective, which could consider the female labor force (real and potential) in the forecasts on employment, unemployment, and underemployment. Novella also shed light on one of the most critical aspects of women's employment trends during the boom years: women's relatively low participation in respect to overall employment growth, a critical aspect confirmed by the census data.[39]

The economic plan's neglect of the role of women workers also triggered criticisms by key female leaders of the Communist Party, starting with the MP Nilde Iotti. At the Second National Conference of Communist Women (1962), Iotti highlighted the "inhuman exploitation of women's labor" caused by the lack of respect for contracts and social security norms, dismissals for marriage, the excessive expansion of home-based work, the abuse of apprenticeships and temporary contracts, the very low level of vocational training, and the widespread use of seasonal work.[40] A few years later, when the favorable conditions of the economic boom had come to an end, Iotti harshly criticized the economic plan launched by Minister of the Budget Giovanni Pieraccini and the concept of "full employment," which was formulated exclusively with male workers in mind. The communist MP stressed that women could no longer be considered a "reserve army" but instead had to be included in the labor force, for which full employment should be sought.[41]

During the Third National Conference of the Factory Communists, promoted by the Communist Party, the Women's Commission of the PCI linked the problem of precarity to the low evaluation of women's work.[42] The latter was strongly associated with lower occupational status and the persistence of wage differentials between male and female workers. Communist women shared with the UDI the strategic goal of a more "stable and qualified" access for women to the paid labor market.[43] For the communists, the problem of precarity and its opposite—that is, the quest for stability—was solvable. The Central Women's Commission of the PCI's criticism of the "Pieraccini Plan" focused on the growth forecasts, which did not consider either the underemployment of women or the recent increase in female unemployment.

37. UDI National Archive, Thematic Section, DILA, f. 82, sf. 1, UDI, *Petizione al Parlamento. "Per il diritto delle donne al lavoro stabile e qualificato."*

38. Novella, "Conclusioni."

39. ISTAT, *Sommario di statistiche storiche.*

40. Iotti, *Intervento.*

41. *IV Conferenza nazionale delle donne comuniste.*

42. *Rafforzare il PCI nelle fabbriche per l'unità.*

43. *Rafforzare il PCI nelle fabbriche per l'unità.*

Furthermore, the plan did not address the issue of social services, which were considered fundamental to promoting women's stable access to the labor market.

The critique of economic planning from a gender perspective led the UDI in 1966 to promote a national conference titled "Il lavoro della donna e la programmazione" ("Women's Work and Planning").[44] The UDI demanded that women's associations be represented in the regional economic planning committees and become special advisers on issues related to women's employment. In her closing speech, Giglia Tedesco emphasized that women's right to work cannot be left "to the spontaneous development of our country" but requires specific intervention at the social and political levels.[45] The association promoted the organization of conferences dedicated to the issue of women's employment at the provincial and regional levels.[46] At the 1967 National Assembly of Female Worker Delegates, analysis of the negative dynamics of female employment was accompanied by an explicit demand by the UDI for policies aimed at achieving "full employment for women."[47]

On the eve of 1968, Italian women finally succeeded in opening a public discussion on women's employment and economic development. As a result of lobbying by left-wing women's associations, political parties, and trade unions, along with mass political mobilization, including marches and petitions, the Ministry of Economic Planning organized a National Conference on the Problems of Women's Employment in March 1968.[48] The influence of the transformation of the Italian factory system, developed in the second half of the 1960s, was discussed, revealing the negative impact on women's employment, which had dropped by hundreds of thousands. Despite their different positions in government, both socialist and communist women called for structural reforms to increase women's participation in the labor market.[49] They discussed not only the quantitative aspect of women's employment but also the quality of women's work. The goal of increasing women's skilled work and its stability was shared by participants from different political backgrounds. The role of the women's movement within the Christian Democrats was also relevant to the conference, which demonstrated the change in attitudes toward women's work that had occurred among Catholic women in the aftermath of the economic boom.[50]

44. UDI, *Il lavoro della donna e la programmazione economica*.
45. Tedesco, "Conclusioni."
46. Tedesco, "Conclusioni."
47. UDI Archive of Bologna, b. 6 "1967," c. III, f. 8, *Occupazione femminile in Emilia-Romagna: realtà e prospettive. Convegno di studio indetto dalle presidenze dell'Unione Donne Italiane dell'Emilia-Romagna* (Bologna, November 21, 1967).
48. "La conferenza nazionale sull'occupazione femminile."
49. "Creare 750.000 posti di lavoro per le donne."
50. For the role of Catholic women, see, e.g., Taricone, *Il Centro italiano femminile*; Pojmann, *Italian Women*.

## Beyond the Male Breadwinner Model: Italian Women's Struggle for Gendering Welfare Services

Between the 1950s and 1960s, Italian women sought to create a welfare system that was more inclusive and focused on women's caring responsibilities.[51] It should be remembered that in the Italian left-wing political milieu until the late 1960s, many women officials experienced forms of double or even triple affiliation, being communist or socialist MPs and at the same time holding key positions in the Union of Italian Women or as trade unionists in the CGIL.[52] This enhanced the impact of the women's political agenda, which was particularly strong on labor and social rights.[53] Not surprisingly, communist and socialist women in Parliament introduced, more than once, bills that had been previously discussed and agreed upon with the UDI leadership.

In 1955, the communist MP Nilde Iotti promoted a bill to guarantee pension rights for housewives, while the UDI promoted petitions, marches, and new forms of sit-ins.[54] In 1957, delegations of housewives from all over Italy (around 1,500 women) attended a conference in Rome to discuss pension rights for housewives and marched with hundreds of these women.[55] In the early 1960s, the struggle reached a peak in terms of putting pressure on Parliament and the government. On March 8, 1961, the housewives organized a picket in front of Parliament, wearing aprons and banging pots in order to obtain pension rights, a form of conflict they repeated in several housewives' demonstrations that took place in many Italian cities, including Rome, Naples, and Palermo.[56] The struggle for housewives' pension rights lasted from 1955 to 1963, when a law was passed. Although the UDI bill was not approved as such, the UDI campaign created the basis for a new law that granted pension rights to the elderly regardless of their working condition.

In the 1960s, women's organizations, often in conjunction with trade unions and other organizations, sponsored a number of studies and conferences on women's working and social conditions, addressing a wide range of issues, as outlined in the previous sections. Among them, particular attention was paid to the relationship between working and family life, which led the leftist UDI to draft a specific agenda on welfare services. In 1960, the association promoted a national inquiry into "women's work and family," through which it collected six hundred thousand questionnaires. The results, presented in a national conference, revealed women's everyday struggles to strike a balance between their caregiving duties at home and their exploitative and low-paid jobs.[57] Even though women's dual burden was not termed as such, the conference explicitly addressed the issue of work-life balance, paying particular attention

51. Gagliani, *Welfare state come umanesimo e antipatronage.*
52. See, for instance, Strazzeri, "Beyond the Double Blind Spot"; Bonfiglioli, "Red Girls' Revolutionary Tales."
53. Betti, "Generations of Italian Communist Women."
54. *Noi Donne*, 1955.
55. *Noi Donne*, 1957.
56. *Noi Donne*, March 8, 1961.
57. UDI, *Il lavoro della donna e la famiglia.*

to the relationship between work and motherhood. The UDI's policies in the early 1960s also led the association to dialogue with architects and urban planners who were invited to a national UDI conference to address women's needs.[58]

The most important campaign in the area of social welfare regarded childcare services. In 1962, UDI organized a national conference titled "Women's Work and the Safeguarding of Early Childhood."[59] It proposed creating nurseries, kindergartens, and daytime care to alleviate women's fatigue and to facilitate family life. Two years later, the association promoted a parliamentary bill aimed at launching a national plan for creating nursery schools across Italy.[60] Within the UDI's political strategy the latter was crucial to guarantee women, especially working women, the freedom of choice to become mothers. Working mothers in the 1960s Italian labor market had to put up with a considerable amount of discrimination. Clauses written into their labor contract allowed employers to fire them once they got married, something that women's associations and trade unions strongly opposed. A 1963 law finally banned those unfair practices.[61]

Protests grew more militant in 1968, when about two thousand women filled the streets of Rome with prams, demanding a law to create a network of nursery schools. The UDI organized this national demonstration under the title "Nursery School and Safeguards for Working Mothers."[62] Prams soon became the icon for the demands of Italian working mothers for new and more inclusive social services and a more gendered welfare state. The UDI launched a national campaign to support new legislation; another demonstration with prams was held in Rome in 1971; and in the same year, the nursery school law was passed, along with a new law for working mothers.[63]

Looking briefly at the role played by the UDI helps to highlight that not only the trade unions but also some women's associations advanced the discussion on women's work in Italy from the late 1960s through the mid-1970s. On the whole, the forms of protest, the language, and the UDI's approach was certainly affected by the new feminist thinking, which permeated a new generation of UDI women born in the 1940 and 1950s and who joined the association in the late 1960s.[64] While the 1968 UDI Congress explicitly reasserted women's work as a key aspect of female emancipation, it also addressed the relationship between women's paid work and women's reproductive labor. The latter was brought into the discussion by intellectuals such as

58. UDI, *Obbligatorietà della programmazione dei servizi sociali*; see also Renzoni, "Una città su misura."

59. UDI, *Il lavoro della donna e la tutela della prima infanzia: Atti del Convegno nazionale (Roma, 3–4 luglio 1962)*.

60. UDI, *Un servizio sociale di asili nido programmati dagli enti locali*.

61. "Processo ai licenziamenti per matrimonio"; Law No. 7, January 9, 1963, *Divieto di licenziamento delle lavoratrici per causa di matrimonio e modifiche alla legge 26 August 1950, n. 860: "Tutela fisica ed economica delle lavoratrici madri."*

62. UDI, *Le donne aprono la vertenza per gli asili nido*.

63. "Siamo stanche di aspettare. le donne aprono la vertenza nazionale sugli asili nido."

64. On second-wave feminism in Italy, see Bracke, *Women and the Reinvention of the Political*.

the communist Luciana Castellina, a UDI leader at the time and afterward cofounder of the radical left magazine and political movement *Il Manifesto*.[65] A few years later, at the 1973 UDI Congress, titled "The Female Dimension: New Values, New Structures Within Society," the tension existing between continuity and change in the association's political thinking under the influence of second-wave feminism clearly emerged.[66]

The effects of the international economic crisis triggered by the oil shock (1973), which according to most interpretations ended the so-called golden age, led the UDI to explicitly address the defense of women's employment as a key aspect of its political strategy. The defense of women's employment through the improvement of women's quality of work and stability were proposed as the main actions to tackle the economic crisis.[67] In 1974 the UDI National Conference, titled "Women as Protagonists of a New Model of Development," addressed the relationship between women's new place in Italian society and the necessity for a new model of development affirming the need for a massive expansion of women's paid work to ensure the progress and development of Italian society as a whole.[68] In 1976 a national demonstration was organized in Rome, attended by fifty thousand women, where slogans such as "Women's emancipation will change our quality of life," "Women's employment is a must for economic development," and "We don't want to be forced to be housewives, we want to work" clearly summed up the new approach to women's work in the 1970s proposed by the UDI and other groups.[69]

## Conclusion

The construction of Fordism during the so-called golden age of the twentieth century left women on the margins, as they did not experience the same job opportunities as men and the quality of their work was considered inferior to that of their male counterparts. Though there were positive features to the system, rethinking the golden age through women's work requires confronting the dark sides of the so-called glorious thirty and the Fordist model. These downsides included job precarity, women's secondary role in economic planning, women's exclusion from the welfare state, and a general lack of social services women workers needed, such as childcare.

To what extent did the stabilization of the male breadwinner and men's full employment during the golden age require maintaining women workers in subordinate conditions through discriminatory practices, low wages, and precarious work?[70]

65. *Le indicazioni di lavoro emerse dall'VIII Congresso. Relazione di Luciana Castellina.*

66. UDI, *Dimensione Donna.*

67. Wolleb, "Mutamenti nei rapporti di produzione nella crisi."

68. UDI National Archive, Thematic Section, Diritto al lavoro, b. 26, f. 148, sf. 2, *No al lavoro dequalificato, no al tempo parziale, no all'emarginazione della donna "Le donne protagoniste del nuovo modello di sviluppo." Note in preparazione del Convegno dell'Unione donne italiane. Genova, March 23, 1974.*

69. UDI National Archive, Thematic Section, Diritto al lavoro, b. 26, f. 16, sf. 4, *Manifestazione nazionale dell'Unione donne italiane February 11, 1976 [Conclusioni Mergherita Repetto].*

70. See Komlosy, "Work and Labor Relations."

The analysis provided here has shown that women workers were certainly considered secondary in the booming labor market of the 1950s and 1960s and again after 1973, when unemployment peaked. Women's precarity was normalized as an outcome of their dual role as workers and mothers. While male workers were seen as the natural breadwinners, female workers were explicitly seen as a reserve army of cheaper labor to be used when needed. This was the social role assigned to them by businessmen, politicians, and, until the boom, even some trade unionists, precisely to favor male employment.

On the other hand, the article shows that women in postwar Italy were not passive subjects, unaware of the discrimination they experienced within Italian society and the labor market.[71] The mobilization of female leaders within different (leftist) organizations, both mixed and women-only, was crucial to attaining influence at an institutional level, especially within the Italian government, and to promoting more equal and inclusive economic and public policies. The end of the golden age abruptly interrupted the positive path toward a more woman-friendly model of society, threatening women's paid work and their role in the labor market. Nevertheless, the new attention to women's work did not end in the 1970s, as the role of long-standing associations such as the UDI demonstrates, and the struggles of the following decades were fortified by the new language and concepts introduced by second-wave feminists. ∎

ELOISA BETTI holds a PhD in European history from the University of Bologna. She is currently assistant professor (RTD/A) at the Department of Political Science, Law and International Studies of the University of Padua, having previously been adjunct professor of labor history at the University of Bologna. In 2014–15 she was a Visiting Fellow at the School of Advanced Study (University of London), and in 2015–16 she was awarded the EURIAS Fellowship at the Institute for Human Sciences in Vienna. Her recent publications in English include the monograph *Precarious Workers: History of Debates, Political Mobilizations and Labor Reforms in Italy* (2022) and the edited volume (with L. Papastefanaki, M. Tolemelli, and S. Zimmerman) *Women, Work and Activism: Chapters of an Inclusive History of Labor in the Long Twentieth Century* (2022).

## References

Badino, Anna. *Tutte a casa: Donne tra migrazione e lavoro nella Torino degli anni Sessanta.* Rome: Viella, 2008.

Bagnoli, Jone. "Cicogna contro le donne." *Il Lavoro*, May 27, 1956.

Barca, Fabrizio. *Storia del capitalismo italiano: Dal dopoguerra a oggi.* Rome: Donzelli, 1997.

Bartolini, Francesco. *La Terza Italia: Reinventare la Nazione alla fine del Novecento.* Rome: Carocci, 2015.

Beau, Anne-Sophie. *Un siècle d'emplois précaires.* Paris: Decitré, 2004.

Becattini, Giacomo. "Il distretto industriale marshalliano come concetto socio-economico." *Stato e mercato*, no. 25 (1989): 111–128.

71. This generation of women activists have been termed "the lost wave"; see Tambor, *Lost Wave.*

Becattini, Giacomo. "Riflessioni sullo sviluppo socio-economico della Toscana in questo dopoguerra." In *Storia d'Italia: Le regioni dall'Unità a oggi. La Toscana*, edited by Giorgio Mori, 899–924. Turin: Einaudi, 1986.

Bergonzini, Luciano. "Casalinghe o lavoranti a domicilio?" *Inchiesta*, no. 10 (1973): 50–54.

Berta, Giuseppe. *L'Italia delle fabbriche: Ascesa e tramonto dell'industrialismo nel Novecento*. Bologna: Il Mulino, 2001.

Betti, Eloisa. "Gender and Precarious Labor in a Historical Perspective: Italian Women and Precarious Work Between Fordism and Post-Fordism." In "Precarious Labor in Global Perspective," edited by Sara Mosoetsa, Chris Tilly, and Joel Stillermann, special issue, *International Labor and Working-Class History*, no. 89 (2016): 64–83.

Betti, Eloisa. "Generations of Italian Communist Women and the Making of a Women's Rights Agenda in the Cold War (1945–68): Historiography, Memory, and New Archival Evidence." In *Gender, Generations and Communism in Central and Eastern Europe and Beyond*, edited by Anna Artwińska and Agnieszka Mrozik, 82–101. New York: Routledge, 2020.

Betti, Eloisa. "Gli archivi dell'UDI come fonti per la storia del lavoro femminile." In *Il genere nella ricerca storica*, edited by Saveria Chermotti and Maria Cristina La Rocca. Padua: Il Poligrafo, 2015.

Betti, Eloisa. "Historicizing Precarious Work: Forty Years of Research in the Social Sciences and Humanities." *International Review of Social History*, no. 2 (2018): 273–319.

Betti, Eloisa. "Industrial Homework and Fordism in Western Europe: Women's Agency, Labour Legislation and Trade Unions' Action in Golden Age Italy (1945–1975)." In *Homebased Work and Homebased Workers 1800–2021*, edited by Malin Nilsson, Indrani Mazumdar, and Silke Neunsinger, 227–44. London: Brill, 2021.

Betti, Eloisa. *Le ombre del fordismo: Sviluppo industriale occupazione femminile e precarietà del lavoro nel trentennio glorioso (Bologna, Emilia-Romagna, Italia)*. Bologna: Bologna University Press, 2020.

Betti, Eloisa. *Precarious Workers: History of Debates, Political Mobilizations and Labor Reforms in Italy*. Budapest: Central European University Press, 2022.

Betti, Eloisa, Leda Papastefanaki, Marica Tolomelli, and Susan Zimmermann, eds. *Women, Work and Activism: Chapters of an Inclusive History of Labor in the Long Twentieth Century*. Budapest: Central European University Press, 2022.

Bonfiglioli, Chiara. "Red Girls' Revolutionary Tales: Antifascist Women's Autobiographies in Italy." *Feminist Review*, no. 106 (2014): 60–77.

Bonucci. "Il lato forte." *Noi Donne*, June 26, 1965.

Boris, Eileen. "The Gender of Labor History: The Difference It Makes." *Genesis* 25, no. 2 (2016): 147–66.

Boris, Eileen. *Making the Woman Worker: Precarious Labor and the Fight for Global Standards, 1919–2019*. New York: Oxford University Press, 2019.

Boris, Eileen, and Leigh Dodson. *Working at Living: The Social Relations of Precarity*. Santa Barbara: University of California, Santa Barbara, Department of Feminist Studies, 2013.

Boris, Eileen, and Angelique Janssens. "Complicating Categories: An Introduction." *International Review of Social History*, no. 44 (1999): 1–13.

Bracke, Maud Anne. *Women and the Reinvention of the Political: Feminism in Italy, 1968–1983*. London: Routledge, 2014.

Bravo, Anna, Margherita Pelaja, Alessandra Pescarolo, and Lucetta Scaraffia. *Storia sociale delle donne nell'Italia contemporanea*. Rome: Laterza, 2001.

Breman, Jan, and Marcel Van der Linden. "Informalizing the Economy: The Return of the Social Question at a Global Level." *Development and Change* 45, no. 5 (2014): 920–40.

Brusco, Sebastiano. "The Emilian Model: Productive Decentralisation and Social Integration." *Cambridge Journal of Economics*, no. 6 (1982): 167–84.

Capuzzo, Paolo. *Genere, generazione e consumi: L'Italia degli anni Sessanta*. Rome: Carocci, 2003.

Causarano, Pietro. "La fabbrica fordista e il conflitto industriale." In *Il Novecento, 1945–2000: La ricostruzione, il miracolo economico, la globalizzazione*, edited by Stefano Musso, 55–101. Rome: Castelvecchi, 2015.

Commissione parlamentare d'inchiesta sulle condizioni dei lavoratori in Italia. *Relazioni della Commissione parlamentare di inchiesta sulle condizioni dei lavoratori in Italia*. Vol. 3, *Qualifiche e carriera del lavoratore, trattamento e tutela delle lavoratrici*. Rome: Segretariati generali della Camera dei deputati e del Senato della Repubblica, 1963.

Commissione parlamentare d'inchiesta sulle condizioni dei lavoratori in Italia. *Relazioni della Commissione parlamentare di inchiesta sulle condizioni dei lavoratori in Italia*. Vol. 8, *Rapporti particolari di lavoro: Contratto a termine, lavoro in appalto, lavoro a domicilio, apprendistato*. Roma: Segretariati generali della Camera dei deputati e del Senato della Repubblica, 1959.

"La conferenza nazionale sull'occupazione femminile." *Noi Donne*, March 18, 1968.

"Creare 750.000 posti di lavoro per le donne." *L'Unità*, March 3, 1968.

Curli, Barbara, and Alessandra Pescarolo. "Genere, Lavori, 'Etichette statistiche': I censimenti in una prospettiva storica." In *Differenze e disuguaglianze: Prospettive per gli studi di genere in Italia*, edited by Franca Bimbi, 65–100. Bologna: Il Mulino, 2003.

De Rosa, Luigi. *Lo sviluppo economico dal dopoguerra ad oggi*. Rome: Laterza, 1997.

Felice, Emanuele. *Divari regionali e intervento pubblico: Per una rilettura dello sviluppo in Italia*. Bologna: Il Mulino, 2007.

Fudge, Judy, and Rosemary Owens, eds. *Precarious Work, Women and the New Economy: The Challenge to Legal Norms*. Oxford: Hart, 2006.

Gabrielli, Patrizia. *La pace e la mimosa: L'unione donne italiane e la costruzione politica della memoria (1944–1955)*. Roma: Donzelli, 2005.

Gagliani, Dianella. "Welfare state come umanesimo e antipatronage: Un'esperienza delle donne nel secondo dopoguerra." In *La sfera pubblica femminile: Percorsi di storia delle donne in età contemporanea*, edited by Dianella Gagliani and Mariuccia Salvati, 163–78. Bologna: Clueb, 1992.

Galbraith, John Kenneth. *The Affluent Society*. Boston: Houghton Mifflin, 1958.

Graziani, Augusto. *Lo sviluppo dell'economia italiana: Dalla ricostruzione alla moneta europea*. Turin: Bollati Boringhieri, 1998.

Hatton, Erin. *The Temp Economy: From Kelly Girls to Permatemps in Postwar America*. Philadelphia: University of Pennsylvania Press, 2011.

Hobsbawm, Eric J. *The Age of Extremes: The Short Twentieth Century, 1914–1991*. London: Michael Joseph, 1994.

Hudson, Pat. "The Historical Construction of Gender: Reflections on Gender and Economic History." In *Frontiers in the Economics of Gender*, edited by Francesca Bettio and Alina Verashchagina, 21–41. New York: Routledge, 2008.

"Le indicazioni di lavoro emerse dall'VIII Congresso: Relazione di Luciana Castellina al Comitato nazionale (23–24 novembre 1968)." In Maria Michetti, Margherita Repetto, and Luciana Viviani, *UDI: Laboratorio di politica delle donne*, 397–401. Rome: Cooperativa libera stampa, 1985.

Iotti, Nilde. Intervento. In *3ª Conferenza nazionale donne comuniste: Atti (Roma, 30–31 marzo-1° aprile 1962)*, 8–28. Rome: Seti, 1962.

ISTAT. *Sommario di statistiche storiche 1861–1975*. Rome: ISTAT, 1976.

IV Conferenza nazionale delle donne comuniste. *Atti (Roma, 26–27–28–29 giugno 1965).* Rome: Seti, 1966.

Komlosy, Andrea. "Work and Labour Relations." In *Capitalism: The Re-Emergence of a Historical Concept,* edited by Jürgen Kocka and Marcel Van der Linden, 33–69. London: Brill, 2016.

Liguori, Maria Chiara. "Donne e consumi nell'Italia degli anni Cinquanta." *Italia contemporanea,* no. 205 (1996): 665–89.

Loreto, Fabrizio. "'Ma j'òm a i capissu nèn!': Le donne nei settori del tessile e dell'abbigliamento." In *Mondi femminili in cento anni di sindacato,* vol. 1, edited by Gloria Chianese, 143–207. Rome: Ediesse, 2008.

Merlin, Lina. *Libro bianco sui licenziamenti per causa di matrimonio in Italia: Situazioni e documentazione.* Rome: Tip. L. Morara, 1961.

Neilson, Bret, and Neil Rossiter. "Precarity as a Political Concept, or, Fordism as Exception." *Theory, Culture and Society* 25, nos. 7–8 (2008): 51–72.

Novella, Agostino. "Conclusioni." In *I diritti della donna lavoratrice nella società nazionale e il riconoscimento del valore obiettivo del suo lavoro: III Conferenza nazionale delle donne lavoratrici (Roma, 9–11 novembre 1962),* 153–75. Rome: Stampagraf, 1962.

Pacini, Monica. *Donne al lavoro nella Terza Italia: San Miniato dalla ricostruzione alla società dei servizi.* Pisa: Edizioni ETS, 2009.

Papanek, Hanna. "Family Status Production: The 'Work' and 'Non-Work' of Women." *Signs,* no. 4 (1979): 775–81.

Pescarolo, Alessandra. *Il lavoro delle donne nell'Italia contemporanea.* Roma: Viella, 2019.

Pesenti, Antonio. "Sottoretribuzione e miseria." In *Atti della Commissione parlamentare d'inchiesta sulla miseria e sui mezzi per combatterla,* vol. 7. Milan: Unione tipografica, 1973.

Pojmann, Wendy. *Italian Women and International Cold War Politics, 1944–1968.* New York: Fordham University Press, 2013.

"Processo ai licenziamenti per matrimonio." *Noi Donne,* March 12, 1961.

Puar, Jasbir, ed. "Precarity Talk: A Virtual Roundtable with Lauren Berlant, Judith Butler, Bojana Cvejic, Isabell Lorey, Jasbir Puar, and Ana Vujanovic." *TDR: The Drama Review* 56, no. 4 (2012): 163–77.

*Rafforzare il PCI nelle fabbriche per l'unità e l'autonomia della classe operaia: III Conferenza nazionale dei Comunisti nelle fabbriche (Genova, 28–29–30 maggio 1965).* Rome: Gate, 1965.

Regione, Emilia-Romagna. *Una politica di riforme economiche e sociali per un nuovo tipo di sviluppo che qualifichi l'occupazione femminile: Atti della conferenza regionale (Casalecchio di Reno, 13–14 aprile 1973).* Bologna: Ica, 1973.

Renzoni, Cristina. "Una città su misura: Servizi sociali e assetto urbano nella pubblicistica e nei congressi dell'Unione donne italiane (1960–1964)." *TRIA International Journal of Urban Planning* 6, no. 10 (2013): 121–34.

Ruffolo, Giorgio, and Maurizio Parasassi. *La disoccupazione in Italia: Relazione sintetica delle indagini e degli studi promossi dalla Commissione parlamentare d'inchiesta sulla disoccupazione.* Bologna: Zanichelli, 1954.

Sabel, Charles F., and Jonathan Zeitlin, eds. *Worlds of Possibilities: Flexibility and Mass Production in Western Civilization.* Cambridge: Cambridge University Press, 1997.

Salvatici, Silvia. *Storia delle donne nell'Italia contemporanea.* Rome: Carocci, 2002.

Saraceno, Pasquale. *L'Italia verso la piena occupazione.* Milan: Feltrinelli, 1963.

Saraceno, Pasquale. *Rapporto del Vice Presidente della Commissione Nazionale per la Programmazione Economica.* Rome: Servizio Informazioni della Presidenza del Consiglio, 1964.

Sarti, Raffaella, Anna Bellavitis, and Manuela Martini, eds. *What Is Work? Gender at the Crossroads of Home, Family, and Business from the Early Modern Era to the Present*. Oxford: Berghahn Books, 2018.

Scrivano, Paolo. "Signs of Americanization in Italian Domestic Life: Italy's Postwar Conversion to Consumerism." *Journal of Contemporary History* 40, no. 2 (2005): 317–40.

Settis, Bruno. *Fordismi: Storia politica della produzione di massa*. Bologna: Il Mulino, 2016.

Shaukat, Saffia Elisa. "Emigrer et travailler en Valais au rythme des saisons: Une histoire d'exclusion." In *Mémoire ouvrière*, edited by Luc Van Dongen and Grégoire Favre. Sierre: Editions Monographic, 2011.

"Siamo stanche di aspettare: Le donne aprono la vertenza nazionale sugli asili nido." *Noi Donne*, March 14, 1970.

Signorelli, Amalia. "Il pragmatismo delle donne: La condizione femminile nella trasformazione delle campagne." In *Storia dell'agricoltura italiana in età contemporanea, vol. 2: Uomini e classi*, edited by Piero Bevilacqua, 635–60. Venice: Marsilio, 1990.

Strazzeri, Victor. "Beyond the Double Blind Spot: Relocating Communist Women as Transgressive Subjects in Contemporary Historiography." *Gender and History*, no. 2 (2022): 755–74.

Tambor, Molly. *The Lost Wave*. Oxford: Oxford University Press, 2014.

Taricone, Fiorenza. *Il Centro italiano femminile: Dalle origini agli anni Settanta*. Milan: Angeli, 2001.

Tedesco, Giglia. "Conclusioni." In UDI, *Il lavoro della donna e la programmazione economica: Atti della Conferenza nazionale (Firenze, 23–34 aprile 1966)*, 191–208. Rome: UDI, 1966.

Tommasetta, Leonardo. *Il lavoro a domicilio nell'Emilia-Romagna*. Bologna: Ica, 1977.

UDI. *Dimensione Donna: Nuovi valori nuove strutture nella società: Atti del IX Congresso nazionale dell'Unione donne italiane (Roma, 1–3 novembre 1973)*. Rome: UDI, 1973.

UDI. *Il lavoro della donna e la famiglia: Atti della Conferenza nazionale (Roma, 18–19 giugno 1960)*. Rome: UDI, 1960.

UDI. *Il lavoro della donna e la programmazione economica: Atti della Conferenza nazionale (Firenze, 23–34 aprile 1966)*. Rome: UDI, 1966.

UDI. *Il lavoro della donna e la tutela della prima infanzia: Atti del Convegno nazionale (Roma, 3–4 luglio 1962)*. Rome: Tip. Sates, 1962.

UDI. *Le donne aprono la vertenza per gli asili nido e per le scuole per l'infanzia: Atti del convegno nazionale (Rome, 18 February 1970)*. Rome: Seti, 1970.

UDI. *Obbligatorietà della programmazione dei servizi sociali in un nuovo assetto urbanistico: Atti del Convegno nazionale (Rome, 21–22 March 1964)*. Rome: UDI, 1964.

UDI. *Un servizio sociale di asili nido programmati dagli enti locali finanziato dallo stato: Assemblea nazionale per la consegna delle firme sotto la proposta di legge di iniziativa popolare. Bologna, 13 dicembre 1964*. Bologna: Tip. Sates, 1964.

Vosko, Leah F. *Temporary Work: The Gendered Rise of a Precarious Employment Relationship*. Toronto: University of Toronto Press, 2000.

Wilson, Perry. *Women in Twentieth-Century Italy*. Basingstoke, UK: Palgrave Macmillan, 2009.

Wolleb, Enrico. "Mutamenti nei rapporti di produzione nella crisi: Ascesa e tracollo del fordismo in Italia." In *La flessibilità del lavoro in Europa*, edited by Robert Boyer and Enrico Wolleb, 57–94. Milan: Franco Angeli, 1987.

# Social Democracy at High Tide: The Humanization of Work in Postwar West Germany

Stefan Müller

In West Germany, humanization of work was closely linked to the federal government's research and action program "Humanization of Working Life" from 1974 to 1989. Initially, this program combined demands for improved occupational health and safety (OHS) and for more workers' participation in companies. The program ran until 1989 and thus outlasted the change in government from Helmut Schmidt to Helmut Kohl in 1982–83. In this essay I discuss the emergence and the framework of the government program "Humanization of Working Life" but also pursue a broader goal. Since the 1960s there had been a discussion on the quality of life. At that time, humanization of work was part of a transatlantic discourse about the "good life," which challenged the future of industrial society and consumption. The demand for better quality of life was a response to the effects of the post-1945 boom, including its destructive effects on the environment, the cities, and much more—it was nothing less than the all-encompassing questioning of industrial modernity. Quality of work and OHS were thus indicators of the quality of life.

To analyze humanization of work and OHS discussions in postwar Germany, three proceeding and/or coincident developments must at least be mentioned. First, since the 1920s there had been a discussion around problems of OHS. Second, labor and scientific management research had played a role since the end of the nineteenth century. This new science focused on rationalization of production, but also on workers' motivation and the integration of workers' production knowledge into operational processes. By the 1920s at the latest, this approach became institutionalized.[1] Third, the desire for democratization of the workplace had a direct impact on the debates on humanization of work. In particular, the immediate context preceding the reformed Works Constitution (*Betriebsverfassungsgesetz*) in 1972 can already be

---

1. See Becker, *"Menschenökonomie"*; Uhl, *Humane Rationalisierung?*; Swiniartzki, *Der Deutsche Metallarbeiter-Verband 1891–1933*.

*Labor: Studies in Working-Class History* Volume 22 • Issue 1
DOI 10.1215/15476715-11521398 © 2025 by Labor and Working-Class History Association

understood as part of the discussion on the humanization of work, although I will only touch lightly on this element in this article.

Across the Western world, humanization-of-work initiatives accumulated in the 1960s and 1970s and led to different policies in different regions and states. In Scandinavia, a central keyword was "industrial democracy"; in Italy, the social discussion on humanization came up against a field of militant trade union initiatives; in the United States, the discussion was closely linked to health protection;[2] and in West Germany, with its social-democrat-oriented trade unions and a governing Social Democratic Party (SPD, Sozialdemokratische Partei Deutschlands), which began after 1945 and focused on social reform initiatives, questions of OHS became part of an expanded social policy.

## OHS After 1945

In view of the devastation after World War II, OHS was not a priority. Trade union demands focused mainly on the reduction of working hours and positive wage development. The underlying goals ranged from material participation in the boom to challenging capitalism via expansive wage demands.[3] In cases where OHS was considered, protection of working people from accidents and mechanical impacts, protection from noise and gases or dust, and the recognition of occupational diseases were paramount. OHS served the health of the individual, the preservation of the labor force, and the family income, and was thus ultimately also recognized as an important economic factor.[4] State initiatives on OHS focused especially on *Unfäller*, workers who supposedly suffer an accident at work through their own fault and who might be predestined to cause accidents through their behavior or character.[5] In the 1960s, OHS received more attention because the economic boom in the Federal Republic had led to an unusually high number of occupational accidents, with a peak of 2.8 million cases in 1961. But even with the beginning of the social-liberal coalition, 2.3 million occupational accidents were still reported.[6]

In his 1969 government declaration, Willy Brandt already formulated the "humanization of working life" in terms of OHS as an important task of the new government.[7] The initiatives reached their peak in the early 1970s: The reformed Works Constitution of 1972 granted works councils a right of workers' participation in the design of workplaces; the Youth Employment Protection Act was revised; in 1973,

2. See Isacson, "Humanization of Work in Scandinavia, 1960–1990"; Lange, *Aufstand in der Fabrik*; and US Department of Health, Education, and Welfare, *Work in America*.

3. See Angster, "Der Zehnerkreis." See also the debate about expansionary wage policy at the end of the 1940s in Jünke, "Remigranten in der westdeutschen Arbeiterbewegung der 1950er Jahre."

4. See DGB (Deutscher Gewerkschaftsbund) und Arbeitsschutz, *Anregungen für die Praxis aus der Arbeitsschutz-Ausstellung des DGB*.

5. Kleinöder, "Humanisierung durch Arbeitssicherheit?!"

6. Remeke, *Gewerkschaften und Sozialgesetzgebung*, 64–65.

7. "Abgabe einer Erklärung der Bundesregierung durch Willy Brandt, 28.10.1969. Deutscher Bundestag, Plenarprotokoll 06/5," 20–34, https://dserver.bundestag.de/btp/06/06005.pdf.

the Occupational Safety Act came into force, followed in 1975 by the Ordinances on Workplaces and on Hazardous Substances.[8] Also as early as 1972, the Federal Institute for Occupational Safety and Accident Research in Dortmund was founded and given a kind of supervision and research mandate. OHS was understood by the federal government as part of social policy, and the reforms mentioned above accompanied the program "Humanization of Working Life."[9]

## Workplace Democracy

The history of worker participation is of course as old as the modern labor movement, and its history in Germany can be traced back to the 1890s and the introduction of the first workers' committees. In the following, I use the term *codetermination*, which has its own history in Germany and is reflected in various laws. Works councils, for example, have legally protected rights to influence company decisions, including hiring and firing, along with the organization of workplaces. A right of codetermination also applies to union and company representatives on supervisory boards—a body that does not exist in US companies. After the 1918 revolution, the Reich Works Councils Act was created, which for the first time established codetermination rights for workers at the workplace level.[10] After World War II, criticism of capitalism and criticism of the workplace as the largest social institution, which was still under patriarchal rule, intensified. The Works Constitution of 1952 (in the tradition of the 1920 law) and the Co-Determination Act of 1951 hammered down stakes of workers' rights, though they were often considered inadequate by contemporary trade unionists and activists. The unions favored the parity codetermination introduced by the British occupation authorities in the coal and steel industry, which was reflected in the 1951 Co-Determination Act for the steel industry and mining companies.[11] If this law was still a trade union success, the Works Constitution Act of 1952 was seen more as a defeat, because only "one-third parity" was achieved for the management of large companies—in Germany the supervisory board, which differs from the executive board in its control functions. Additionally, trade unions were not given automatic rights of access to the companies.

The lack of trade union rights in the workplace and the lack of parity codetermination at the company level had been an issue again ever since the late 1960s. With the 1969 social-liberal government it was clear that the Works Constitution and the Co-Determination Act would be reformed. One proposal was the formation of working groups at the factory level, with their own elected spokespersons. These bodies would have their own rights and would operate alongside the established works councils. The catchphrase was "codetermination at the workplace." The proposal

---

8  See Bethge, "Arbeitsschutz."

9  See also Süß, "Sozialpolitische Denk- und Handlungsfelder in der Reformära."

10. Milert and Tschirbs, *Die andere Demokratie*; Däubler, Kittner, and Cerny, *Geschichte und Zukunft der Betriebsverfassung*.

11. Lauschke, *Die halbe Macht*.

came from an activist wing of the metalworkers' trade union (IG Metall), which in turn was closely linked to the SPD. One of these protagonists was Hans Matthöfer. He headed the Education Department of IG Metall until 1972 and became minister for research and technology in 1974, making him one of the main people responsible for the humanization program.[12] However, the trade unions opposed "codetermination at the workplace" and countered that there was a danger of a fragmentation of workers' interests.[13] Due to this rejection it did not find its way into the law, but it came up again in the state program on humanization. Regarding OHS, the reform of 1972 was a step forward, as it gave works councils the right to have a say in the design of workplaces.[14]

## Quality of Life

The term *quality of life* framed the discussion on OHS and humanization from the late 1960s onward. The term itself probably first appeared in the 1920s and described, generally, the material and immaterial circumstances for an individual to live a satisfying life. In the 1960s, the meaning shifted toward a critique of social inequality, which came to the fore again after two decades of boom and in the face of an "affluent society" (as it was also contemporarily called).[15]

The term entered the German debate via the United States. In 1964, US president Lyndon B. Johnson used it in his election campaign to describe a comprehensive reform program. In Germany, Willy Brandt, who famously transferred methods from the US election campaigns to Germany, was among the first to take up this formulation.[16] The importance of the term became obvious when it appeared in the 1972 SPD election campaign, which was titled "With Willy Brandt for Peace, Security and a Better Quality of Life."[17]

Behind the demand for a better quality of life was a social exhaustion: the exhaustion of working bodies; the exhaustion of the environment and natural resources; the exhaustion of public goods such as education or health, which had not grown along with private prosperity; the exhaustion of cities, which were clogged with cars and flooded with toxins from the exhaust pipes of individual mobility, no longer offering their inhabitants an attractive place to live; the exhaustion of the future, previously thought to be plannable and now contingent again; and finally, consumption, which had exhausted itself as a compensation for the hardships to be endured under industrial modernity. After a twenty- to twenty-five-year economic boom and an increase in prosperity never thought possible for the working people,

---

12. For the background of Matthöfer, see Müller, *Heinz Dürrbeck*.

13. See Lenk, "Mitbestimmung am Arbeitsplatz."

14. "Bundesgesetzblatt, Teil 1, 2/1972, 18.1.1972," http://www.bgbl.de/xaver/bgbl/start.xav?startbk =Bundesanzeiger_BGBl&jumpTo=bgbl172s0013.pdf.

15. Hockerts, "Rahmenbedingungen."

16. On Brandt's election campaign see the commentary by Süß, *Der seltsame Sieg*, 54–57.

17. SPD, *Mit Willy Brandt für Frieden, Sicherheit und eine bessere Qualität des Lebens*.

the society focused on quantities, we might say, went into crisis. While the 1950s and partly the 1960s were still characterized by state and social planning optimism, a series of crises accumulated at the end of the decade. The immense growth in consumption, especially for the working class, could no longer absorb these crises.

For example, cities were perceived as a "Moloch," as something that constantly and relentlessly demands sacrifices from its inhabitants. The cities had become too big to be experienced as reasonable and satisfying for the people: They became too big spatially and were populated by too many people. A core problem was traffic. The growth of cities increased car traffic by increasing the physical distance between home and workplace. All this was publicly discussed as a media topic and part of public opinion about the trope of dying cities.[18] Not only were the material effects of industrial society criticized; the cultural and aesthetic effects were also. Closely linked to this issue was pollution and other environmental problems. The mass consumption of the 1950s and 1960s was possible only due to the immense expansion of industry and the intensified exploitation of natural resources. The London smog of 1964, the accident of the oil tanker Torres Canyon off the English coast in 1967, or the great "fish kill" in the river Rhine in the summer of 1969 became symbols of environmental pollution. Environmental pollution was a permanent topic in the press and thus also in the social discussion.[19]

As it was a societal topic, quality of life was also taken up by the trade unions. Since 1963, IG Metall had organized international conferences around the topics of automation and rationalization.[20] The background to the congresses was the dynamics in computer development, the technological-economic utopias, and, of course, social fears associated with them. The trade unions undoubtedly welcomed technical progress and hoped for the liberation of people from heavy physical labor. The flip side of this, however, was the fear that up to half of all people in the Western world would lose their jobs (according to forecasts at the time).[21] However, in April 1972 the union held its fourth conference under a different motto and with different aims: "Future Task: Quality of Life."[22] The conference was attended by prominent personalities (e.g., the German federal president Gustav Heinemann, the Swedish prime minister Olof Palme, and Tony Benn from the Labour Party), and there was a discursive atmosphere that went far beyond the world of work and the trade unions. Approximately 1,200 guests from twenty-two countries came to Oberhausen,

18. See the front pages of *Der Spiegel* on February 3, 1969 ("Future Obstructed: Living in Germany"), April 23, 1971 ("New York: Death of a Metropolis?"), and June 6, 1971 ("Can the Cities Still Be Saved?").

19. See Uekötter, *Umweltgeschichte*.

20. The presentations and discussions of the conferences were subsequently documented in three works by Friedrichs: *Automation und technischer Fortschritt in Deutschland und den USA; Automation;* and *Computer und Angestellte.*

21. See, for the fantasy of a factory devoid of people, Uhl, "Eine lange Geschichte"; Roth, "Die automatische Fabrik."

22. The German phrase in the title, *aufgabe Zukunft*, emphasizes more strongly the requirement for the trade union to understand the future as a task that can be shaped. It is a mandate to act.

including 170 scientists. Unlike at the first three conferences, only a few topics revolved around work. Instead, life in all facets became the focus: The fifty-eight papers in total dealt with transport and environmental problems, the future of the education system, health issues, and even regional development. The concept of quality was very broad. Tony Benn understood it as nothing less than "the creation and maintenance of a social order that enriches all people and gives them the greatest possible prospects for a satisfying life."[23] The German trade unionists argued more moderately but along similar lines. The president of the German Trade Union Confederation, Heinz Oskar Vetter, criticized the contradiction between private prosperity and public poverty: He said, "We treat ourselves to long and luxurious holiday trips and are unable to build hospitals and schools.... We pride ourselves on the fast car, even the second car for the family, and suffocate in exhaust fumes on congested roads."[24] Vetter addressed the gap between increased private wealth and the lack of funding for public goods, and he conflated this criticism with the criticism of environmental pollution and the destruction of cities. The German trade union leader concluded his analysis with a call for a radical social break from the "dominant principles of private profit and uncritically viewed growth."[25] Remarkably, and to be understood as a sign of the times, even Federal President Gustav Heinemann echoed this theme. "We are in the midst of a stormy industrial revolution and increasing prosperity of our civilization," Heinemann said in his greeting to the conference, and he asked whether Western industrial societies had not "passed on some of the costs of our prosperity . . . to the environment for far too long" and were now "threatening to suffocate" from the consequences.[26]

### The Federal Program "Humanization of Working Life"

The developments mentioned above—quality of life, demands for more workplace codetermination, and the changes in OHS itself—accompanied the efforts to shape work in a more humane way.[27] However, state agencies, trade unions, and employers took part in the debate on the humanization and quality of work with their own interests in mind. In the trade unions, attention to qualitative issues began to show up in labor-management negotiations.[28] One example was a collective agreement for the metalworkers in Baden-Württemberg in 1973, which was about a paid five-minute rest break per hour for assembly line workers.[29] Although the collective agreement was about a material (quantitative) improvement, the trade union arguments related to

23. Friedrichs, *Aufgabe Zukunft*, 1:27.

24. Quoted in Friedrichs, *Aufgabe Zukunft*, 1:17.

25. Friedrichs, *Aufgabe Zukunft*, 1:17–18.

26. Friedrichs, *Aufgabe Zukunft*, 1:14.

27. See, for more on this section, Müller, "Das Forschungs- und Aktionsprogramm."

28. Sauer, "Von der 'Humanisierung der Arbeit' zur 'Guten Arbeit'"; Oehlke, *Arbeitspolitik zwischen Tradition und Innovation*, 16.

29. See IG Metall, *Werktage werden besser*.

human satisfaction at the workplace. The federal government saw its initiatives confirmed by such industrial action.[30]

On the company side, the growing need for more flexible production in order to react to rapidly changing product types with smaller production lines became important. Against this background, experiments with (semi-autonomous) work groups as an alternative to assembly line production were in demand, especially in the 1970s; motivational issues came into focus as well.[31] The employers' interest in rationalization was unmistakable. The metal, electrical, and car industries in particular felt that new work organization structures and management concepts were necessary to make production more flexible and market-oriented. The sociologist Werner Fricke, who was involved in the humanization program, commented that the profit motive sometimes led to the "granting of at least enclaves of limited autonomy and self-control in the work process."[32] For the trade unions, a close connection between decent work and quality of life was obvious. It was remarkable, however, that the employers' side also participated in this discourse and had to do so. One can see the importance of the quality-of-life discourse, among many other things, in a title from employer-related research that speaks of the "quality of life at work."[33]

In 1974, the Federal Ministry of Labor and the Federal Ministry of Research and Technology finally launched the Action and Research Program "Humanization of Working Life." By 1989, more than 1,600 individual measures had been funded under this program.[34] From the beginning and already before the program's start, the minister of labor invited the scientific community to participate.[35]

The humanization program was designed in such a way that companies applied for funding for projects; a few years later this also became possible for employers' organizations and trade unions. Scientists could apply for projects too but needed company support. Companies were reimbursed up to 50 percent of the cost price, while scientific institutions usually received 100 percent. The Federal Ministries pursued four goals with the program for which funding was available.[36] First, guideline values (new standards) were to be developed for machines and systems that served OHS. Second, projects for the development of humane work technologies could be applied for. These two objectives served to reduce harmful work stressors, whether physical or mental. The third objective concerned work organization. Projects in this category had a technical effect on the organization of work, but particularly of group work; a

30. See Ehmke, "Forschung und Entwicklung zur Humanisierung des Arbeitslebens."

31. See Arbeitskreis, "Neue Arbeitsstrukturen der deutschen Automobilindustrie."

32. Fricke, "Drei Jahrzehnte Forschung und Praxis," 145.

33. Schlaffke, Rühl, and Weil, *Qualität des Lebens am Arbeitsplatz*.

34. For the figures see Projektträger, "Humanisierung des Arbeitslebens," "Projektstatusbericht 1988/89," 11.

35. See Bethge, "Arbeitsschutz," 304; Ulich, "Erfahrungen aus dem VW-Projekt."

36. Bundesminister für Arbeit und Sozialordnung / Bundesminister für Forschung und Technologie, *Forschung zur Humanisierung des Arbeitslebens*. For funding see "Deutsche Forschungs- und Versuchsanstalt für Luft- und Raumfahrt/Projektträger HdA, Grundsätze zur Förderung der Forschung und Entwicklung auf dem Gebiet 'Humanisierung des Arbeitslebens,' 1.7.1976," in Bundesarchiv Koblenz, B 196/31220.

few projects also concerned management and personnel planning. Finally, the fourth funding area served to transfer findings from the accompanying scientific research.

At the beginning, about a quarter of the projects carried out consisted of OHS measures, especially in noise or dust control; another quarter of all projects in this early phase (until 1978–79) dealt with new work structures. The latter program line can be described as the characteristic feature of the program in the 1970s. In the early years, mining also occupied a dominant position in the program, accounting for a quarter of all projects.[37] In general, the first projects were awarded to large industrial companies used to dealing with the ministry's funding.[38]

To sum up, one can see a strong trade union political focus in the humanization program, which was certainly due to Minister of Labor Walter Ahrend (who had previously been the chairman of the Mining and Energy Trade Union); his parliamentary state secretary, Helmut Rohde (the chairman of the Labor Group in the SPD); Hans Matthöfer (who once headed the education department of IG Metall); and the head of the project-executing agency, Willi Pöhler, who had also previously been active in the education work of IG Metall.[39]

### Trade Union Skepticism and Crisis of the Humanization Program

Although the humanization program took up a number of trade union demands for improved occupational health and safety, and important former trade unionists now even held ministerial positions, the program met with skepticism in the trade unions. The trade unions were very skeptical about the technological focus of the program, and they criticized the democratic impulse, as they saw their rights in the form of collective agreement law and the Works Constitution Act endangered. Two key factors explain this trade union criticism. First, the trade unions claimed to be the motor of labor humanization and accused the program of being too accommodating toward the rationalization interests of the companies. Second, the program started after the onset of the 1973 energy price crisis. For example, the president of the German Trade Union Federation (DGB, Deutscher Gewerkschaftsbund), Heinz Oskar Vetter, expressed strong doubts about the "people-friendliness" of the proposed technological solutions, fearing instead performance increases and new burdens.[40] Vetter also criticized the lack of trade union involvement in the program. The government took this up and changed the project conditions. Companies now had to obtain the consent of the works council to carry out a project, and an expert committee consisting of scientists, employers, and trade unionists was set up at the ministry. This was a big step for the ministry, as there had never been such labor participation before.[41]

37. See Poplawski, "Humanisierung unter Tage?"
38. See Peter and Pöhler, "Umsetzungskonzepte."
39. See, for Willi Pöhler, Müller, *Heinz Dürrbeck*, 357–59.
40. Vetter, "Referat," 27–28.
41. Bundesminister für Forschung und Technologie/Bundesminister für Arbeit und Sozialordnung, *Forschung zur Humanisierung des Arbeitslebens*, 21–22; Kleinöder, *Humanisierung der Arbeit*, 14–15; Peter and Pöhler, "Umsetzungskonzepte," 105.

Criticism of the humanization program was particularly strong in IG Metall. This was the union most affected in the 1970s, since more than half of the projects funded in the 1970s took place in its organizational area.[42] Reimar Birkwald, who was involved in the ministry's committee on behalf of IG Metall, drew a "sobering" conclusion at the end of 1978, some four and a half years after the program's start: "To sum up briefly: The declared objective of humanizing working conditions has largely remained on paper in practice."[43] Birkwald criticized the projects on work organization in particular. As already outlined above, the 1960s ideas about code-termination in the workplace flashed up again in the humanization program. Just as had occurred following the works council constitution in 1972, when trade unions resisted undermining the rights of works councils through additional workplace bodies, they now objected to the humanization program. This time it was the semi-autonomous work groups that provoked the unions' opposition. In a pilot project at the car manufacturer Volkswagen (1975 to 1977), the economic efficiency in engine production by classic assembly line work was compared with that by semi-autonomous work groups. In contrast to the assembly line, a group of employees in a production island produced an engine completely on their own. As there were still foremen (but with unclear tasks), the production method was described as semi-autonomous.[44] The conflict revolved around the tasks of the group spokespersons and the extent of the work group's autonomy. The works council insisted that the autonomous organization of working time and the distribution of tasks in the group represented an encroachment on its codetermination rights. The works council's criticism took place against the background of significant rationalization cuts made by the company: In the first half of 1975, the local workforce in Salzgitter (where the project took place) had been reduced from about 9,000 to around 5,500 employees through severance agreements and transfers to Wolfsburg.[45] It is therefore not surprising that the works council regarded the project with skepticism. Finally, it withdrew from the project.

The conflict over the (semi-)autonomous work groups was inherent in the goals of the humanization program. The expert committee at the ministry, with equal representation of employers, trade unions, and academics, explicitly considered the democratization of the workplace a goal. In a joint statement, it stipulated that the "employees should be involved in the determination of their work tasks and work relations," which meant questions of working time and performance density as well

42. "Udo Blum, Entwurf für ein IG Metall-HdA-Beratungsprojekt, 7.11.1978," in Archiv der sozialen Demokratie, 5/IGMA150847.

43. "Reimar Birkwald, Humanisierungs- und Technologieförderung durch den BMFT, Frankfurt am Main, November 1978," in Archiv der sozialen Demokratie, 5/IGMZ210421.

44. Volkswagenwerk AG, Institut für Arbeits- und Betriebspsychologie der ETH Zürich, and Institut für Arbeitswissenschaft der TH Darmstadt, *Gruppenarbeit in der Motorenmontage*. For a historiographical perspective, see Fuhrich, *Humanisierung oder Rationalisierung?*

45. See Barth, "Projektgeschichte aus der Sicht der Begleitforschung," 40–41.

as the "operational decision-making structure [and] personnel planning."[46] So while companies such as Volkswagen, for example, were primarily interested in the potential profitability of experiments with group work in production, the expert committee was aiming for more self-determination in the workplace. The committee thus formulated its claim to want to intervene extensively in the competencies of works councils, management, and collective bargaining parties. On the trade union side, the committee was made up of supporters of this approach. Within the union itself, however, this position did not command a majority.[47] The role of the group spokespersons was unclear and overlapped with the rights of the works councils, but without a legal basis. The majority of trade unionists feared that this new body would operate at the expense of the works councils' powers, which had only been considerably expanded in 1972. In IG Metall's functionary newspaper, the industrial sociologist Horst Kern even characterized the "autonomous working groups" as "nonsense" and argued that Scandinavian models could not be transferred to West Germany.[48]

At the end of the 1970s, the humanization program fell into a deep crisis. The project-executing agency was publicly accused of lacking efficiency. In particular, it was criticized for not transferring project results to other companies. The criticism was carried by the conservative opposition in Parliament and the Federal Audit Office, which both said that the funding of 100 million Deutsche Marks per year was not in efficient proportion to the results.[49] The protagonists of the humanization program were well aware of the seriousness of the accusations and the fractured field. By the end of 1977, they felt that signs of fatigue were already evident; the impetus provided by the program had "more or less worn off."[50] When Hans Matthöfer moved to the Ministry of Finance in 1978, the humanization program lost its mainstay at the government. However, at the very time that the program was in crisis, the trade unions, especially IG Metall, came to terms with the program and carried out projects themselves. In a project lasting from 1979 to 1984, IG Metall advised works councils with the aim of getting them to take the initiative and complete company projects. This did not succeed. According to their own assessment, this was because the works councils were mainly occupied with defensive struggles.[51]

With the change of government in 1982, the project line on work organization was finally discontinued, even though the program as a whole continued until 1989.

46. "Deutsche Forschungs- und Versuchsanstalt für Luft- und Raumfahrt/Projektträger HdA, Grundsätze zur Förderung der Forschung und Entwicklung auf dem Gebiet 'Humanisierung des Arbeitslebens,' 1.7.1976," in Bundesarchiv Koblenz, B 196/31220.

47. See Ulich, "Erfahrungen aus dem VW-Projekt."

48. Kern, "Vom Unfug mit der 'autonomen Arbeitsgruppe.'"

49. See Bethge, "Arbeitsschutz"; Kleinöder, Humanisierung der Arbeit, 17.

50. "Ergebnisprotokoll der 13. Sitzung des Fachausschusses 'Humanisierung des Arbeitslebens' am 2.12.1977 in Bonn vom 6.12.1977," 2, in Bundesarchiv Koblenz, B 196/31216.

51. "IG Metall: Abschlußbericht zum 'HdA-Beratungsprojekt der IG Metall zur Unterstützung von Arbeitnehmern und deren Interessenvertretern im Rahmen des Förderschwerpunktes Umsetzung des Aktionsprogramms HdA,' 1.7.1979–31.12.1984," in Archiv der sozialen Demokratie, 5/IGMZ220602.

Instead of questions of work organization, the topics of "production" and "office and administration" were now included in the funding.[52] This reflected not only a political change but also the increasing influence of computer-assisted production in the 1980s More importantly, the concept of innovation was introduced into the program, and questions of participation were replaced by categories of competition. From now on, human-centered work design was regarded as an intrinsic "entrepreneurial task."[53]

## Conclusion

The Research and Action Program "Humanization of Working Life" was part of a future-oriented debate on the quality of life, which resulted from multiple sources. Through this program, social democracy sought answers to the problems of industrial work for the health and well-being of working people. With its far-reaching OHS goals as well as its goals for the expansion of workplace democracy, the program still breathed the spirit of the late 1960s and early 1970s. Characteristic of the 1970s were the work-structuring projects, with their search for alternatives to assembly line work. Central actors in the program also came from a specific trade-union-dominated wing of the SPD, whose political orientation I have described elsewhere as "social democratic operaismo."[54] This refers to an orientation toward political work in the companies and the efforts to encourage their own organization (trade union, party) to take more initiative by mobilizing its own rank and file. The social and political goals of these German social democrats were of course not comparable with the Italian operaist movement, although similar methods can be found in workplace mobilization, for example.

After a short time, the initial reform impulse was exhausted. This went hand in hand with the great economic crisis in Western societies in the 1970s. The humanization program thus fared similarly to other social democratic reform initiatives undertaken during the decade, whose reforming zeal wore off in the coming crises.[55] The positive reference in the discourse to "humanization of labor" continued throughout these crisis years—at least during the 1980s. The government under Helmut Kohl still had to hold on to the term, even if it was eventually interpreted differently in the program.

The actors in the ministries, the trade unions, and the business camp were well aware of the antagonistic interests in the program. It was probably easier for the individual companies to formulate their interests. As applicants, the initiative lay with them. The trade unions, on the other hand, were conflicted from the beginning, with the advocates of a state-supported approach in the minority. The difficulties of the program lay in the areas of friction between humanization and rationalization and

---

52. Fricke, "Drei Jahrzehnte Forschung und Praxis," 149.

53. Bundesminister für Forschung und Technologie/Bundesminister für Arbeit und Sozialordnung, *Forschung zur Humanisierung des Arbeitslebens*, 8, 9.

54. See Müller, "Linkssozialistische Erneuerung," 164.

55. See Faulenbach, *Das sozialdemokratische Jahrzehnt*.

were obvious from the beginning. The ruling social democracy tried to use the program to implement its economic modernization ideas of the time, which to a certain extent constituted a fork in the road between trade union and company interests and provided the framework for a compromise for a few years. Under the slogan of a "modernization of the national economy," the focus in the 1970s was on the development of key technologies that were poor in raw materials and on overcoming labor-intensive sectors for low-skilled workers.[56] In this duet of the two policy fields, social policy stood for the social cushioning of technology-driven social change.

Finally, one desideratum should be mentioned: We basically know nothing about the long-term effects of the program—not at the company level, not in the associations, and not in research and technology policy. According to their own statements, the trade unions entered a lost decade in labor policy in the 1990s.[57] Similarly, both labor sociologists and labor historians are only just beginning to deal with questions of work organization. ■

STEFAN MÜLLER is head of the Public History Department in the Archive of Social Democracy at the Friedrich-Ebert-Stiftung. His research focuses on trade union history, the history of détente, and oral history. Among other things, he has published on relations between West German trade unions and Eastern Europe as well as on the West German state program for occupational health and safety in the 1970s.

### References

Angster, Julia. "Der Zehnerkreis: Remigranten in der westdeutschen Arbeiterbewegung der 1950er Jahre." *Exil: Forschung, Erkenntnisse, Ergebnisse* 18 (1998): 26–47.

Arbeitskreis. "Neue Arbeitsstrukturen der deutschen Automobilindustrie." In *Gestaltung der menschlichen Arbeit: Beispiele aus der deutschen Automobilindustrie.* Stuttgart: Daimler Benz, 1976.

Barth, Hans Rudolf. "Projektgeschichte aus der Sicht der Begleitforschung." In *Arbeits- und sozialpsychologische Untersuchungen von Arbeitsstrukturen im Bereich der Aggregatefertigung der Volkswagen AGs,* vol. 1, edited by Hans Rudolf Barth, Manfred Muster, and Eberhard Ulich, 29–97. Bonn: BMFT, 1980.

Becker, Frank. *"Menschenökonomie": Arbeitswissen und Arbeitspraktiken in Deutschland 1925–1945.* Frankfurt am Main: Campus, 2021.

Bethge, Dietrich. "Arbeitsschutz." In *Geschichte der Sozialpolitik in Deutschland seit 1945, vol. 5: Bundesrepublik Deutschland 1966–1974,* edited by Hans Günther Hockerts, 277–330. Baden-Baden: Nomos, 2006.

Bundesminister für Arbeit und Sozialordnung, Bundesminister für Forschung und Technologie. *Forschung zur Humanisierung des Arbeitslebens: Aktionsprogramm des Bundesministers für Arbeit und Sozialordnung und des Bundesministers für Forschung und Technologie.* Bonn: BMFT/BMAS, 1974.

---

56. See Witt-Barthel, *Chancen sozialorientierter Technikgestaltung,* 20. For the debate on technology and modernization, see SPD, *Ökonomisch-politischer Orientierungsrahmen.*

57. Pickshaus and Urban, "Perspektiven gewerkschaftlicher Arbeitspolitik."

Bundesminister für Forschung und Technologie, Bundesminister für Arbeit und Sozialordnung, eds. *Forschung zur Humanisierung des Arbeitslebens: Dokumentation 1987*. Bonn: BMFT/BMAS, 1987.

Däuber, Wolfgang, Michael Kittner, and Josef Cerny. *Geschichte und Zukunft der Betriebsverfassung*, vol. 2. Frankfurt am Main: Bund, 2022.

Delamotte, Yves. *Recherches en vue d'organisation plus humaine du travail industriel*. Paris: La Documentation Française, 1972.

DGB (Deutscher Gewerkschaftsbund) und Arbeitsschutz. *Anregungen für die Praxis aus der Arbeitsschutz-Ausstellung des DGB*. Frankfurt am Main: DGB, 1954.

Ehmke, Horst. "Forschung und Entwicklung zur Humanisierung des Arbeitslebens." *Bulletin des Presse- und Informationsamt der Bundesregierung*, no. 35 (1974): 331–36.

Faulenbach, Bernd. *Das sozialdemokratische Jahrzehnt: Von der Reformeuphorie zur neuen Unübersichtlichkeit. Die SPD 1969–1982*. Bonn: Dietz, 2011.

Fricke, Werner. "Drei Jahrzehnte Forschung und Praxis zur Humanisierung der Arbeit in Deutschland—eine Bilanz." In *Wirtschaft, Demokratie und soziale Verantwortung: Kontinuitäten und Brüche*, edited by Wolfgang G. Weber, 144–68. Göttingen: Vandenhoeck & Ruprecht, 2004.

Friedrichs, Günter, ed. *Aufgabe Zukunft: Qualität des Lebens. Beiträge zur vierten internationalen Arbeitstagung der Industriegewerkschaft Metall für die Bundesrepublik Deutschland, 11.–14. April 1972 in Oberhausen*, vol. 1: Qualität des Lebens. Frankfurt am Main: IG Metall, 1973.

Friedrichs, Günter, ed. *Automation: Risiko und Chance. Beiträge zur zweiten internationalen Arbeitstagung der Industriegewerkschaft Metall für die Bundesrepublik Deutschland über Rationalisierung, Automatisierung und technischen Fortschritt, 16. bis 19. März 1965 in Oberhausen*. 2 vols. Frankfurt am Main: IG Metall, 1965.

Friedrichs, Günter, ed. *Automation und technischer Fortschritt in Deutschland und den USA: Ausgewählte Beiträge zu einer internationalen Arbeitstagung der Industriegewerkschaft Metall für die Bundesrepublik Deutschland*. Frankfurt am Main: IG Metall, 1963.

Friedrichs, Günter, ed. *Computer und Angestellte: Beiträge zur dritten Internationalen Arbeitstagung der Industriegewerkschaft Metall für die Bundesrepublik Deutschland über Rationalisierung, Automatisierung und Technischen Fortschritt, 5. bis 8. März 1968 in Oberhausen*. Frankfurt am Main: IG Metall, 1971.

Fuhrich, Gina. *Humanisierung oder Rationalisierung? Arbeiter als Akteure im Bundesprogramm "Humanisierung des Arbeitslebens" bei der VW AG*. Stuttgart: Franz Steiner, 2020.

Hockerts, Hans Günther. "Rahmenbedingungen: Das Profil der Reformära." In *Geschichte der Sozialpolitik in Deutschland seit 1945*, vol. 5: Bundesrepublik Deutschland 1966–1974, edited by Hans Günther Hockerts, 1–155. Baden-Baden: Nomos, 2006.

IG Metall, ed. *Werktage werden besser: Der Kampf um den Lohnrahmentarifvertrag II in Nordwürttemberg/Nordbaden*. Frankfurt am Main: Bund, 1977.

Isacson, Maths. "Humanization of Work in Scandinavia, 1960–1990: Strategies Against Problems of the Modern Industrial Work." In Kleinöder, Müller, and Uhl, "Humanisierung der Arbeit," 305–27.

Jünke, Christoph. "Das dritte Leben des Viktor Agartz." *Mitteilungsblatt des Instituts für soziale Bewegungen*, no. 40 (2008): 39–60.

Kerr, Horst. "Vom Unfug mit der 'autonomen Arbeitsgruppe.'" *Der Gewerkschafter*, no. 1 (1977): 16–18.

Kleinöder, Nina. *Humanisierung der Arbeit: Literaturbericht zum Forschungsprogramm zur Humanisierung des Arbeitslebens*. Düsseldorf: HBS, 2016.

Kleinöder, Nina. "Humanisierung durch Arbeitssicherheit? Die Reform des Arbeitsschutzes als Ausgangspunkt der 'Humanisierung des Arbeitslebens' zwischen 1963 und 1979/80." In Kleinöder, Müller, and Uhl, *"Humanisierung der Arbeit,"* 91–108.

Kleinöder, Nina, Stefan Müller, and Karsten Uhl, eds. *"Humanisierung der Arbeit": Aufbrüche und Konflikte in der rationalisierten Arbeitswelt des 20. Jahrhunderts.* Bielefeld: Transkript, 2019.

Lange, Dietmar. *Aufstand in der Fabrik: Arbeitsverhältnisse und Arbeitskämpfe bei FIAT-Mirafiori 1962 bis 1973.* Cologne: Böhlau, 2021.

Lauschke, Karl. *Die halbe Macht: Mitbestimmung in der Eisen- und Stahlindustrie 1945 bis 1989.* Essen: Klartext, 2007.

Lenk, Erhard. "Mitbestimmung am Arbeitsplatz durch gewerkschaftliche Vertrauensleute." *Gewerkschaftliche Monatshefte* 21, no. 3 (1970): 143–47.

Milert, Werner, and Rudolf Tschirbs. *Die andere Demokratie: Betriebliche Interessenvertretung in Deutschland 1848 bis 2008.* Essen: Klartext, 2012.

Müller, Stefan. "Das Forschungs- und Aktionsprogramm 'Humanisierung des Arbeitslebens' (1974–1989)." In Kleinöder, Müller, and Uhl, *"Humanisierung der Arbeit,"* 59–88.

Müller, Stefan. *Heinz Dürrbeck (1912–2001): Gewerkschafter, Sozialist und Bildungsarbeiter.* Essen: Klartext, 2010.

Müller, Stefan. "Linkssozialistische Erneuerung in der IG Metall? Eine neue Konzeption von Arbeiterbildung in den 1960ern." In *Linkssozialismus in Deutschland: Jenseits von Sozialdemokratie und Kommunismus?*, edited by Christoph Jünke, 153–70. Hamburg: VSA.

Oehlke, Paul. *Arbeitspolitik zwischen Tradition und Innovation: Studien in humanisierungspolitischer Perspektive.* Hamburg: VSA, 2004.

Peter, Gerd, and Willi Pöhler. "Umsetzungskonzepte im Humanisierungsprogramm—und was man daraus für heute lernen könnte." *Zeitschrift für Arbeitswissenschaft* 63, no. 2 (2009): 104–7.

Pickshaus, Klaus, and Hans-Jürgen Urban. "Perspektiven gewerkschaftlicher Arbeitspolitik: Plädoyer für eine neue Humanisierungsoffensive." *Gewerkschaftliche Monatshefte,* nos. 10/11 (2002): 631–39.

Poplawski, Martha. "Humanisierung unter Tage? Das HdA-Programm und seine Umsetzung im westdeutschen Steinkohlenbergbau." In Kleinöder, Müller, and Uhl, *"Humanisierung der Arbeit,"* 215–31.

Projektträger "Humanisierung des Arbeitslebens." *Projektstatusbericht 1988/89: Bericht zur Fördermaßnahme des BMFT im Rahmen des Bundesprogramms "Forschung zur Humanisierung des Arbeitslebens."* Bonn: BMFT, 1989.

Remeke, Stefan. *Gewerkschaften und Sozialgesetzgebung: DGB und Arbeitnehmerschutz in der Reformphase der sozialliberalen Koalition.* Essen: Klartext, 2005.

Rohde, Helmut. "Zur Strategie der Humanisierung des Arbeitslebens." *Neue Gesellschaft* 21, no. 3 (1974): 201–7.

Roth, Ralf. "Die automatische Fabrik als Zukunft in der Vergangenheit." *Zeitschrift für Weltgeschichte,* no. 1 (2018): 125–56.

Sauer, Dieter. "Von der 'Humanisierung der Arbeit' zur 'Guten Arbeit.'" *Aus Politik und Zeitgeschichte* 61, no. 15 (2011): 18–24.

Schlaffke, Winfried, Günther Rühl, and Reinhold Weil. *Qualität des Lebens am Arbeitsplatz.* Cologne: Deutscher Institut-Verlag, 1974.

SPD (Sozialdemokratische Partei Deutschlands). *Mit Willy Brandt für Frieden, Sicherheit und eine bessere Qualität des Lebens: Beschlossen vom Außerordentlichen Parteitag der SPD, Dortmund, 13.10.1972.* Bonn: SPD, 1972.

SPD (Sozialdemokratische Partei Deutschlands). *Ökonomisch-politischer Orientierungsrahmen für die Jahre 1975–1985, in der vom Mannheimer Parteitag der SPD am 14.11.1975 beschlossenen Fassung.* Bonn: SPD, 1976.

Süß, Dietmar. *Der seltsame Sieg: Das Comeback der SPDS und was es für Deutschland bedeutet.* Munich: Beck, 2022.

Süß, Winfried. "Sozialpolitische Denk- und Handlungsfelder in der Reformära." In *Geschichte der Sozialpolitik in Deutschland seit 1945*, vol. 5: Bundesrepublik Deutschland 1966–1974, edited by Hans Günther Hockerts, 157–221. Baden-Baden: Nomos, 2006.

Swiniartzki, Marco. *Der Deutsche Metallarbeiter-Verband 1891–1933: Eine Gewerkschaft im Spannungsfeld zwischen Arbeitern, Betrieb und Politik.* Cologne: Böhlau, 2017.

Ueköter, Frank. *Umweltgeschichte im 19. und 20. Jahrhundert.* Munich: Oldenbourg, 2007.

Uhl, Karsten. *Humane Rationalisierung? Die Raumordnung der Fabrik im fordistischen Jahrhundert.* Bielefeld: Transkript, 2014.

Uhl, Karsten. "Eine lange Geschichte der 'menschenleeren Fabrik': Automatisierungsvisionen und technologischer Wandel im 20. Jahrhundert." In *Marx und die Roboter: Vernetzte Produktion, künstliche Intelligenz und lebendige Arbeit*, edited by Florian Butollo and Sabine Nuss, 74–90. Berlin: Dietz, 2019.

Ulich, Eberhard. "Erfahrungen aus dem VW-Projekt." *Zeitschrift für Arbeitswissenschaft* 63, no. 2 (2009): 119–22.

US Department of Health, Education, and Welfare. *Work in America: Report of a Special Task Force to the Secretary of Health, Education and Welfare.* Cambridge, MA: MIT Press, 1973.

Vetter, Heinz-Oskar. "Referat." In *Humanisierung der Arbeit als gesellschaftspolitische und gewerkschaftliche Aufgabe: Protokoll der Konferenz des Deutschen Gewerkschaftsbundes vom 16. und 17. Mai 1974 in München*, edited by Heinz-Oskar Vetter, 25–38. Frankfurt am Main: Bund, 1974.

Volkswagenwerk AG, Institut für Arbeits- und Betriebspsychologie der ETH Zürich, and Institut für Arbeitswissenschaft der TH Darmstadt, eds. *Gruppenarbeit in der Motorenmontage: Ein Vergleich von Arbeitsstrukturen.* Frankfurt am Main: Campus, 1980.

Wilson, Norman A. B. *On the Quality of Working Life: A Report Prepared for the Department of Employment.* London: HMSO, 1973.

Witt-Barthel, Annegret. *Chancen sozialorientierter Technikgestaltung: Politische Ansätze und Gestaltbarkeit der Informationstechnik in der sozialen Sicherung.* Wiesbaden: VS Verlag für Sozialwissenschaften, 1992.

# Rethinking Shop-Floor Power in Postwar Europe: Participation Versus Mobility in East and West

Jan de Graaf

## Introduction

The idea of opportunity has a strong resonance in the historiography of the working class in postwar Europe. Historians have observed how various opportunities for workers opened up at the moment of liberation and organized labor built on that momentum to wrest real concessions from capital in the decades to follow. This interpretation shapes our perception of the golden age of social democracy to this day. In the wake of World War II, explained Geoff Eley, there was an "opportunity for radical democratic change" in Europe, as the participatory socialism espoused by workers' councils seemed to point to a "third way" beyond capitalism and communism.[1] If the radical aspirations of these bodies were sacrificed on the altar of the Cold War, it has become common wisdom that the war fundamentally changed the balance of power between capital and labor. According to Wolfgang Streeck, "postwar democratic capitalism" represented a "historic compromise between a then uniquely powerful working class and an equally uniquely weakened capitalist class," under which the labor movement agreed to restore the "capitalist hunting license" only at the "high price" of full and stable employment, rising living standards, redistributive measures, collective bargaining, and the establishment of a comprehensive welfare state.[2] This went hand in hand with the creation of a more meritocratic society. "During the decades that followed World War II," argues Thomas Piketty, "inherited wealth lost much of its importance, and for the first time in history, perhaps, work and study became the surest routes to the top."[3]

The historiography of the golden age of social democracy has identified opportunities for workers at both the political and the social level. This article focuses on

1. Eley, "Legacies of Antifascism," 79.
2. Streeck, "Comment," 53.
3. Piketty, *Capital*, 302.

*Labor: Studies in Working-Class History*   Volume 22 • Issue 1
DOI 10.1215/15476715-11521382   © 2025 by Labor and Working-Class History Association

the two interconnected sets of opportunities that have dominated academic debates. The first set revolves around opportunities for workers to participate in the postwar settlement. There is a wide body of scholarship on direct shop-floor participation in the aftermath of the war. As collaborationist owners and managers fled the advancing Allied armies, workers placed their factories under self-management, relaunching production under the aegis of elected works councils.[4] If this experiment with worker self-management proved short-lived, it left a lasting legacy not only in the formalization of shop-floor codetermination but also in protest forms that stressed worker control over the workplace.[5] Worker participation in the postwar settlement went beyond the workplace, though. Historians have underlined that through the intermediaries of trade unions and mass parties, workers also managed to make their voice heard in the political arena. The postwar era was the "heyday" of trade unions, during which the threat of strikes alone sufficed to obtain higher wages and a larger share of the national income for workers.[6] "Mass ideological political parties," for their part, "acted as channels for citizen participation,"[7] translating the "popular democratic momentum of . . . wartime mobilization" into a durable social contract.[8]

The second set of opportunities revolves around mobility. It has become customary to describe the postwar era as a period during which workers were on the move, both literally and figuratively. Mobility offered workers in postwar Europe opportunities on three levels. First, it enabled millions, especially in Eastern and Southern Europe, to escape semifeudal servitude in the countryside and move to industrializing cities. Historiography has documented how postwar migration not only represented a transformative experience for those who left behind poverty and illiteracy to become industrial workers, but also increased the life chances of the established urban working-class communities.[9] Second, the aftermath of the war provided workers with unprecedented job mobility. The extreme labor shortages of the reconstruction era enabled workers to sell their services to the highest bidder; the headhunting or poaching of skilled workers was common.[10] Third, workers are taken to have benefited disproportionately from the postwar "golden age of social mobility." Even if most of postwar society experienced upward mobility as a consequence of what Ulrich Beck described as the "elevator effect,"[11] its impact was more keenly felt among those at the bottom, as skilled industrial workers and public sector employees became the "central carriers" of the aspirations of the golden age.[12]

4. Horn, *Moment of Liberation*; Heumos, *"Vyhrňme si rukávy, než se kola zastaví!"*; Mencherini, *La libération.*

5. Lauschke, *Die halbe Macht*; De Graaf, "Occupational Strikes"; De Graaf, "No Italian Stalingrads."

6. Kaelble, "Abmilderung," 605.

7. Della Porta, "For Participatory Democracy," 609.

8. Eley, "Corporatism," 40.

9. Horváth, *Stalinism Reloaded*, chap. 3; Mattes, "Wirtschaftliche Rekonstruktion," 841.

10. Pittaway, "Reproduction of Hierarchy," 751.

11. Beck, *Risikogesellschaft.*

12. Vogel, *Staatsbedürftigkeit*, 86.

The historiography of the golden age of social democracy has generally understood participation and mobility as mutually reinforcing tendencies. That is, the spoils
of worker participation in economic and political decision-making facilitated the geographical and social mobility of workers, and vice versa. In fact, questions of vertical
and horizontal mobility have been identified as one of the core issues of worker participation at plant level.[13] This is often linked to what Gøsta Esping-Andersen called
the "decommodification of labor,"[14] the job security and social safety net that meant
that workers were no longer at the mercy of market forces to sustain a decent standard
of living. Decommodification also allowed workers to be more mobile. "Guaranteed
a certain level of welfare," notes Sheri Berman in her overview of twentieth-century
European social democracy, "workers became less deferential to employers and found
it less necessary to hold on to particular jobs."[15] The securities of the golden age thus
opened up altogether new horizons to working-class families, enabling "many, especially male skilled workers, to independently plan their lives"[16] while providing their
children with "possibilities for individual development that had previously been
unknown."[17] It is these social democratic ideals of autonomy, elevation, and self-
fulfillment that are often seen as the main casualties of the demise of the golden age.
Even if the welfare state, albeit in slimmed-down form, still exists in Europe today,
the "elevator" of the postwar era has been replaced by the "revolving door" of the
neoliberal age.[18]

This article challenges the assumption of mechanical links between participation and mobility under the golden age of social democracy. It demonstrates that
workers and trade unionists in postwar Europe often exploited the opportunities
offered by participation to curtail geographical and social mobility. To make this
argument, the article takes a pan-European approach, engaging with the communist
East and the capitalist West in an integrated account. Insofar as the historiography
of the golden age of social democracy has dealt with the communist bloc at all, it is
mostly to claim that the specter of "actually existing socialism" in Eastern Europe
frightened the Western European capitalist class into granting the welfare state.[19] By
shifting the focus to workers and lower-level trade unionists, this article shows that
labor's participation in the postwar settlement had strong antimobility overtones

13. Pries, "Workers' Participation," 44.
14. Esping-Andersen, *Three Worlds of Welfare Capitalism*.
15. Berman, *Primacy of Politics*, 181.
16. Brinkmann and Nachtwey, "Industrial Relations, Trade Unions and Social Conflict in German Capitalism."
17. Nachtwey, *Germany's Hidden Crisis*, 4.
18. Beck, *Brave New World of Work*, 53.
19. The original version of this argument was formulated by Eric Hobsbawm, who argued that "whatever
Stalin did to the Russians, he was good for the common people in the West" as the "fear of an alternative that
really existed and that could really spread" was at the root of Western efforts "of saving capitalism concentrated
on welfare and social security." Hobsbawm, "Goodbye to All That," 21.

across the continent. In fact, the East-West comparison illustrates how worker participation had a similar impetus even under the initially radically different mobility regimes that were imposed by the Stalinist and bourgeois states.

## Participation

To properly understand the dynamics of postwar worker participation, we have to go back to 1945. The works councils that took charge of factories at the moment of liberation have mostly been understood as a bottom-up challenge to capitalism, but their brief dominance of industrial life also represented a victory of shop-floor activists over trade unions. That was because worker participation in the wake of World War II saw the return of many practices that trade union leaders had decried during the 1930s. Their vision of the planned economy required the labor movement to be centralized, disciplined, and united. In practice, that meant that wage bargaining was to take place on the national rather than the factory level, spontaneous industrial action had to be avoided at all costs, and sector-based unions were to be submerged into general confederations. The emerging war economies of the late 1930s had already been conducive to these objectives. "Confronted by countries subjected to strict discipline, organised for war, [and] masters of their economy," trade union leaders in democratic nations had called for economic planning as "a method, a discipline imposed on everyone" and managed to push radical sector-based unions in the same direction.[20]

If the postwar era saw trade union leaders also realize their dreams of establishing (more) united labor confederations,[21] the reality that returning trade unionists found on the ground in liberated Europe was radically different from what they had left behind. The war had done much to break the bonds between trade union leaders and the shop floor. As independent unions were repressed and/or submerged into collaborationist labor fronts, workers had been left to fend for themselves and had grown distrustful of nominal labor leaders preaching discipline and hard work. This atmosphere of distrust toward trade unions continued into the postwar years, when trade union leaders once again called on workers to show restraint and make sacrifices for the greater good (this time the reconstruction effort), enabling shop-floor activists to claw back important powers that had been lost to trade unions during the interwar years. First, this concerned the return of shop-floor bargaining, much resented by trade union leaders but highly popular among workers weary of the compromises made in their name.[22] Second, the power of the shop floor was reflected in the wave of wildcat strikes that swept postwar Europe, which often saw worker delegations reject trade union intervention and demand direct negotiations with management or

20. Imlay, "Democracy and War," 11–12.
21. Pasture, "Window of Opportunities or Trompe l'Oeil?"
22. Kössler, "Arbeiter und Demokratiegründung."

the authorities.[23] Third, the postwar years were characterized by what trade unionists denounced as "syndicalism" or "company egoism," in which shop-floor activists put the interests of workers at their own factories before the overall interests of the labor movement as defined by national trade union leaders.[24]

Contrary to conventional wisdom about organized labor in postwar Europe, trade unions were thus hardly all-powerful organizations that could mobilize and demobilize the working class at the snap of a finger. In their attempts to regain control over their rank and file, and restore their credibility as negotiation partners for employers and the state, trade union leaders were forced to make important concessions to the shop-floor veterans who had represented the workforce during and immediately after the war. In practice, that meant that in return for restoring the national prerogative exercised by trade union leaders, skilled workers were granted a significant measure of control over the workplace. This did not entail actual worker self-management; the principle that directors, irrespective of whether they represented the capitalist class or the state, had the final say in questions of investment and production remained untouched across postwar Europe. Yet the golden age of social democracy did enable skilled workers to shape their own work rhythm, regulate their pay and conditions, and make their voice heard on shop-floor recruitment and promotion policies. To start with these first two dimensions, the postwar "politics of productivity" helped skilled workers restore hierarchies of remuneration within industry.[25] The war itself had already seen strong wage leveling across the continent,[26] and developments in its aftermath further eroded the preferential position that skilled workers had once enjoyed. The abolition of piece rates in many companies at the moment of liberation, although a widely shared desire after the Nazis had imposed extortionate rates,[27] made it more difficult for skilled workers to translate their higher productivity into higher wages. The rationed economy, even if workers with specific expertise or in key sectors were in receipt of higher rations, was likewise a source of considerable discontent among skilled workers. This was linked to the general depreciation of earned wages in a barter economy dominated by the black market, in which street smarts often mattered more than performance at work.

The economic stabilization that accompanied the onset of the Cold War spelled the end for the postwar egalitarian moment. The scientization of the production process, as planners in East and West sought to emulate the Soviet and American models respectively, saw the intensification of performance measuring and reintroduction of piecework. It is important to stress that the pressure for piecework often came from below, with skilled workers demanding (individual) piece rates to boost

---

23. De Graaf, "Strikes as Revolutionary History?"
24. Boldorf, "Social Movements," 61; Kenney, *Rebuilding Poland*, 60–63.
25. Maier, "Politics of Productivity."
26. Piketty, *Capital*, 360; Gazeley, "Levelling of Pay."
27. Kopstein, "Chipping Away at the State," 401–2.

their wages. As one trade unionist at the Fiat Mirafiori plant in Turin described the postwar evolution of attitudes toward piecework,

> At the outset, we were fighting for equality. But then the skilled workers started to argue: "but, wait a minute, equality . . . we have more responsibilities." So instead of a [collective] rate for the entire plant, they requested a piece rate at shop level. Afterward they requested that shop rates would be replaced by team rates. And then they demanded the introduction of individual piecework, as: "In total, there are 40 of us, but should I compare myself to him?"[28]

Why did skilled workers cling to this despised method of prewar and wartime capitalist exploitation under the golden age? The answer lies at least partly in shop-floor participation. Through processes of informal shop-floor bargaining with foremen and rate setters, skilled workers were able to exercise collective control over their targets.[29] This not only gave them a direct say in their pay but also allowed them to structure their own pace of work. Secure in the knowledge of a manageable target, and of preferential access to the best tools and machinery, they could divide their time without much supervision.[30]

### Mobility

In the wake of the war, the position of older and experienced workers at the top of the shop-floor hierarchy had been undercut not only by wage leveling but also by geographical and social mobility. With millions displaced, disabled, or deceased as a result of the war, key industries across the continent suffered from enormous labor shortages. This forced companies into indiscriminate recruitment strategies, which saw the employment of, for example, prisoners of war, displaced persons, or refugees.[31] Increasingly, the state also stepped into the void both by setting up campaigns to direct labor from the countryside to industrial regions and by implementing forms of labor conscription.[32]

The impact of this vast turnover of personnel on established working-class communities remains understudied, especially for postwar Western Europe. The arrival of thousands of newcomers, many of whom were ill equipped for industrial work, had profoundly disrupting effects on the core workforce. The organs of shop-floor participation, as the mouthpiece of skilled workers, complained bitterly about the attitudes that the new recruits took toward their job and their colleagues. First, this concerned their perceived lack of respect for their superiors or mentors (i.e., more experienced workers), who felt that their advice went unheeded and that newcomers

28. Quoted in Antoniello, *Da Mirafiori alla S.A.L.L.*, 124.
29. McKinlay and Melling, "Shop Floor Politics."
30. Grama, "Antinomy."
31. Diamond, "'Prisoners of the Peace'"; Zahra, "'Prisoners of the Postwar'"; Roseman, "Refugees and Ruhr Miners."
32. De Graaf, "Meaning of Free Labor."

did not show hierarchies of skill proper reverence.[33] Second, the frequent absenteeism and job-hopping of new recruits did much to sour the mood toward them on the shop floor, as it interfered with the flow of work (and the making of performance targets) and robbed companies of valuable equipment and work clothing.[34] Third, newcomers found themselves accused of taking an instrumental attitude toward work, in which everything was geared toward obtaining the same benefits as skilled workers and/or getting access to goods that could be traded on the black market.[35]

The experience of the first postwar years thus instilled in skilled workers a deep desire to keep new workers in their place, both literally and metaphorically. On the one side, this was formulated as a demand for more control over who was coming in. In the context of the postwar housing shortage, there was often a conflict over which groups could legitimately call themselves (industrial) workers. That is, "real workers"—for example, miners who had been expelled from the Sudetenland— were welcome to flock to industrial regions like the Ruhr, but "nothing good was to be expected" of rural recruits from "foreign provinces" (*fremde Provinzen*) like Bavaria and Schleswig-Holstein.[36] In fact, working-class polities were not afraid to bar unwanted newcomers access to the urban area. The city of Turin invoked the fascist-era (and technically unconstitutional) "law against urbanization" to deny rural migrants residency well into the 1950s.[37] If the communist regimes in Eastern Europe initially promoted rural-to-urban migration in the context of the industrialization drive, the overcrowding of cities forced them to apply the brake as well. Romania introduced a system of residency permits to relieve pressure on industrial centers as late as 1975, which complemented the stick of restrictions on geographical mobility with the carrot of better commuting links.[38] This also helps explain why social dem-ocrats in postwar Western Europe became champions of campaigns to combat rural exodus, historically a conservative crusade, by bringing urban amenities to the coun-tryside.[39]

On the other side, skilled workers insisted on exercising tight control over upward mobility on the shop floor. This was achieved as a side effect of Cold War stabilization in Western Europe, where the interests of skilled workers, trade unions, and employers were closely aligned in restoring traditional hierarchical routes to

33. Pittaway, "Reproduction of Hierarchy," 753–57; Gritti, "In Search of Unanimity," 304.

34. Situational report of the Bergamt Herne, December 1946, Landesarchiv Nordrhein-Westfalen, Abtei-lung Westfalen, Münster, M550/Bergämter Nr. 7579.

35. Position paper of the IVB Dortmund on *Arbeitsverpflichtung*, 15 November 1946, Archiv der sozialen Demokratie, Bonn, Archiv des Deutschen Gewerkschaftsbundes, Bestand Deutscher Gewerkschaftsbund (Britische Zone), 5/DGA000449.

36. Speeches by Heinrich Jochem, leader of the Oberhausen chapter of the Mining Union, at several pits in 1946. All translations are my own unless otherwise noted.

37. Sparschuh, "Citizens and Non-Citizens," 37.

38. Cucu, "Going West." On state restrictions on geographical mobility in communist Eastern Europe, see also Brunnbauer and Nonaj, "Finding Workers," 82–83.

39. Hall, "Classrooms of Democracy."

shop-floor promotion through apprenticeship.[40] In Eastern Europe, conversely, the full-fledged Stalinist regimes that were installed from 1947 to 1948 initially stepped up campaigns to advance the fortunes of young newcomers to the industrial workforce like women, rural migrants, and ethnic minorities.[41] Their aims in doing so were both ideological and practical. These groups were considered less corrupted by interwar bourgeois society and served as a blank slate for the socialist "new" man and woman that the regimes were seeking to foster. But they were also sent to industrial regions, fresh on the back of receiving crash courses in Soviet production methods, to break resistance to such methods (labor competition, shock work, Stakhanovism, etc.) within established working-class communities. To give these workers a foothold in industry, the state accorded them preferential treatment in several ways: The traditional apprenticeship was abolished to allow new workers to jump the queue when it came to promotions; women and ethnic minorities were trained for and employed in hitherto unthinkable positions as skilled worker or foreman/forewoman; and shock workers were provided with the best possible conditions to outperform their targets and collect monetary bonuses. In Eastern Europe's preexisting industrial heartlands, skilled workers fought these social mobility programs tooth and nail and often worked successfully with the organs of shop-floor participation to fend off the Sovietization of the workplace.[42] From the mid-1950s onward, in the wake of the upheavals that shook the Eastern bloc, the communist regimes mostly abandoned these programs and started showing shop-floor hierarchies the respect that skilled workers craved.

In both Eastern and Western Europe, therefore, the golden age saw the valorization of the "core workforce," experienced workers who had been with the company for several decades and who could, by virtue of their skill and influence on the shop floor, help shape their own workflow and pay as well as recruitment and promotion policies. These workers were in many ways the master of their own fate, independent from employers, trade unions, and the state. In fact, many shop-floor practices that we associate with trade union or (state-)employer policy can actually be traced back to the interests of skilled workers. Consider the issue of "overmanning." The fact that companies in both the capitalist West and the communist East employed workers in excess to their productive needs has often been attributed to forces beyond the shop floor. In Western Europe, overmanning is understood as emblematic of trade unions' power (i.e., their successful resistance to redundancies even under conditions of full employment). In Eastern Europe, overmanning is linked to the exigencies of the centrally planned economy (i.e., managerial need to keep workers in reserve to "catch up with the plan" once raw materials finally arrived).[43] Yet from the perspective of skilled workers, overmanning also held significant appeal. This appeal lay not so much in the caricature of workers reading newspapers or playing board games on the job as in the

40. Roseman, *Recasting the Ruhr*.
41. Fidelis, *Women, Communism, and Industrialization*; Donert, *Rights of the Roma*, 48–83.
42. Heumos, "'Der Himmel ist hoch und Prag ist weit!'"
43. Jarosz, "Food, Housing, Work, Retirement," 45.

stability that overmanning offered.[44] It shielded workers from some of the most griev-
ous aspects of the postwar experience—the rapid turnover of personnel, the deployment of outsiders at peak times, and the attendant "ruralization" of the urban space.
It also kept workers in their place in a literal sense, making sure that no one would
jump the queue of professional advancement. Skilled workers, moreover, stood to lose
almost nothing from overmanning, as efforts to tackle it mostly affected their unskilled
colleagues.[45] And of course, *man* is the operative part of overmanning, as the backlash
against excess employment in industry almost exclusively targeted female workers.[46]

Much as becoming part of the "core workforce" was a key aspiration and source
of pride for many workers—the factory morphed into family life as "factory dynasties"
of husbands, wives, brothers, sisters, and their sons and daughters devoted their working
lives to one and the same factory—achieving core worker status did not usher in upward
mobility for working-class families.[47] The best that new arrivals could hope for, even if
they began at the bottom of the ladder and patiently awaited their turn, was on-the-job
training and shop-floor promotion, with limited opportunities outside their sector.[48]
Even for skilled workers, a clear class ceiling remained in place. Although companies
would accord their most experienced and loyal blue-collar workers the respect of the
title of "honorary white-collar worker" (*Ehrenangestellte*) at the height of the economic
miracle, this was still a far cry from actually joining the ranks of the professional salariat.[49]

## Conclusion

The golden age of shop-floor participation and geographical as well as social immobility lasted a little over a decade. In the course of the 1960s, those groups of workers that
had been on the sharp end of the postwar settlement began to take a more assertive
attitude. This was reflected in a fresh wave of wildcat strikes and industrial protests,
led mostly by newcomers to the industrial working class who had been shut out of the
formal organs of shop-floor participation.[50] The most immediate effect of this was a
weakening of the influence that skilled workers could exert over wage arrangements.
In both Eastern and Western Europe, individual piece rates were gradually replaced
by team rates that covered a longer period and a larger group of workers. This enabled
many female, migrant, and young workers to boost their meager base incomes with
performance bonuses for the first time, leading to an overall leveling of wages.[51]

If participation in industrial struggle enabled new workers to finally reap
some of the (monetary) rewards of the golden age during the 1960s, the underlying

44. Saunders, *Assembling Cultures*, 42–44.

45. Plumpe, *German Economic and Business History*, 278.

46. Jarska, "Gender and Labour," 63–66.

47. Tóth, "Shifting Identities," 87. On the fortunes of working-class children in the postwar school system see Todd, *People*, chap. 10.

48. Beyers, "From Class to Culture," 49.

49. Wurster, "Angestellte h.c."

50. Birke, *Wilde Streiks*.

51. Majchrzak, *Arbeit-Produktion-Protest*; Grama, "Antinomy," 184–85.

assumption of most research on the period seems to be that the same was true for mobility. These accounts acknowledge that it was mostly skilled male workers who benefited from the opportunities opening up in the golden age, while female and migrant workers were still trapped in commodified labor relations.[52] This is, however, often brushed off as a side effect of the conservative reconstruction in Western Europe, which would have been swept away in the wake of the cultural revolution of the 1960s had it not been for the incoming neoliberal tide ending the golden age of social mobility altogether.[53] In a sign of the gender-blindness of this sort of research, the question of how women were going to exploit career opportunities without decommodification being accompanied by what feminist scholars called "defamilialization" is left unexplored. This notion—stipulating that decommodification should not only cover worker independence from market forces but also "the degree to which individuals can uphold a socially acceptable standard of living independently of family relations"—would be adopted by Esping-Andersen in his later work.[54] Yet he was still criticized for his "taken-for-granted assumptions about what women want": jobs that would be facilitated by state or market provision of childcare but not necessarily careers.[55]

The comparison with Eastern Europe undertaken in this article confirms that the restriction of geographical and social mobility was a feature rather than a bug of worker participation in the golden age. In the maelstrom of Stalinist modernization, the state actively promoted the mobility of newcomers to the industrial working class, but still foundered on the resistance of skilled workers who exploited shop-floor participation to block the opportunities that had been offered to female and migrant workers. In fact, the Eastern European experience shows that mobility was weaker there where participation was stronger and vice versa.[56] In Western Europe too, shop-floor participation was seemingly more successful at hampering mobility than at preventing equality. For even if piece rates had been reformed to the disadvantage of skilled workers, the recession of the 1970s and 1980s showed that their interests still shaped mobility regimes. In the first place, geographical mobility was restricted once more as guest worker agreements were abruptly ended, with migrant workers either told to return to their countries of origin or confronted with enormous administrative and legal hurdles in securing basic rights of family reunion.[57] Second, the retraining schemes that trade unions demanded in return for agreeing to wage moderation had strong biases; while skilled male workers were prepared for the challenges of the technological age, younger, female, and/or migrant workers were condemned to long-term unemployment or precarious work at best.[58]

Taking a broader perspective, two general conclusions about the nature and eventual demise of the golden age of social democracy can be drawn from the oppo-

---

52. See, e.g., Brinkmann and Nachtwey, "Industrial Relations, Trade Unions and Social Conflict in German Capitalism."

53. Nachtwey, *Marktsozialdemokratie*, 147.

54. Lister, "'She Has Other Duties,'" 37.

55. Orloff, review of *Social Foundations*, 1180.

56. See the comparison between the Łódź and Wrocław in Kenney, *Rebuilding Poland*.

57. Stokes, *Fear of the Family*.

58. Raphael, *Jenseits von Kohle und Stahl*.

sition of participation and mobility. The first concerns the enduring importance of shop-floor participation under the golden age and beyond. In the historiography on postwar Europe, worker participation is either described as irrelevant to the wider process of economic reconstruction or ascribed a great radical potential that was cut short by the onset of the Cold War.[59] This article has shown that meaningful shop-floor participation not only had a much longer lifespan than commonly assumed and was often successful in frustrating the plans (both lower- and uppercase) of Cold War technocrats, but also had a conservative rather than a radical impetus. The second conclusion revolves around the role of mobility in the demise of the golden age. Some scholars speak with barely disguised contempt about the younger generations of the 1970s and 1980s, who rejected the securities of the postwar settlement for a more adventurous lifestyle, both career-wise and in their everyday lives.[60] Their embrace of the more flexible working arrangements on offer under neoliberalism is sometimes dismissed as if it were the product of false consciousness.[61] If we understand participation and mobility as conflicting forces, it becomes more understandable that those workers for whom geographical and/or social mobility was unavailable (or decades away) were keen to move on from the golden age. This approach also suggests that within present-day European social democracy, the pendulum might be shifting from mobility to participation once more. From the British Labour Party abandoning its long-standing commitment to social mobility to the German Social Democratic Party campaigning on "respect for work," social democratic parties seem to have set their sights on a new golden age of worker participation (and immobility).[62] ∎

JAN DE GRAAF is Junior Professor of European History at the Institute for Social Movements of the Ruhr-Universität Bochum and member of the Young Academy of Europe. As holder of the Sofja Kovalevskaja Award of the Alexander von Humboldt Foundation, he leads the junior research group "Europe's Postwar Consensus: A Golden Age of Social Cohesion and Social Mobility?" He was a postdoctoral researcher at the KU Leuven from 2015 to 2019, where he worked on wildcat strikes between 1945 and 1953 as a pan-European phenomenon. He obtained his PhD from the University of Portsmouth in 2015. A revised and extended version of that thesis was published in 2019.

59. Steinhouse, *Workers' Participation*; Eley, *Forging Democracy*, 271; Chapman, *France's Long Reconstruction*.

60. For this general criticism of the generation of 1968 see Judt, *Postwar*.

61. Streeck, *Buying Time*, 31.

62. For the British Labour Party, see Labour, "Labour to Put Social Justice at the Heart." For the German Social Democratic Party, see the chapter titled "Eine Gesellschaft des Respekts" in the 2021 program of the SPD: https://www.spd.de/programm/respekt (accessed March 24, 2023). The specific slogan of "respect for work" was used on campaign posters by the SPD in Germany's most populous Bundesland of Northrhine-Westphalia for the May 2022 Land elections.

## References

Antonello, Donato. *Da Mirafiori alla S.A.L.L.: Una Storia operaia*. Milan: Editoriale Jaca, 2004.

Beck, Ulrich. *The Brave New World of Work*. Cambridge, UK: Polity, 2000.

Beck, Ulrich. *Risikogesellschaft: Auf dem Weg in eine andere Moderne (Risk Society: Toward a New Modernity)*. Frankfurt am Main: Suhrkamp, 1986.

Berman, Sheri. *The Primacy of Politics: Social Democracy and the Making of Europe's Twentieth Century*. Cambridge: Cambridge University Press, 2006.

Beyers, Leen. "From Class to Culture: Immigration, Recession, and Daily Ethnic Boundaries in Belgium, 1940s–1990s." *International Review of Social History* 53, no. 1 (2008): 37–61.

Birke, Peter. *Wilde Streiks im Wirtschaftswunder: Arbeitskämpfe, Gewerkschaften und soziale Bewegungen in der Bundesrepublik und Dänemark (Wildcat Strikes During the Economic Miracle: Industrial Disputes, Trade Unions and Social Movements in West Germany and Denmark)*. Frankfurt am Main: Campus Verlag, 2007.

Boldorf, Marcel. "Social Movements and the Change of Industrial Elites in East Germany." In *Social Movements and the Change of Economic Elites in Europe After 1945*, edited by Marcel Boldorf and Stefan Berger, 43–62. Cham, Switzerland: Palgrave Macmillan, 2018.

Brinkmann, Ulrich, and Oliver Nachtwey. "Industrial Relations, Trade Unions and Social Conflict in German Capitalism." *La Nouvelle Revue du Travail*, no. 3 (2013). http://journals.openedition.org/nrt/1382.

Brunnbauer, Ulf, and Visar Nonaj. "Finding Workers to Build Socialism: Recruiting for the Steel Factories in Bulgaria and Albania." In *Labor in State-Socialist Europe, 1945–1989: Contributions to a History of Work*, edited by Marsha Siefert, 73–98. Budapest: Central European University Press, 2020.

Chapman, Herrick. *France's Long Reconstruction*. Cambridge, MA: Harvard University Press, 2018.

Cucu, Alina-Sandra. "Going West: Socialist Flexibility in the Long 1970s." *Journal of Global History* 17, no. 1 (2022): 1–19.

De Graaf, Jan. "The Meaning of Free Labor After the Second World War: Worker Protest Against Arbeitsverpflichtung and Mobilisation Civile in Postwar Germany and Belgium." *Moving the Social* 69 (2023): 15–32.

De Graaf, Jan. "No Italian Stalingrads: The C.G.I.L. and the Working Class in the Northern Industrial Heartlands, 1945–1955." *Journal of Modern Italian Studies* 23, no. 5 (2018): 620–39.

De Graaf, Jan. "The Occupational Strikes in the Dąbrowa Basin of April 1951: Stalinist Industrialization Against the Polish Working Class." *International Labor and Working Class History*, no. 98 (2020): 22–42.

De Graaf, Jan. "Strikes as Revolutionary History? Probing the Potential for a Revolution in Post-1945 Europe Through Wildcat Strikes." *Archiv für Sozialgeschichte*, no. 59 (2019): 229–52.

Della Porta, Donatella. "For Participatory Democracy: Some Notes." *European Political Science*, no. 18 (2019): 603–16.

Diamond, Hanna. "'Prisoners of the Peace': German Prisoners-of-War in Rural France, 1944–48." *European History Quarterly* 43, no. 3 (2013): 442–63.

Donert, Celia. *The Rights of the Roma: The Struggle for Citizenship in Postwar Czechoslovakia*. Cambridge: Cambridge University Press, 2017.

Eley, Geoff. "Corporatism and the Social Democratic Moment: The Postwar Settlement, 1945–1973." In *The Oxford Handbook of Postwar European History*, edited by Dan Stone, 37–59. Oxford: Oxford University Press, 2012.

Eley, Geoff. *Forging Democracy: The History of the Left in Europe, 1850–2000*. Oxford: Oxford University Press, 2002.

Eley, Geoff. "Legacies of Antifascism: Constructing Democracy in Postwar Europe." In "Legacies of Antifascism," special issue, *New German Critique*, no. 67 (1996): 73–100. https://doi.org/10.2307/827778.

Esping-Andersen, Gøsta. *Three Worlds of Welfare Capitalism*. Cambridge, UK: Polity, 1990.

Fidelis, Malgorzata. *Women, Communism, and Industrialization in Postwar Poland*. Cambridge: Cambridge University Press, 2010.

Gazeley, Ian. "The Levelling of Pay in Britain During the Second World War." *European Review of Economic History* 10, no. 2 (2006): 175–204.

Grama, Adrian. "The Antinomy of Workers' Control in Socialist Eastern Europe." In *Worlds of Labour Turned Upside Down*, edited by Pepijn Brandon, Peyman Jafari, and Stefan Müller, 169–98. Leiden: Brill, 2020.

Gritti, Andrea Umberto. "In Search of Unanimity: Human Relations at the Falck Steelworks, 1948–1962." In *Labour History in the Semiperiphery: Southern Europe, 19th–20th Centuries*, edited by Leda Papastefanaki and Nikos Potamianos, 297–320. Berlin: De Gruyter, 2021.

Hall, Kevin T. "Classrooms of Democracy: Cultivating Change and Social Cohesion Through Rural Community Centres in Postwar Hesse." *Rural History* 33, no. 2 (2022): 207–30.

Heumos, Peter. "'Der Himmel ist hoch und Prag ist weit!': Sekundäre Machtverhältnisse und organisatorische Entdifferenzierung in tschechoslowakischen Industriebetrieben (1945–1968)" ("'The Sky Is the Limit and Prague Is Far!': Secondary Power Relations and Organisational De-Differentiation in Czechoslovakian Industrial Companies"). In *Vernetzte Improvisationen: Gesellschaftliche Subsysteme in Ostmitteleuropa und in der DDR (Interconnected Improvisations: Societal Subsystems in Eastern Central Europe and the GDR)*, edited by Annette Schuhmann, 21–41. Cologne: Böhlau, 2008.

Heumos, Peter. *"Vyhrňme si rukávy, než se kola zastaví!": Dělníci a státní socialismus v Československu 1945–1968 ("Let's Roll Up Our Sleeves, Before the Wheels Come to a Halt!": Workers and State Socialism in Czechoslovakia, 1945–1968)*. Prague: Ústav pro soudobé dějiny AV ČR, 2006.

Hobsbawm, Eric. "Goodbye to All That." *Marxism Today*, October 1990, 18–23.

Horn, Gerd-Rainer. *The Moment of Liberation in Western Europe: Power Struggles and Rebellions, 1943–1948*. Oxford: Oxford University Press, 2020.

Horváth, Sándor. *Stalinism Reloaded: Everyday Life in Stalin-City, Hungary*. Bloomington: Indiana University Press, 2017.

Imlay, Talbot. "Democracy and War: Political Regime, Industrial Relations, and Economic Preparations for War in France and Britain up to 1940." *Journal of Modern History* 79, no. 1 (2007): 1–47.

Jarosz, Dariusz. "Food, Housing, Work, Retirement: Resourcefulness in Everyday Life as an Element of the Functioning of Society and the Economy in the People's Republic of Poland (Selected Aspects)." *Studia Historiae Oeconomicae* 41, no. 1 (2023): 29–52.

Jarska, Natalia. "Gender and Labour in Post-War Communist Poland: Female Unemployment 1945–1970." *Acta Poloniae Historica* 110 (2014): 49–85.

Judt, Tony. *Postwar: A History of Europe Since 1945*. London: Penguin, 2005.

Kaelble, Hartmut. "Diskussionsforum: Abmilderung der sozialen Ungleichheit? Das westliche Europa während des Wirtschaftsbooms der 1950er bis 1970er Jahre" ("Discussion Forum: Mitigation of Social Inequality? Western Europe During the Economic Boom of the 1950s to 1970s"). *Geschichte und Gesellschaft (History and Society)* 40, no. 4 (2014): 519–609.

Kenney, Padraic. *Rebuilding Poland: Workers and Communists, 1945–1950*. Ithaca, NY: Cornell University Press, 1997.

Kopstein, Jeffrey. "Chipping Away at the State: Workers' Resistance and the Demise of East Germany." *World Politics* 48, no. 3 (1996): 391–423.

Kössler, Till. "Arbeiter und Demokratiegründung in Westdeutschland nach 1945: Das Beispiel der kommunistischen Bewegung" ("Workers and the Foundation of Democracy in West Germany After 1945: The Example of the Communist Movement"). *Zeithistorische Forschungen / Studies in Contemporary History* 3, no. 2 (2006): 188–209.

Kössler, Till. "Confrontation or Cooperation? The Labour Movement and Economic Elites in West Germany After 1945." In *Social Movements and the Change of Economic Elites in Europe After 1945*, edited by Stefan Berger and Marcel Boldorf, 21–42. Cham, Switzerland: Palgrave Macmillan, 2018.

Labour. "Labour to Put Social Justice at the Heart of Everything a Labour Government Will Do with New Social Justice Commission." *Labour Party*, June 7, 2019. https://labour.org .uk/press/labourput-social-justice-heart-everything-labour-government-will-new-social -ustice-commission/.

Lauschke, Karl. *Die halbe Macht: Mitbestimmung in der Eisen- und Stahlindustrie 1945 bis 1989 (Half the Power: Co-Determination in the Iron and Steel Industry 1945 to 1989)*. Essen: Klartext, 2007.

Lister, Ruth. "'She Has Other Duties': Women, Citizenship and Social Security." In *Social Security and Social Change: New Challenges to the Beveridge Model*, edited by Sally Baldwin and Jane Falkingham, 31–44. New York: Harvester Wheatsheaf, 1994.

Maier, Charles S. "The Politics of Productivity: Foundations of American International Economic Policy After World War II." *International Organization* 31, no. 4 (1977): 607–33.

Majchrzak, Sarah Graber. *Arbeit-Produktion-Protest: Die Leninwerft in Gdańsk und die AG "Weser" in Bremen im Vergleich (1968–1983) (Labor-Production-Protest: The Lenin Shipyard in Gdańsk and the AG "Weser" in Bremen in Comparison [1968–1983])*. Cologne: Böhlau, 2020.

Mattes, Monika. "Wirtschaftliche Rekonstruktion in der Bundesrepublik Deutschland und grenzüberschreitende Arbeitsmigration von den 1950er bis zu den 1970er Jahren" ("Economic Reconstruction in West Germany and Cross-Border Labor Migration from the 1950s to the 1970s"). In *Handbuch Staat und Migration in Deutschland seit dem 17. Jahrhundert (Handbook of State and Migration in Germany since the 17th Century)*, edited by Jochen Oltmer, 815–52. Berlin: De Gruyter, 2016.

McKinlay, Alan, and Joseph Melling. "The Shop Floor Politics of Productivity: Work, Power and Authority Relations in British Engineering, c. 1945–57." In *British Trade Unions and Industrial Politics: The High Tide of Trade Unionism, 1964–1979*, edited by John McIlroy, Nina Fishman, and Alan Campbell, 238–57. 1999. Reprint, London: Routledge, 2018.

Mencherini, Robert. *La libération et les entreprises sous gestion ouvrière: Marseille 1944–1948 (The Liberation and Companies Under Worker Management: Marseille 1944–1948)*. Paris: L'Harmattan, 1994.

Nachtwey, Oliver. *Germany's Hidden Crisis: Social Decline in the Heart of Europe*. London: Verso Books, 2018.

Nachtwey, Oliver. *Marktsozialdemokratie: Die Transformation von SPD und Labour Party (Market Social Democracy: The Transformation of the SPD and the Labor Party)*. Wiesbaden: VS Verlag für Sozialwissenschaften, 2009.

Orloff, Ann Shola. Review of *Social Foundations of Postindustrial Economics*, by Gøsta Esping-Andersen. *American Journal of Sociology* 106, no. 4 (2001): 1178–81.

Pasture, Patrick. "Window of Opportunities or Trompe l'Oeil? The Myth of Labor Unity in Western Europe After 1945." In *Transnational Moments of Change: Europe 1945, 1968, 1989*, edited by Gerd-Rainer Horn and Padraic Kenney, 27–50. Lanham, MD: Rowman & Littlefield, 2004.

Piketty, Thomas. *Capital in the Twenty-First Century*. Cambridge, MA: Belknap Press of Harvard University Press, 2014.

Pittaway, Mark. "The Reproduction of Hierarchy: Skill, Working-Class Culture, and the State in Early Socialist Hungary." *Journal of Modern History*, no. 74 (2002): 737–69.

Plumpe, Werner. *German Economic and Business History in the 19th and 20th Centuries*. New York: Palgrave Macmillan, 2016.

Pries, Ludger. "Workers' Participation at Plant Level in a Comparative Perspective." In *The Palgrave Handbook of Workers' Participation at Plant Level*, edited by Stefan Berger, Ludger Pries, and Manfred Wannöffel, 37–62. New York: Palgrave Macmillan, 2019.

Raphael, Lutz. *Jenseits von Kohle und Stahl: Eine gesellschaftsgeschichte Westeuropas nach dem Boom (Beyond Coal and Steel: A Social History of Western Europe After the Economic Boom)*. Frankfurt am Main: Suhrkamp, 2019.

Roseman, Mark. *Recasting the Ruhr, 1945–1959: Manpower, Economic Recovery and Labour Relations*. New York: Berg, 1992.

Roseman, Mark. "Refugees and Ruhr Miners: A Case Study of the Impact of the Refugees on Post-War German Society." In *Refugees in the Age of Total War*, edited by Anna C. Bramwell and Michael R. Marrus, 184–97. 1988. Reprint, London: Routledge, 2021.

Saunders, Jack. *Assembling Cultures: Workplace Activism, Labour Militancy and Cultural Change in Britain's Car Factories, 1945–1982*. Manchester: Manchester University Press, 2019.

Sparschuh, Olga. "Citizens and Non-Citizens: The Relevance of Citizenship Status in Labour Migration within Italy and to Germany from the 1950s to 1970s." *Journal of Contemporary History* 49, no. 1 (2014): 28–53.

Steinhouse, Adam. *Workers' Participation in Post-Liberation France*. Lanham, MD: Lexington Books, 2001.

Stokes, Lauren. *Fear of the Family: Guest Workers and Family Migration in the Federal Republic of Germany*. Oxford: Oxford University Press, 2022.

Streeck, Wolfgang. *Buying Time: The Delayed Crisis of Democratic Capitalism*. London: Verso, 2014.

Streeck, Wolfgang. "Comment on Wolfgang Merkel: 'Is Capitalism Compatible with Democracy?'" *Zeitschrift für vergleichende Politikwissenschaft (Journal for Comparative Political Science)* 9, nos. 1–2 (2015): 49–60.

Todd, Selina. *The People: The Rise and Fall of the Working Class, 1910–2010*. London: John Murray, 2014.

Tóth, Eszter Zsófia. "Shifting Identities in the Life Histories of Working-Class Women in Socialist Hungary." *International Labor and Working-Class History* 68 (2005): 75–92.

Vogel, Berthold. *Die Staatsbedürftigkeit der Gesellschaft (Society's Need for the State)*. Hamburg: Hamburger Edition, 2007.

Wurster. "Angestellte h.c." *Der Spiegel*, November 22, 1960. https://www.spiegel.de/politik/angestellte-h-ca-28401119-0002-0001-0000-000043067669?context=issue.

Zahra, Tara. "'Prisoners of the Postwar': Expellees, Displaced Persons, and Jews in Austria After World War II." *Austrian History Yearbook* 41 (2010): 191–215.

# Inflation, Wage Policy, and the End of the New Deal Order

## Andrew Elrod

Throughout the post–World War II era—and indeed up to the present day—inflation has consistently proved a major obstacle to would-be social democratic regimes. Economic growth through tight labor markets, trade union rights, and entrepreneurial profits defined the framework for postwar economic steering. An intolerance for continuously rising prices, however, threatened the simultaneous pursuit of these goals, fracturing governing coalitions and auguring irresolvable political conflicts that would transform these countries during the 1970s. When democratic countries were unable to abandon one or more of them, the power behind these competing interests compelled a transformation of economic institutions and policy instruments and radicalized the nature of reform. National wage policies offered one of the more prevalent and enduring forms of this transformation necessary to tame inflationary pressures without abandoning full employment or private discretion over prices. Yet bringing wage determination under public oversight proved a demanding and politically volatile process. This essay telescopes the major national attempts of liberal policymakers and labor leaders to hammer out a public wage policy in the United States to contend with the problem of rising prices without sacrificing employment or working-class incomes.

Across the Western world, new strategies of growth and development during the 1940s assumed a prior and necessary centralization of wage bargaining and stabilization of wage growth—the US included. Organized labor's responsibility for preventing inflation, however, presented a paradox. Having wrested wages from both markets and employers, unions now confronted governments that asked them to relinquish the hard-won prize in exchange for participation in a supposedly pluralist political economy. The implications were at once practically conservative and potentially transformative, as labor's power to restrain rather than accelerate wage growth entered broader negotiations on legislation and business policy.[1]

---

1. "So long as freedom of collective bargaining is maintained," William Beveridge explained during the war, "the primary responsibility of preventing a full employment policy from coming to grief in a vicious spiral of wages and prices will rest on those who conduct the bargaining on behalf of labor.... But it would be unrea-

*Labor: Studies in Working-Class History*  Volume 22 • Issue 1
DOI 10.1215/15476715-11521326   © 2025 by Labor and Working-Class History Association

Wage policy therefore entailed larger political bargains over the shape and direction of economic growth. Repeat experiments with national wage policies over the first four postwar decades compelled states to expand the scope of political bargains to include adjustments to the social structure itself: the distribution of income between labor and capital, administered prices, and the business cycle itself. The new practice of "macroeconomic management"—those projects of maintaining high employment and stabilizing prices that separate governments of the twentieth century from those of earlier epochs—thus put the legal foundations of the mixed economy up repeatedly for debate. Alarm over "wage inflation" invited investigation of variously privately or publicly controlled prices, the adequacy of profits, sources of tax revenue in fiscal restraint, the coverage and benefits of social insurance programs, the content of collective bargaining rights, minimum wage and prevailing wage laws, and the sources of investment driving growth. The history of national wage policies is thus a vector along which to trace the renegotiation of labor's rights and privileges in the era of social democracy, and the extent to which the industrial system could transform itself to accommodate labor's power.

The United States did not escape this dilemma. From the end of World War II until 1980, the country experienced six distinct waves of inflation in which negotiations over the "political wage"—what Charles Maier has described as the "implicit negotiation over the broader social role of labor" influencing the real value of the pay envelope—brought organized labor into political exchange with successive governments from the Truman through Carter administrations.[2] The history of the political wage can be divided into three periods. The first, between World War II and the end of the Truman administration, saw a prolonged struggle over standby controls culminate in the conflictual economic planning of Korean War. In the second, between the beginning of the Eisenhower administration and the Watergate investigations, organized labor's economic and political power plateaued as it sought to regain legal terrain conceded during the 1940s. Able to defend—or augment—real wages against inflation and to focus national politics on the era's unemployment and on corporate profits, organized labor had transmuted the Depression-era problems of working-class political inclusion into new kinds of conflict within the state over the tools of economic policy. The final period after Watergate saw organized employers unify behind the protection and expansion of nonunion labor markets and unilateral wage determination—rather than political bargains—as the preferred instrument for wage stabilization.

The decisive shifts in position and power occurred in the second of these periods, when economists began to reconsider the significance of the "wage-price

---

sonable to expect the trade unions from using their bargaining strength to the full, unless the Government can give them some assurance that it is pursuing a policy of stable prices. This is … why price policy must be an integral part of a full employment policy" (Beveridge, *Full Employment in a Free Society*, 200–2). See also Hansen, "Wages and Prices: The Basic Issue."

2. Maier, "Preconditions for Corporatism," 39, and *Project State and Its Rivals*, 228–29.

spiral" in theories of inflation. The spiral's significance inverted during the employer offensive of the late 1960s and 1970s. Employers began to mobilize the image of the spiral, which workers had invoked to demand more progressive taxation and price controls, rhetorically in arguments for new restrictions on collective bargaining and tolerating higher unemployment. In the politically pregnant era that followed Watergate and the OPEC oil-shock inflations of 1973 and 1979, the very continuation of collective bargaining for wide swaths of the economy was at stake. Yet labor's critical defeat in Washington over domestic stabilization of the Vietnam War economy foreclosed the continuation of the kinds of statist solutions invited by its earlier economic power, exacerbating the decade's rising prices in prolonged political stalemate.

### The Roosevelt and Truman Era: The Growth Programs That Mobilized Labor

Wage policy in the Truman era hinged on the possibility of formal political bargains, national in scope, between the leaders of the new industrial unions, the large corporate manufacturers, and the government in Washington, DC. Such a wage policy had been hammered out, at times violently, under the National War Labor Board (NWLB). In exchange for "union security," labor had pledged to adhere to NWLB orders and not to strike. While unions grew under the policy by four million members (50 percent of the prewar membership), the erosion of real wages by wartime inflation undermined union leaders' authority over their members and introduced an explosive volatility to bargaining. Rather than allow further wage increases, the New Dealers and loyal CIO leaders sought expanded price-control powers from the Congress, empowering the Office of Price Administration (OPA) to fix agricultural prices, subsidize production, and require grade labeling to ensure the quality of controlled commodities. But by November 1943, the pressure of illegal strikes had succeeded in breaking the "Little Steel Formula" wage policy and provoked a conservative bloc in Congress to authorize imprisonment of strike leaders.

With national election campaigns underway in 1944, Congress began debating the future of the postwar economy—in particular the future role of the federal budget, which had grown to more than $100 billion in FY 1945 (from $9 billion in FY 1940). Comprising half of a total national output then estimated around $200 billion, this level of government spending appeared to New Dealers and the CIO critical to maintaining high employment after the war.[3] The struggle for a reconversion wage policy began in this context of the broader CIO–New Deal push for postwar planning. As Director of Economic Stabilization William H. Davis told the Advisory Board to the Office of War Mobilization and Reconversion (OWMR) in March 1945, it was "fundamental that the real wages of workers—standards of living—must

---

3. Annual Report of the Secretary of the Treasury (1946), 362; Minutes of the Advisory Board of the Office of War Mobilization and Reconversion, August 21, 1945, box 5, George W. Taylor Papers, Ms. Coll 1210, Kislak Center for Special Collections, University of Pennsylvania (hereafter OWMR minutes).

rise else a $150,000,000,000 national income cannot be consumed."[4] At the same meeting, CIO president Philip Murray argued that "it would be difficult to maintain the confidence of labor organizations in" the OPA and NWLB "without reassuring them that the agencies had V-E Day plans ready or in process of preparation for early announcement." The preferred program among the New Dealers, as OPA director Chester Bowles later put it, was "that the government should take the leadership and make an adjustment, or propose an adjustment, of wages up to about 10 percent on wage rates on the promise from the unions that they would not strike before a period of, say, 18 months, and they would stick to their jobs."[5] In January 1945, after six months of debate, Montana senator James Murray introduced his Full Employment Act in Congress to obligate annual spending at levels administratively determined as capable of maintaining full employment. In late September, the Senate passed the proposal 71–10.

On August 16, 1945, however, the day after the Japanese surrender, President Truman announced a reconversion wage policy that imperiled any attempt at an orderly conversion and jeopardized plans for a permanently enlarged public sector. On the recommendations of Stabilization Director Davis and NWLB chairman George Taylor, the president called for a national conference of labor and employer leaders at an undetermined date to deliberate the future of NWLB policy. Yet in an impulsive accommodation to Labor Secretary Lewis Schwellenbach and assistant John Steelman, the president also declared that the NWLB would expire after the conference.[6] This vitiated the Davis-Taylor program—employers and unions needn't adhere to temporary NWLB rules and procedures.

The result was the historic strike wave of the winter of 1945–46, in which labor and business openly challenged existing wage-price relationships. In this struggle business had the advantage of the looming expiration of OPA funding on the last day of June 1946. The cost of any wage increases granted through strike pressure might be recouped so long as price-control authority was not renewed. Firms might even sit idle, as tax rebates written into the excess profits tax were reimbursed. When the national labor-management conference finally met in November 1945, there was little hope of achieving an agreement on wage policy: John L. Lewis of the mine workers, who had led his union to break the Little Steel Formula, voted together with William

4. OWMR minutes, March 6, 1945.

5. Reminiscences of Chester Bowles (1963), Oral History Archives at Columbia, Rare Book and Manuscript Library, Columbia University in the City of New York, 195–96.

6. "Plans Given as Controls Are Reduced," *Hartford Courant*, August 15, 1945, 1; "Truman Lays Down Policy for Return to Free Economy," *New York Times*, August 19, 1945, 1; "Truman Gives Authority to Raise Wages," *Los Angeles Times*, August 17, 1945, 1; Harry S. Truman, "Statement by the President Proposing Measures to Insure Industrial Peace in the Reconversion Period," in Gerhard Peters and John T. Woolley, American Presidency Project, https://www.presidency.ucsb.edu/node/231272; Harry S. Truman, Executive Order 9599, in Gerhard Peters and John T. Woolley, American Presidency Project, https://www.presidency.ucsb.edu/node/278117.

Greer of the AFL and Benjamin Fairless of US Steel to dissolve the NWLB against the votes of the CIO and administration representatives.[7]

At OPA, Chester Bowles became inundated with petitioned price increases on the grounds of ungranted wage demands. Organized or large employers, eyes toward the summer appropriations process in the Congress, delayed or refused the financial disclosures OPA needed for its price determinations. Gesturing fecklessly toward an organized solution, Truman ordered the establishment of several industry-specific fact-finding boards to delay national strikes set for December and rule on specific wage-price settlements. Unable to lift prices, many firms, notably the meatpacking industry, withheld product. Compounded by strikes interrupting production and by a growing volume of exports to occupied Europe, the United States experienced widespread shortages in food, fuels, clothing, and electrical equipment between the autumn of 1945 and the summer of 1946.[8] During the first half of the year, the wartime wage bargain dissolved decisively into decentralized conflict.

Amid this disorganized wage pressure, the controlling bloc of Republican Party and southern Democratic legislators mastered the second session of the Seventy-Ninth Congress. In January 1946, the Conference Committee on Senator Murray's Full Employment Act stripped the labor-backed law of its budget authority, just as the uncoordinated strike wave took off. As passed in February, the Employment Act of 1946 established only a new advisory office, the president's Council of Economic Advisers (CEA), and a new congressional committee, the Joint Economic Committee. By June 1946, the poor public image of retail shortages had emboldened Congress to write into the OPA renewal immediate removal of all prices from control. Truman vetoed this legislation, but this meant expiration. For twenty-five days OPA operated without statutory authority. Annualized inflation, which hovered between 2 and 3 percent between January and June 1946, rose rapidly to 9.4 percent in July. Although a second bill passed restoring the agency's powers, Congress again removed all but a few specific commodities from control; inflation accelerated to 17.7 percent in November and peaked at 19.7 percent in March 1947. In the disorder of the conflict, the employers' focused public relations message and House majority suffocated the social democratic opportunity. Republicans won large majorities in the November 1946 elections.

Political victory masked the economic failure of the conservative program of decentralized price determination amid widespread, but likewise decentralized collective bargaining. The wage-price spiral of 1946–48 forced this problem onto the new CEA, an agency originally devised for budget policy. "Since no other measures of public

7. "CIO's Resolution Assailed by Lewis," *Baltimore Sun*, November 9, 1945, 1; "Lewis and Murray Clash over Wages at Labor Meeting," *New York Times*, November 9, 1945, 1; "Lewis Demands Early End to Price Controls, Attacks CIO Wage Stand at Labor-Management Conference," *Wall Street Journal*, November 9, 1945, 2; Bernstein, "Walter Reuther and the General Motors Strike of 1945–1946," 261. A summary of the conference is in James Livingston, "Was a Labor Crisis Necessary?," November 21, 1945, folder 2, box 2, George W. Taylor Papers.

8. Reminiscences of Chester Bowles (1963), Oral History Archives at Columbia, Rare Book and Manuscript Library, Columbia University in the City of New York, 160–62.

policy [than continuing high taxes] were put into effect to damp the ensuing inflation," the CEA staff reflected on the problem, "it was clear that . . . the measures which could restrain it would have to be based upon voluntary self-restraints by those with power to determine wages, prices." Whether "labor can properly be admonished to forgo wage increases to prevent inflation" and "a similar admonition [can be made] applicable to business management" would depend on voluntary educational conferences.[9]

Events intervened as the administration began this voluntarist stabilization program. First, the onset of the Cold War superimposed onto the class struggle a new labor law regime—the Taft-Hartley Act of July 1947. This represented a long-sought conservative goal that dated to original debates over the Wagner Act in 1935, was refined in the strike-limitation bills of the Seventy-Eighth and Seventy-Ninth Congresses, and consolidated in the Eightieth into a new omnibus reform to the nation's labor law: outlawing secondary strikes, requiring anti-Communist affidavits of board petitioners, allowing the board to declare union activity "unfair," and inserting into federal law an exemption (Section 14[b]) for states to outlaw federally protected union-security contract language. Second, the Cold War simulated exports and injected new sources of investment around politically influential centers of business initiative—the Marshall Plan and the Defense Production Act of 1950. This represented a new force unleashed by the war. For the next two years, as the Marshall Plan stiffened markets and with the campaign for its Foreign Assistance Act providing a forum for economic planning, powerful labor unions in both the AFL and CIO went to Washington to support the emerging Cold War. Truman had opened the door to this alliance in late 1947, realizing his need for a new political formula against a hostile Congress and continuing inflation (still 12.7 percent that September). Facing intensifying political crisis in Europe, a third "round" of wage demands to "catch up" to inflation, and a presidential election year, Truman called two special sessions of the Congress in November 1947 and July 1948 to approve spending on foreign aid and new inflation-control measures. From $33 billion in FY 1948, the Marshall Plan had raised government spending to $40 billion in FY 1949. Centering the Republican Party's continued opposition to price control during this export drive, Truman's "Fair Deal" campaign openly championed a host of additional federal spending and reform ideas, including national health insurance, federal rent control, and civil rights. The campaign worked. In November, the Democrats recaptured both houses of Congress, and Truman kept the White House.[10]

With help from labor, the Fair Deal's defense spenders ultimately saw their program through. But electoral victory followed by the belated arrival of the postwar recession in 1949 (the last to see prices falling significantly along the pattern of prewar business cycles) appeared to sap the White House of whatever domestic reform energies it had harnessed in the campaign. Senator Murray again produced

9. Paul T. Homan, "An Approach to Wage and Price Policies," April 27, 1949, 3, 33, in Homan Folder, box 1, Edwin G. Nourse Papers, Truman Library.

10. On the internationalist alliance with labor, see Barker, "Cold War Capitalism," 100–109.

full-employment legislation, and the Cabinet eventually lobbied Congress for the Fair Deal. But the anticommunist rhetoric both the AFL and the CIO embraced as part of the Marshall Plan coalition was now mobilized against the administration proposals for government steel plants and "socialized" medicine. The business downturn reduced tax revenues and, combined with the Marshall Plan, produced a $3 billion deficit in FY 1950. White House toleration of this unplanned deficit, rather than pursuit of much larger planned ones, again foreclosed the domestic reform agenda.

It was instead the Korean War in June 1950 that accomplished the fiscal breakthrough and reopened the negotiation of labor's rights and the nation's obligations. During the Eighty-First Congress's second session, with prospect of a third world war against communism in Asia, such economic planning as Truman and the CIO had proposed in January now served an arguably capitalist purpose. In July 1950, the administration rewrote Murray's capacity-expansion bill as the Defense Production Act (DPA). Passed in September 1950, the DPA oversaw a near doubling of federal spending over the next two years, peaking at $74 billion in FY 1953 ($9.5 billion deficit). It was paired with the McCarran Act that expanded anticommunist affidavits and loyalty boards beyond the NLRB across all federal employees.

The Korean War transformed the Fair Deal's social democratic program. The road to the military-Keynesian Sunbelt development that would reshape the geography of capitalist power by the 1970s and stimulate the growth of nonunion labor markets ironically passed through the agency of newly powerful labor unions engaged in Washington with repealing Taft-Hartley. More immediately, however, wartime panic buying and a vigorous return to full employment reinvigorated the wage-price spiral and gave urgency to the labor movement's demands for price stabilization. Though Congress raised tax rates and symbolically cut civilian spending by $2 billion in FY 1951, these anti-inflation measures were unable to arrest the rising cost of living. Between September 1950 and January 1951, annualized inflation jumped from 2 percent to 8 percent. Wage increases likewise accelerated; the rise in nonsupervisory manufacturing workers' average hourly earnings increased from 6.4 percent to 10.2 percent (annualized). By December 1950, after much resistance, the Congress reestablished an excess profits tax. In January, the administration finally acceded to price-wage controls, ordering a freeze at the end of the month.

The Korean War inflation peaked at 9.3 percent in February 1951. For the next two years, the cost of living stabilized as government spending ballooned. Inflation fell to 2.3 percent in February 1952 (when the prefreeze months exited the annual calculation). Stabilization, however, was politically tumultuous. Labor fought hard to shape the Korean War wage-price bargain, the AFL and the CIO overcoming their domestic disagreements to lobby for single labor interest within the new economic controls agencies. When defense mobilization director Charles Wilson (CEO of General Electric) declared that the new tripartite Wage Stabilization Board (WSB) would not hear labor disputes, depriving it of the powers enjoyed by the World War II labor board, a United Labor Policy Committee won expanded authority for the wage board only after a five-week boycott of union participation in the stabilization agencies. The prize was "annual improvement factors" and "cost-of-living adjustments" awarded by the reconstituted WSB. The World War II wage policy had bequeathed private health and pension "fringe" benefits; the Korean War wage policy standardized inflation adjustments to current pay.

But the full implications of the stabilization regime—and capital's intolerance for it—soon became clear. In late 1951, US Steel refused to grant a wage increase under existing price-control standards. Having established the authority of the WSB to determine wage increases, and maneuvered the employer to defy that authority, the steelworkers pulled a page from John L. Lewis's book and turned business and government against each other. The White House faced a decision: allow a strike in the critically important steel industry over a government-approved but employer-rejected settlement or impose a labor agreement that under price control reduced corporate profits. On April 8, 1952, Truman seized the industry's properties to pay the wage increase and avoid a strike.[11] Wilson resigned. Though the Supreme Court quickly invalidated the seizure, the experience demonstrated the radicalizing nature of inflation in a pluralist economy—and the importance of business organization to command the government in the contest.

### From Eisenhower to Nixon: A Growth Experiment Mobilizes Capital

The Korean War's stimulation of what had been a dampening post–World War II wage-price spiral, so that only a return to price control achieved stability, confirmed for many liberal economists a structural dilemma produced by the rise of organized labor. "Uncontrolled collective bargaining, full employment, and stable prices are probably incompatible," Harvard's Sumner Slichter had explained in 1948, arguing for a "national wage policy" among unions, employers, and government. But if the wage-price spiral set off by Korea hardened this conclusion, the threat to the corporate order of the politics of wage policies brought a newfound tolerance for inflation. "At the risk of being called an irresponsible and dangerous thinker," Slichter wrote in 1952, drawing very different conclusions from four years earlier, "let me say that in the kind of economy possessed by the United States a slowly rising price level is actually preferable to a stable price level." After Korea, post–World War II designs for price stability melted into positive arguments for passivity in the face of "creeping inflation." John Kenneth Galbraith put the same problem more forcefully: "If maximum current production is taken as an imperative, then the only paths are either to have open inflation or to remove to central authority the power of decision over prices and wages."[12]

The observed incompatibility of full employment, price stability, and privately determined wages and prices produced a political and intellectual puzzle during Eisenhower's second term that would shape historical possibilities during social democracy's so-called golden age. Creeping inflation returned after the short

11. McConnell, *Steel Seizure of 1952*; Marcus, *Truman and the Steel Seizure Case*.
12. Slichter, *American Economy*, 43, and "How Bad Is Inflation?"; Galbraith, *American Capitalism*, 205.

post–Korean War recession of 1953–54, pushed by a round of pattern-setting union wage contracts (the seventh in auto and steel) followed by an investment boom in the capital-goods industries in 1956–57. The president publicly urged wage and price restraint and threatened price control. As prices rose in 1956, the administration pursued an anti-inflation policy of budget surpluses ($1.6 billion each in FYs 1956 and 1957), while the Federal Reserve also raised its short-term interest rate. This fiscal-monetary contraction pushed up unemployment in the second half of 1957, passing 7 percent by April 1958. Yet curiously as joblessness rose in winter and spring 1958, the inflation it had been intended to dampen remained around 3.6 percent—then felt too high. It would not fall below 2 percent until the following winter. Unemployment, having not fallen below 5 percent, began to rise again in July 1959, peaking above 7 percent in summer 1961.[13]

Economic historians have revised our understanding of the rising prices from 1956 to 1961 as the successful achievement of "low inflation."[14] For contemporaries, however, any inflation amid rising unemployment was a disquieting development. Senator Hubert Humphrey spoke of the White House's "planned, premeditated, pre-designed recession"; in the 1958 midterms, the Democrats flipped thirteen seats in the Senate and forty-seven in the House. By 1959, the professional social scientists studying inflation had developed a host of explanations, not mutually exclusive, competing for dominance among political and policy priorities: cost-push, demand-pull, "seller's inflation," demand-shift, and the early modern quantity theory of money. Though the late Eisenhower inflation was low by the standards of those before and after—plateauing between 1.3 and 1.7 percent between September 1959 and November 1960—its occurrence provoked a reconsideration of the post–Korean War intellectual settlement in favor of "macroeconomic" steering and "creeping" inflation. "There is a growing consensus," the editorial board of the *Washington Post* declared in March 1959, "that the present fiscal and monetary controls of the government simply cannot cope with the administered price sector of the economy where concentrated industries like steel can . . . defy sagging demand, increase prices and profits, and thus seriously retard economic growth." Woodlief Thomas, staff economist to the Federal Reserve Board of Governors, acknowledged "unstabilizing forces in pricing actions of the private economy—on the part of both management and labor—that cannot be effectively controlled or corrected by governmental actions in the area of fiscal and monetary policies."[15]

The economists affiliated with the Democratic Party and its internationalist commitments confronted Eisenhower's dilemma directly. The long recession not

13. On Eisenhower's price control threats, see "Eisenhower Asserts Inflation May Result in Economic Control," *Baltimore Sun*, February 7, 1957, 1.

14. Romer and Romer, "Rehabilitation of Monetary Policy."

15. Humphrey in Sundquist, *Politics and Policy*, 21, 28. On inflation theories, see the committee prints prepared for Joint Economic Committee, 86th Cong., 1st sess., in particular Charles L. Schultze, "Recent Inflation in the United States," Study Print No. 1, "The Price Issue Is Joined," and Woodlief Thomas, "Those Administered Prices," *Washington Post*, March 12, 1959, A24–25.

only undermined the country's economic competition with the Soviet Union; the inflation it failed to arrest also jeopardized the world position of the dollar. Accelerating peacetime growth without the galloping wage-price spiral of the late 1940s or the creeping inflation of the late 1950s was therefore their domestic and geopolitical quest. The "heart" of the nation's "inflation problem," Walt Rostow wrote for the Democrat's 1960 campaign, was that "as a society, we have no agreed norm for wage and price policy." Though the new Kennedy administration would debate the appropriate sources of growth—tax cuts or government spending—there was consensus well before the inauguration that the new administration would pair growth with some form of wage-price stabilization. Because "in essential ways the wage-price spiral was beyond the reach of fiscal and monetary policy," Arthur Schlesinger Jr. explained, the new government's growth program needed "new institutions assuring a greater public role in wage-price settlements." Paul Samuelson put the new conventional wisdom clearly for President-Elect Kennedy: "Just as we pioneered in the 1920s in creating potent monetary mechanisms and in the 1930s in forging the tools of effective fiscal policy, so may it be necessary in the 1960s to meet head on the problem of a price creep."[16]

The search for Schlesinger's "new institutions" proved the defining political and organizational challenge for every labor-aligned political party of the North Atlantic during the 1960s. The reason was the long-observed tendency of employers to raise prices at the beginning of business-cycle expansions, creating the profits on which capitalist investment depended. Rising prices elicited demands for higher wages, which, where organized labor was able, turned the spiral. During the late 1940s, liberal economists had prescribed a wage policy while President Truman proclaimed the need for price controls; conservatives urged restrictions on organized labor and a return to pre–New Deal levels of government spending. The onset of the Cold War had shifted these coalitions toward favoring a high level of (military) spending but opposing controls. Reflecting this consensus, the Kennedy CEA proposed a middle ground between controlled mobilization and free market: "guideposts for noninflationary wage and price behavior." Published annually in the president's economic report beginning in 1962, this guideline consisted of a single concept—the annual rate of increase of output-per-manhour nationally—and a set of rules for how it would be used in evaluating the "inflationary pressure" of different industries' wage and price decisions. Where industry productivity was above national productivity, prices should fall. Where an industry was contracting, prices might increase above the guidepost. Wage increases should not outpace national productivity unless the industry was unable to attract labor. To invite unions and management to adhere to these

16. Walt W. Rostow, "The Problems of Inflation and Productivity in the United States," in Papers of John F. Kennedy, Presidential Papers, President's Office Files, Staff Memoranda, "Rostow, Walt W., 1960," https://www.jfklibrary.org/asset-viewer/archives/JFKPOF/064a/JFKPOF-064a-007; Paul Samuelson, "Prospects and Policies for the 1961 American Economy, a Report to President-Elect Kennedy," in US Congress, Joint Economic Committee, *January 1961 Economic Report of the President and the Economic Situation and Outlook*, 87th Cong., 1st sess., 1961, Committee Print, 703–11; Schlesinger, *Thousand Days*, 647.

ambiguous rules, Kennedy (at the suggestion of Labor Secretary Arthur Goldberg, former general counsel for the steelworkers) established the President's Advisory Committee for Labor-Management Policy, a twenty-one-member group cochaired by the secretaries of labor and commerce and composed of business and labor leaders from across the economy, in February 1961.[17]

Between 1961 and the first half of 1965, the Kennedy administration successfully secured wage restraint as it deliberated how to reduce unemployment. Total spending (administrative budget) jumped in Kennedy's first year to $81.5 billion (from Eisenhower's $76.6 billion austerity budget) and crept steadily upward by around $5 billion per year over the next three years, reaching $97.7 billion in FY 1964. Collectively bargained wage increases were 2.9 percent in 1962, 3.0 percent in 1963, and 3.2 percent in 1964—exactly in line with the guideposts. So long as inflation remained around 1 to 1.3 percent, as it would until July 1965, labor's participation in "guideposted" settlements was easily achievable.[18] But even as the program restored business expansion with stable prices, it faced grumbling criticism from both capital and labor. The unemployment rate, which fell to 5.5 percent in the first year, resisted further reductions after February 1962. And basic industry, at a moment when profits were usually to be taken, found its price policy in sharp conflict with that of the administration.

The signal for capitalist discontent was the public April 1962 dispute between the White House and the steel industry over prices. Having received a personal visit from US Steel chairman Roger Blough announcing a 3.5 percent price increase—after a presidentially negotiated 2.5 percent wage settlement—the executive office mobilized to move the market to force the company to rescind its increase or lose market share. Wall Street felt victimized; in late May, the Dow Jones lost more than $20 billion in value in one day. "Anti-business governmental attitudes," wrote economic advisers Robert Solow and Paul Samuelson, now presented the possibility of a "Kennedy recession." The public celebrated the conflict as trustbusting along the old New Deal pattern—Marilyn Monroe's feting of the president for besting US Steel captured the mood. But this popularity did not lessen the administration's horror at the resulting business sentiment. The politics of the wage-price bargain was loosening on the price side.[19]

The businessmen who had come to power under Eisenhower considered Kennedy's administration hostile to their interests and overly deferential to organized labor. Their evidence was not just the price policy that had led to the steel dispute. Commerce Secretary Luther Hodges had in 1961 attempted to reform his department's Business Advisory Council (BAC). Described by Harper's as "Ameri-

17. Stebenne, *Arthur Goldberg*, 253–56; "Labor in 1961," *Monthly Labor Review* (January 1962).

18. The administration published ranges in 1962 and 1963 before settling, in 1964, on 3.2 percent. *MLR* "current labor statistics" Labor in 1961, Labor in 1962.

19. McConnell, *Steel and the Presidency*; Goodwin, *Exhortation and Controls*, 172, 178; Okun, *Political Economy of Prosperity*, 45. Marilyn Monroe's words: "Happy Birthday, Mr. President / For all the things you've done / The battles that you've won / The way you deal with U.S. Steel / And our problems by the ton / We thank you so much."

ca's most powerful private club," the BAC's opposition to more direct public participation in collective business decision making prompted BAC president Blough to
pull the group out of the government and reconstitute itself as the private Business
Council (BC). Most deeply motivating business organization were the president's
appointments to the NLRB, which began to tip the balance in collective bargaining
back toward labor.[20] Control of the board was a decisive business issue because the
AFL-CIO's primary legislative goal remained repeal of Section 14(b), which would
deprive regional employer associations of the tools in state legislatures they had used
to halt labor's progress.[21] Lyndon Johnson's landslide victory in November 1964, and
the supermajorities won by his Great Society Democratic Party, ensured a hearing for
14(b) in the Eighty-Ninth Congress. In his January 1965 State of the Union address,
Johnson pledged to tackle the issue.

Historians tend to locate the political mobilization of business that remade
the postwar United States in the 1970s Sunbelt, in response to President Nixon's price
controls or the stagflation that followed.[22] But it was labor's participation as a junior
partner in the Kennedy-Johnson coalition that fertilized the growth of decisive institutions such as the Business Roundtable that would shape the neoliberal transition
from New York and Chicago. Business, alert to challenge on the labor-law status quo,
responded now to harden the wage side of the national settlement. Led by Douglas Soutar of American Smelting and Refining, Virgil Day of General Electric, and
Fred Atkinson of Macy's, leading labor relations executives formed a private strategy
group including their counterparts at AT&T, Ford, US Steel, Union Carbide, General
Dynamics, B. F. Goodrich, Humble Oil and Refining, Columbia Gas, and Sears Roe-
buck. Twelve in all, the group hired two former members of Eisenhower's NLRB and
began meeting with the law offices of Vedder, Price, Kaufman & Kammholz (Theophil Kammholz had served as the chief counsel of Eisenhower's NLRB), whose law
clients included such leading BC firms as General Electric and Campbell's Soup.[23]
Their purpose, as Soutar later recalled, was "exorcism of the NLRB."[24]

Thus the renegotiation of the terms of the nation's wage-price settlement was
already underway when the Vietnam War intervened. On the same day the House
passed labor's Section 14(b) repeal in July 1965, the president publicly announced an
increase in the US troop presence to 125,000 soldiers, a doubling of draft inductions,
and a request for supplemental military spending. Unemployment finally fell to 4 percent in December. Wage restraint, however, which had succeeded with stability in the
cost of living, now confronted a challenge. Inflation ran at 1.9 percent throughout the

20. Rowen, *Free Enterprisers*, 62–71; Gross, *Broken Promise*, 163–91.

21. Goulden, *Meany*, 349–57; Bernstein, *Guns or Butter*, 426–38; Gross, *Broken Promise*, 147.

22. Waterhouse, *Lobbying America*; Vogel, *Fluctuating Fortunes*; Stein, *Pivotal Decade*; Plotke, "Political
Mobilization of Business."

23. Gross, *Broken Promise*, 366n75; "Theophil C. Kammholz Dies at 83; Lawyer an Expert in Labor
Issues," *New York Times*, July 1, 1992, 21.

24. *The War on Wage Protection: The Business Offensive*, Center to Protect Worker's Rights (1979), 10–11;
Payne, "Plot to Subvert Labor Standards"; Gross, *Broken Promise*, 201; Waterhouse, *Lobbying America*, 79–80.

second half of 1965 and rose to 2.6 percent in February 1966. Just as labor's legislative reward for four years of wage restraint began to glimmer on the horizon, accelerating inflation returned for the fourth time in postwar history. To labor's opponents in Congress, the AFL-CIO's lobbying campaign for Section 14(b) repeal now took on a new, aggressive, and inflationary meaning. In the closing months of 1965, the bill stalled against Senator Everett Dirksen's filibuster. In January 1966, as the Senate reconvened to test the issue, transit workers illegally struck New York City's metro system for twelve days for an above-guidepost settlement, winning 6.3 percent and dispelling any illusions of labor's docility.[25]

The wage-price spiral began turning in 1966. But whereas in 1948 and 1959 the Democratic Party's alliance with organized labor elicited proposals to break the spiral with controls on prices and profits, labor and the Democratic Party now split over macroeconomic planning. An extraordinary mobilization of White House staff, led by a young Joe Califano, enforced the administration's price policy on key sectors. But the cost of living was now increasing, eating away at guidepost settlements. The AFL-CIO urged the reestablishment of an excess-profits tax, which Paul Douglas and Albert Gore threatened privately to introduce in Congress.[26] When the president in January did call for a tax increase to slow inflation, the Business Council urged civilian spending cuts as the condition for any revenue increase. Such proposals further antagonized unions chafing at the wage guidelines.

The AFL-CIO's Executive Council called for wartime price control, a fact too often forgotten in accounts of the Vietnam inflation, declaring that the federation would "cooperate [on wages] so long as such restraints are equitably placed on all costs and incomes—including all prices, profits, dividends, rents, and executive compensation."[27] Having desperately maintained alliances with a business lobby defined by its preference for private prices and lower taxes, Lyndon Johnson and his Kennedy advisers refused to publicly countenance labor's proposals. The shape of the expansion therefore favored the private sector over labor's preference for greater public spending; the *Washington Post* had considered the Revenue Act of 1962 a "bitter defeat for the labor movement," while the AFL-CIO's official embrace of the 1964 tax cut was quickly reversed by its calls to restore top-end taxes as inflation picked up. In a promise to business leaders, Johnson maintained federal spending (administrative budget) below $100 billion—$97.7 billion in FY 1964 and $96.5 billion in FY 1965. As total spending rose to $107 billion ($2.3 billion deficit) in FY 1966, ensuring civilian spending did not rise with the war was a key goal of conservative fiscal policy, which Congress achieved: Of the $10 billion increase, $9 billion was for the military operation in Vietnam.

25 Roof, *American Labor, Congress, and the Welfare State, 1935–2010*, 102–3.

26 Hearings on the President's Economic Report, February 1966; Conversations with Edwin Weisl, January 4, 1966: Miller Center citation 9421 and 9416; Oral history transcript, Paul H. Douglas and Emily Taft Douglas, interview 1 (I), 11/1/1974, by Michael L. Gillette, LBJ Library Oral Histories, LBJ Presidential Library, 16.

27 Goulden, *Meany*, 349–51.

The impasse over who would bear the tax increase complicated anti-inflation fiscal policy. The failure of the wage guideposts in 1966 proved the decisive push. Congress did not pass a tax increase until November 1966, after a number of high-profile strikes interrupted business and secured above-guidepost wage settlements. While inflation peaked at 3.8 percent that month and subsided throughout 1967, stabilization eluded the administration so long as the Vietnam War continued: Total expenditure in FY 1967 rose to $125.7 billion, a $19 billion increase, of which $13 billion was for defense. Despite claims of a "mini-recession," growth resumed in 1968. Provoked by 2+ percent inflation rising to 4 percent in summer 1968, wage increases remained elevated. In both the nonunion service sector, where full employment pulled up low wages, and the construction industry, where the local unions mounted an aggressive wage offensive, annual increases in average hourly earnings rose to 11 and 8 percent, respectively—well above the 3.2 percent guidepost.[28] The administration responded with a push for a second tax increase, not achieved until June 1968, while annual military spending increased by another $10 billion in FY 1968.

As the public divided over the war, corporate America unified around a common message for the 1968 elections: "irresponsible" unions. North Carolina senator Sam Ervin staged hearings on labor law reform in his Senate subcommittee in March, assisted by the Soutar-Day-Macy group of Business Council executives and Eisenhower NLRB attorneys, now calling themselves the Labor Law Study Group. "The time is now," proclaimed the National Association of Manufacturers (NAM) during the hearings. "Let it not be said that industry sidestepped the challenge for major labor-law reform when both the need and the opportunity were so clear." By May, Chamber of Commerce president Winton Blount was urging a "showdown" with organized labor. Just days before the election, the Los Angeles Times reported that thirty-five employer associations—including the Chamber, NAM, the National Small Business Association, and the American Retail Federation—had contributed $500,000 to a campaign for labor law reform, joined by corporations such as AT&T, GM, Sears Roebuck, and General Dynamics. "If we can show that inflation is due to the imbalance of strength between labor unions and management, we hope to get changes again [to the labor law] next year," the Chamber's Peter Pestillo told the Los Angeles Times. In addition to reform of the NLRB, the program now included repeal of the Davis-Bacon Act.[29]

This campaign bore rotten fruit in the Nixon White House. Continuing Johnson's tax increases and his restraint on nondefense expenditures, the Republican candidate promised one distinctive change: nonintervention in private business. He

28. "Mini-Recession" is in Hyman Minsky, "The Crunch of 1966," (1968), Hyman P. Minsky Archive (1968), 267, 1. Wage statistics are average hourly earnings of production and nonsupervisory workers in construction and leisure and hospitality.

29. Gross, Broken Promise, 206–11. For NAM, see "Businessmen Complain National Labor Board Shows Pro-Union Bias," Wall Street Journal, March 29, 1968, 1; for Blount, see Linder, Wars of Attrition, 182; Harry Bernstein, "Major Firms Unite to Limit Union's Strength," Los Angeles Times, November 3, 1968, 1; War on Wage Protection, 12–13.

delivered. Inflation, which had risen to 4.7 percent in November 1968, jumped to 5.5 percent in April and 6.2 percent in August 1969. Business had framed the election differently: Rather than embracing laissez-faire, it urged government to disempower labor. But the Democratic Congress of 1969–70 was unwilling to consider such a one-sided program, and after four years of accelerating inflation it finally authorized price-wage controls in the Stabilization Act of 1970, daring the Wall Street-lawyer president to declare controls over the wartime economy.

Political necessity channeled Nixon's stabilization program back toward national wage policy. Unwilling to freeze wages alone, as the administration's business contacts urged, the White House in February 1971 picked the key construction industry—where wage settlements were reported as high as 17 percent, and where the mass-consuming public was not directly exposed to price increases—to convene meetings with national union and business leaders, issuing an executive order to suspend the Davis-Bacon Act to bring labor to the table.[30] In exchange for reinstatement of the prevailing wage law, the unions agreed to join a twelve-member Construction Industry Stabilization Committee, which began to centralize signatory power for labor agreements "to determine whether wages and salaries are acceptable in accordance" with stabilization guidelines.[31]

What began in construction wages soon spread to the rest of the economy. On August 15, 1971, Nixon declared a ninety-day freeze on all wages and prices, to be followed by a phased program of wage and price controls. Having induced a recession in 1969–71 that saw unemployment rise from 3.5 to 6.1 percent, the White House released its fiscal restraint for the controls period. While unemployment fell to 4.6 percent in 1973, the "Phase II" control period of 1972 revealed the administration's stabilization strategy: Holding wages to exact standards, it left prices and profits to vary among size categories of corporations. "The idea of the freeze and Phase II was to zap labor," freeze director Arnold Weber told *Business Week*, "and we did."[32] The result was the strike wave of 1973, the largest since 1946, and the AFL-CIO's turn against controls, which expired in April 1974 without labor's protest.

### After Nixon

Labor had regrouped after the post–World War II reconversion. Both the 1948 campaign and the Korean War defense boom provided an opportunity to press labor's cause in laws governing the structure of the economy and the contest over wages and profits it produced. The Vietnam War appeared to offer a similar chance, at first. But as with the failure of Section 14(b) repeal in 1965, the business coalition that had matured

---

30. Weber, *In Pursuit of Price Stability*, 5; Linder, *Wars of Attrition*, 310.

31. Mills, "Wage Stabilization in the Construction Industry"; Linder, *Wars of Attrition*, 317–19; Richard Nixon, Executive Order 11588—Providing for the Stabilization of Wages and Prices in the Construction Industry Online, by Gerhard Peters and John T. Woolley, American Presidency Project, https://www.presidency.ucsb.edu/node/307118; Palladino, 170–73; Weber, *In Pursuit of Price Stability*, 5, 76.

32. David Gordon, "Recession Is Capitalism as Usual," *New York Times*, April 27, 1975, 241.

in the Cold War was less amenable to the pluralist political order labor thought it had achieved since the 1940s. After Vietnam, political wage restraint hinged on strengthening collective bargaining. In 1975 and 1978, reforms to the NLRB—legalizing secondary strikes, expanding capacity to process cases, enlarging the number of members on the board, and providing greater penalties for employer violations—advanced through Congress, only to face White House vetoes or Senate filibusters. Political defeat was measured not only in organized labor's failure to keep pace with the new geography and sectoral composition of economic growth in the Cold War. It was also measured in continued inflation. Unable to achieve wage restraint, many liberals came to see unions' struggle to defend wages against rising prices as itself the source of economic dysfunction. A political liability through the Nixon years, unemployment and the open shop became positive instruments for achieving the negotiated stability that eluded American politics. ∎

ANDREW ELROD is an editor at the Jain Family Institute and a research consultant for United Teachers Los Angeles. He holds a PhD from the Department of History at University of California, Santa Barbara.

## References

Barker, Tim. "Cold War Capitalism: The Political Economy of American Military Spending, 1947–1990." PhD diss., Harvard University Graduate School of Arts and Sciences, 2022.

Barton, J. Bernstein. "Walter Reuther and the General Motors Strike of 1945–46." *Michigan History* 49, no. 3: September 1965.

Bernstein, Irving. *Guns or Butter: The Presidency of Lyndon Johnson.* New York: Oxford University Press, 1996.

Beveridge, William. *Full Employment in a Free Society.* London: Allen & Unwin, 1944.

Galbraith, John Kenneth. *American Capitalism: The Concept of Countervailing Power.* Boston: Houghton Mifflin, 1952.

Goodwin, Craufurd D., ed. *Exhortation and Controls: The Search for a Wage-Price Policy 1945–1971.* Washington, DC: Brookings Institution, 1975.

Goulden, Joseph C. *Meany: The Unchallenged Strong Man of American Labor.* New York: Atheneum, 1972.

Gross, James A. *Broken Promise: The Subversion of U.S. Labor Relations Policy, 1947–1994.* Philadelphia: Temple University Press, 1995.

Hansen, Alvin. "Wages and Prices: The Basic Issue." *The New York Times Sunday Magazine,* January 6, 1946, 5.

Linder, Marc. *Wars of Attrition: Vietnam, the Business Roundtable, and the Decline of Construction Unions.* Iowa City: Fanpihua Press, 2000.

Maier, Charles. "Preconditions for Corporatism." In *Order and Conflict in Contemporary Capitalism: Studies in the Political Economy of Western Nations,* edited by John Goldthorpe, 39–59. Oxford: Clarendon, 1984.

Maier, Charles. *The Project State and Its Rivals: A New History of the Twentieth and Twenty-First Centuries.* Cambridge, MA: Harvard University Press, 2023.

Marcus, Maeva. *Truman and the Steel Seizure Case: The Limits of Presidential Power*. New York: Columbia University Press, 1977.

McConnell, Grant. *The Steel Seizure of 1952*. Inter-University Case Program no. 52: Bobbs Merrill Company, 1960.

McConnell, Grant. *Steel and the Presidency: 1962*. New York: W. W. Norton, 1963.

Mills, D. Quinn. "Wage Stabilization in the Construction Industry." *Industrial Relations Research Association Spring Meeting*, August 1972, 2–67.

Okun, Arthur. *The Political Economy of Prosperity*. Washington, DC: Brookings Institution, 1970.

Palladino, Grace. *Skilled Hands, Strong Spirits: A Century of Building Trades History*. Ithaca: Cornell University Press, 2005.

Payne, Phillis. "The Plot to Subvert Labor Standards." *The American Federationist*, July 1979, 17–21.

Plotke, David. "The Political Mobilization of Business." In *The Politics of Interests: Interest Groups Transformed*, edited by Mark Petracca, 175–200. Boulder, CO: Westview, 1992.

Romer, Christina D., and David H. Romer. "A Rehabilitation of Monetary Policy in the 1950s." *American Economic Review* (2002): 121–27.

Roof, Tracy. *American Labor, Congress, and the Welfare State, 1935–2010*. Baltimore: Johns Hopkins University Press, 2011.

Rowen, Hobart. *The Free Enterprisers: Kennedy, Johnson and the Business Establishment*. New York: Putnam, 1964.

Schlesinger, Arthur M. *A Thousand Days: John F. Kennedy in the White House*. 1965. Reprint, New York: First Mariner Books, 2002.

Slichter, Sumner. *The American Economy, Its Problems and Prospects*. New York: Knopf, 1948.

Slichter, Sumner. "How Bad Is Inflation?" *Harpers*, August 1952, 52–57.

Steberne, David. *Arthur J. Goldberg*. Oxford: Oxford University Press, 1996, 253–56.

Stein, Judith. *Pivotal Decade: How the United States Traded Factories for Finance in the Seventies*. New Haven, CT: Yale University Press, 2011.

Sundquist, James. *Politics and Policy: The Eisenhower, Kennedy, and Johnson Years*. Washington, DC: Brookings Institution, 1968.

Vogel, David. *Fluctuating Fortunes: The Political Power of Business in America*. New York: Basic Books, 1989.

Waterhouse, Benjamin C. *Lobbying America: The Politics of Business from Nixon to NAFTA*. Princeton, NJ: Princeton University Press, 2013.

Weber, Arnold. *In Pursuit of Price Stability: The Wage-Price Freeze of 1971*. Washington, DC: Brookings Institution, 1973.

## No Harmless Power: The Life and Times of the Ukrainian Anarchist Nestor Makhno
Charlie Allison
Oakland, CA: PM Press, 2023
256 pp.; $21.95 (paper), $8.95 (ebook)

This study charts the life of the famous Ukrainian anarchist Nestor Makhno from his earliest years, through the development of his anarchist views in his youth and in prison, culminating in his command of the Revolutionary Insurgent Army of Ukraine. It is this military endeavor to establish an anarcho-communist state during the Russian Civil War that occupies the bulk of this volume. The years from 1917 through 1922 saw the Makhnovshchina embroiled in brutal battles, and increasingly caught up in often dangerous alliances with the Bolsheviks against the White armies. A cruel and vicious rout of his army by the Bolsheviks caused Makhno to flee to an unhappy and frustrating exile in Paris. He died there at the age of forty-five, his interment at the famous Père-Lachaise cemetery attended by five hundred mourners.

I am uncertain how fair it is to write an academic review of a volume that, rather fittingly given its subject matter, is anarchic in style. This volume is not intended as a formal research work based on original research or innovative methodologies, or even located in a broader set of historiographies. Indeed, it does not go much beyond a small array of key secondary studies of Makhno for its information, and on Makhno's own writings. It consciously eschews a more formal, academic style in favor of a breezy, often tongue-in-cheek riffing on this historical figure and his Black Army of anarchists. It started life as a podcast series, and the author is clearly endeavoring to re-create that genre's accessibility on paper. Unsuspecting readers should be prepared for probably unfamiliar turns of phrase like "by gum," "cheesed off," or "one sidesplitter too many" (10–14). Similarly, the author's folksy renderings of imagined conversations, for example between Makhno and his jailor, and his habit of wandering off on tangents only to suddenly yank his reader back with the phrase "but back to Makhno" will either endear or irritate the reader. Lengthy quotations from secondary authors sometimes stand in for the author's own analysis.

In the final paragraph of his study, the author states that Makhno and the world for which he fought "didn't require heroes" but, rather, "action and responsibility" and "boldness," concluding that this might well be Makhno's life lesson for us even today (180). Yet this study itself tends toward hagiography of man and movement, replete with its pantheon of anarchists "you should know" in its final chapter. This section of minibiographies is furnished with a series of beautifully austere illustrations (the artist Kevin Matthews adds real texture here). The author of this volume elevates Makhno's actions at every opportunity and clearly has his own anarchist axe to grind. Consequently, the often interesting discussion of this complex, contradictory, and not especially well-known anarchist movement in early Soviet Russia is undercut by lazy caricaturing of the broader field of conflict and its protagonists. The antisemitic, opportunistic anticommunist Cossack Ataman Grigoriev, for example, who urges Makhno to "thrash" the Bolsheviks, serves merely as a foil for a joke by the author: "'Thrash them' has also been translated as . . . 'bop them on the head.' . . . I like 'bop them on the head' myself—makes me imagine Grigoriev as the absolute worst version of Little Bunny Foo Foo" (99). An oddly placed grim joke, "'What do you call a pile of dead Chekhists [*sic*]?' 'A good start,'" merely distracts, and would be relevant only if it were a contemporary joke, which it does not appear to have been (111). Similarly, calling the death of the "legendary anarchist" Maria Nikiforova "another turd in the water pipe of bad news for the anarchists" is just crass (37, 111). Makhno's opponents are stripped of any complexity, diminished by throwaway lines and reductive caricatures. "Vladimir 'Terror Is the Only Method I Have of Governing' Lenin" had a "taste for blood" (109, 120). Leon Trotsky was "that bloviating scumbag . . . of the Red Army" (128). The Bolsheviks' "act of bad faith" was "typical" (129). Even Churchill gets an anachronistic jab: "Winston 'I Only Look Good Because Hitler and Stalin Were Also Alive at the Time' Churchill" (101). The style and organization adopted for this book are not bad per se. They irritate (at least this reader) because they substitute for more substantive argument. On the other hand, the description of Makhno by the end of the Civil War as "a patchwork of scars wearing a mustache" is genius (114).

**Frederick Corney, William & Mary**
DOI 10.1215/15476715-11521366

## Precarious Workers: History of Debates, Political Mobilizations, and Labor Reforms in Italy
Eloisa Betti
Budapest: Central European University Press, 2022
268 pp.; $85.00 (cloth)

Most people around the world are not employed in a standard work relationship. Instead, they are employed precariously. The term *precarity* is borrowed from French. It might be translated into a more common English idiom as "insecurity or instability of work." But the difficulties of translating this term into English are not merely linguistic. In the United States, almost all workers are employed *at will*. They are protected against discrimination based on sex, race, or ability; technically, it is also illegal to fire workers in America for unionizing, although firms do so regularly. Beyond that, American workers can be fired at any time, for any reason. In other countries, workers hired on standard contracts are accorded a much greater degree of protection against arbitrary dismissal. After passing through a trial period, they gain a kind of "tenure" not unlike that afforded to professors in American academia. Workers employed on standard contracts cannot be fired without *just cause*. By contrast, workers in other countries who are employed on nonstandard contracts (part-time, temporary, or fixed-duration) lack protections and also pathways to acquiring them. Their situation is more akin to that of American adjunct lecturers. Like adjunct lecturers in the United States, nonstandard workers in other countries argely remain outsiders at their jobs, both objectively and subjectively. This institutional struc-ture makes the "secure versus precarious" (or "standard versus nonstandard") job distinc-tion more meaningful in other countries than in the United States.

Since 1980, precarity has gotten worse. The share of workers employed on stan-dard contracts in wealthy countries has declined somewhat, making work more insecure and unstable (the same has been true, of course, in American academia). But statistics measuring this decline fail to capture the true extent of the transformation underway. Since the 1990s, most newly created jobs in Europe and wealthy East Asian countries have been "nonstandard" in form. Meanwhile, outside of high-income countries, the majority of all jobs are precarious: Worldwide, standard jobs are still accorded a high degree of pro-tection, but most workers are not employed in standard jobs. Most histories of the grow-ing precarity of workers both in rich countries and around the world begin in the 1980s and examine the decline of the standard working relationship. Eloisa Betti, in her excellent book *Precarious Workers: History of Debates, Political Mobilizations, and Labor Reforms in Italy*, argues that this perspective makes the decades since 1980 seem like a deviation from the norm, when in fact those decades mark a return to the previously prevailing norm. "If precarity is inherent to the capitalist system," she explains, "it is the stability known to the Western world during the third quarter of the twentieth century that is actually the exception" (1).

To tell a more adequate history of the precaritization of the workforce, Betti's account begins in the 1950s and focuses on Italy—a particularly good case study for her argument because the fight to standardize employment there unfolded as a legal battle. Italy was a late developer among the rich countries. Its labor force experienced a high degree of employment instability even during the 1950s and '60s boom years. It was only in 1970 that Italian workers achieved legally protected job stability, with the approval of the Statute on Workers' Rights, which shielded workers from arbitrary dismissal. In essence, that was the year that Italy abolished American-style at-will employment. Shortly there-after, in the 1980s, legislators began to undermine these protections, hoping to encourage job creation in an era of persistently high unemployment. Their efforts culminated in the 1997 Treu Package and the 2003 Biagi Law, which made it easier for companies to hire workers on nonstandard contracts. "Unlike in other European countries," Betti explains, "where less restrictive labor legislation permitted the introduction of various types of flex-ible employment, Italy had to deregulate in order to make the labor market more flexible" (113). In focusing on Italy, Betti provides a detailed history of both the standardization of work relationships and their subsequent precaritization.

Betti tells that story as a combined history not just of labor law but also of social movements, social theory, and cultural expressions. The Statute on Workers' Rights, for example, was only approved following the Italian "Hot Autumn" of 1969, which saw mil-lions of workers go out on strike. Later on, protests against the Biagi Law were among the largest in Italy's postwar history. In the late 1990s and early 2000s, Betti argues, "Italy played a leading role in Europe" in the development of social movements against precarity (167). She also argues, rightly, that Italy led Europe in terms of the postwar study of pre-carious work. Italian economist Paolo Sylos Labini had already begun to publish studies of precarious work, in Sicily, in the early 1960s. His work was translated into English and published in the International Labor Organization's flagship journal in 1966. A host of Italian scholars, cooperating at times with the government and with labor unions, extended this work in subsequent decades. Betti's account focuses on the important role of feminist scholars, activists, and union leaders in bringing attention to the plight of precarious workers, a disproportionate share of whom were women. Fighting against nonstandard contracts was one element of a broader fight for women's equality.

*Precarious Workers* is rich and highly relevant for scholars of labor beyond the Italian context. One element of the story that perhaps deserves stronger emphasis is the economic dimension. The Italian economy began to grow at a slower pace in the mid-1970s and 1980s. It has stagnated completely, in per capita terms, for the past quarter century. Betti mentions this trend in passing, but focusing on it more directly would have helped explain the pressures that left-wing politicians and trade unions felt, around the turn of the century, to consider the deregulation of the labor market as a viable if deeply impoverished fix for Italy's persistent problem of slow job creation (more radical solutions to this problem would have required Italian politicians to fight for policy changes at the European Union level). At the same time, while Betti is right to emphasize Italy's priority in the history of scholarly discussion of precarious labor, that is in part a result of focusing narrowly on that term. In the 1950s and '60s, scholars in many other countries engaged in studies of similar phenomena under the headings of "disguised unemployment" or "underemployment." But these are minor quibbles with a great account.

In passing, Betti mentions that she is not only a historian of precarity but also has herself been its victim, in an Italian academic context in which fewer scholars are able to find steady work (among many other things, her book also tells the story of academic precaritization and the movements against it). What a tragedy that such a careful historian, with such an expansive and interesting research program, has—like so many historians in the United States as in Italy—been unable to find a stable home in academia. This situation will not get better without a fight.

Aaron Benanav, Cornell University
DOI 10.1215/15476715-11521390

## The Sons of Molly Maguire: The Irish Roots of America's First Labor War
Mark Bulik
New York: Fordham University Press, 2023
384 pp.; $70.00 (cloth), $19.95 (paper), $18.99 (ebook)

Do we really need another history of the events that took place in Pennsylvania's anthracite district in the 1860s and 1870s, events that Mark Bulik characterizes as "one of the longest and most murderous industrial conflicts the nation has ever seen" (9)? After all, the Molly Maguires, the secretive grouping of Irish American miners that stood at the center of these events, have been the subject of several scholarly books, as well as an Arthur Conan Doyle novel, a shelf of polemics arguing for the guilt or innocence of the twenty men who were eventually hanged, and even a Hollywood movie starring Sean Connery as Pinkerton detective James McParland, who infiltrated the Mollies and provided evidence for their prosecution. With the publication of Kevin Kenny's *Making Sense of the Molly Maguires* (1998), which persuasively analyzed the Mollies as both a "shadowy pattern of actual violence" and an "ambiguous concept in a system of ideological representation" (73), one could be forgiven for assuming that we had learned just about all that we could regarding this dramatic moment in US working-class history.

*The Sons of Molly Maguire*, however, demonstrates that even the most familiar of such moments can be profitably reexamined in the light of previously unexplored sources and new conceptual framings. Bulik, a senior editor at the *New York Times*, proves adept at the historian's craft, conducting substantial research in both Pennsylvania and Irish primary sources and uncovering a great deal that is new. He has also elaborated the transnational approach to the Mollies that Kenny had initiated, while developing a generally persuasive new interpretation of his own. Finally, he has fashioned a vivid and memorable narrative that should engage any reader interested in the subject.

The first part of the study makes good on its subtitle by analyzing the Irish roots of the Mollies, drawing not only on work by some of the most important Irish rural historians and folklorists but also, helpfully, on work by notable scholars of preindustrial protest in England, Wales, and France, such as E. P. Thompson and George Rudé. In four substantial chapters, Bulik traces popular festive traditions that cemented the bonds of rural society; the rise of secret societies like the Defenders and Ribbonmen (who mixed communal defense against the anti-Catholic Orange Order with mutual aid and even a sort of informal trade unionism); and the increasing salience of the land question over the course of the early nineteenth century. These ideas and organizations culminated with the emergence of an Irish underground movement calling itself the Molly Maguires on the eve of the Great Famine in the mid-1840s. Kenny covered some of this ground in his earlier study, but Bulik adds much more detail and goes beyond County Donegal, Kenny's primary focus, to include the Ulster borderland counties of Cavan, Leitrim, and Monaghan. Especially impressive is his careful analysis of the overlap between the festive culture of mummers (young, single men who dressed in women's clothing or straw costumes and traveled door to door near the Christmas, New Year's, and midsummer holidays, performing plays and demanding food or drink) with the more political traditions of Ribbon and Molly Maguire protest. Kenny had mentioned a possible mummery connection, but only briefly—and, in fact, he had cited Bulik's then-unpublished research as the basis of his discussion.

Having established the Mollies' roots, Bulik then explores their branches in Pennsylvania anthracite. At the center of his analysis is the Ancient Order of Hibernians (a neo-Ribbon body, in his telling), which established itself in the United States with an organization in Schuylkill County that by 1845 was deeply involved in trade union activity, Democratic politics, and opposition to emancipation—this last reflecting a deep-seated racism that Bulik attributes somewhat superficially to Irish American fears of Black economic competition.

These threads came to the surface during the Civil War, when, in the first wave of Molly Maguire violence in Pennsylvania, opposition to emancipation and resistance to unequal and punitively enforced conscription laws (along with growing labor conflict) led to several assassinations in 1863. Here Bulik builds on Grace Palladino's important study, *Another Civil War* (1990), while again adding a great deal of new evidence of his own. A second wave of violence came in the wake of the defeat of the miners' new union, the Workingmen's Benevolent Association (WBA), in the Long Strike of 1875. By this time, however, McParland had infiltrated the clandestine movement, and the arrests and trials began the following year. In his discussion of these later events, Bulik does not add much to earlier accounts, but his focus, after all, is on the roots of the phenomenon, not its flowering.

Beyond the transnational reconstruction of Irish roots is a partially new interpretation of the Pennsylvania Mollies that harks back to classic work by Herbert Gutman and Eric Hobsbawm. In different ways, both historians had posited a transition from preindustrial collective behavior to modern labor activity (what Hobsbawm called "learning the rules of the game": *Labouring Men* [1964], 345). Bulik builds on this framework in conceptualizing a dialectic between the retributive violence practiced by the Mollies and the more "forward-looking" WBA: "Just as coal is created from peat pushed underground and subjected to tremendous pressure so were American workers made of Irish peasants and industrial union members of Mollies. The peasant solidarity that served as the bedrock of the Molly Maguires became the industrial solidarity that served as the foundation of the WBA and, later, the United Mine Workers" (301).

Bulik's final chapter moves in several different directions, with a discussion of a mummery / Molly Maguire motif in James Joyce's *Ulysses* and an interesting hypothesis regarding a Molly Maguire legacy that might explain the persistence of labor violence and Irish American support for the IRA in Pennsylvania as late as the 1970s; however, the evidence for this hypothesis is much less substantial than in the rest of the book. Nonetheless, this is a stimulating coda to an important work that does indeed contribute something new to our understanding of the topic.

David Brundage, University of California, Santa Cruz
DOI 10.1215/15476715-11521318

## Black Scare / Red Scare: Theorizing Capitalist Racism in the United States
Charisse Burden-Stelly
Chicago: University of Chicago Press, 2023
344 pp.; $99.00 (cloth), $26.00 (paper), $25.99 (ebook)

In *Black Scare / Red Scare*, Charisse Burden-Stelly seeks to contribute to discussions on "racial capitalism" by exploring how racism and capitalism connect, how repressive government actions sustain class divisions and economic exploitation, and how racial hierarchy shapes economic practices. She accomplishes this by reviving and reinventing "how we speak and think about a Radical Black otherwise" (4). Starting from the point of "US Capitalist Racist Society," a term the author uses to drive at structural racial hierarchies that serve to exploit labor, dominate political discourse, and continue the tradition of racial/colonial subservience, the book successfully merges the Black Scare with the Red Scare. She demonstrates, in convincing fashion, how Blackness was reduced to a label of subordination through the criminalization of anticapitalist ideas, many of which were grounded in race, as un-American and a threat to national security. Thus, the Black Scare informed and served the Red Scare and vice versa.

The book is divided into two parts, the first focused on political economy and how "Radical Blackness" threatened the status quo and the second exploring how American governance of anti-Blackness and anticommunism served to normalize a culture that was openly hostile to ending (or even addressing) inequality based on race and/or class. Burden-Stelly achieves the former feat by outlining the "Structural Local of Blackness," a concept that examines how Blackness is systematically situated and treated within societal structures, influencing access to resources, opportunities, and power. The author highlights how sharecropping and land tenancy served as the bedrock of US capitalist racist society from the Reconstruction period to the early stages of World War I (17). Throughout this same period, Burden-Stelly contends "Wall Street Imperialism," which thrived on maintaining low standards of living in "dependent" countries through financial aid, had allowed US-based corporations to dominate markets both at home and abroad. As the author notes, American corporations benefited from the abhorrent conditions of the American South, which served to keep wages low while undermining the overall conditions of labor. World War I threatened this situation, however. As the Great Migration began to take shape, and Black soldiers enlisted, a new racial assertiveness began to emerge. When combined with mass movements such as the Industrial Workers of the World, there was the potential to upend corporate hegemony. Black activism, especially when it merged with radical white allies, needed a new definition so as to repress the threat posed to the Wall Street order. The convenient "witch word" that emerged was "Bolshevism" (47). Labeling antiracists as radical, un-American, and foreign opened the door to justifiable repression. In this way, labor organizers, pacifists, and, naturally, civil rights advocates came to represent a threat to American national security, and therefore suppression, incarceration, and even violence were justified.

Burden-Stelly points to the persecution of Marcus Garvey as a case in point with respect to this repression. Because his brand of Black nationalism became popular with the masses as it aimed to end lynching and white terrorism under the guise of fighting "fire with hell-fire," it could be characterized as an existential threat. To neutralize this threat, the government branded Garvey, who was openly critical of the Communist Party USA, as a communist (65–69).

Burden-Stelly dedicates the second half of the book to explaining how anticommunism, working through and with white supremacy, discouraged labor solidarity and normalized the repression of civil rights activists. When Congress passed the Smith Act (1940), the Taft-Hartley Act (1947), and the McCarren Internal Security Act (1950), it inadvertently swept "racial militancy, worker agitation, and peace activism into the dragnet of repression" (156). Burden-Stelly points out that the US capitalist racist society viewed union organizers who took up the cause of racial equality and "fought for Black and white labor rights on equal footing" as the most radical and dangerous form of labor activists. This definition, in conjunction to the aforementioned laws, provided an opening to repress this activism by branding it un-American and a threat to national security within the backdrop of the Cold War. Burden-Stelly insists that the passage and enforcement of these laws allowed the system to "imperil the rights and citizenship of, strip rights and citizenship from, or deny rights and citizenship to those who believed in, advocated, or struggled for an alternative to US Capitalist Racist Society" (205).

Burden-Stelly believes that the concept of "True Americanism" helped to legitimize the governance of Black Scare / Red Scare politics. Accordingly, US capitalist racist society conflated "True Americanism" with the "American way of life," which was entirely consistent with free market exchange. Thus, anyone who rejected True Americanism also rejected the "American way" and posed a threat to American life. Black people and those who advocated on their behalf were "un-American" because their critique of the economic and racial order created a "potential opening for outside subversive influence to take hold" (239).

*Black Scare / Red Scare* is a valuable addition to any library focused on American radicalism, anticommunism, civil rights activism, or labor organizing throughout the twentieth century. It does, however, have some minor limitations. Although the author highlights the lives of Angelo Herndon and Ben Fletcher, the role of the labor movement within the broader context of civil rights is underdeveloped. The leftists who comprised the Congress on Industrial Organizations served as some of the fiercest advocates for civil rights, and in their attempts to organize the basic industries of the United States, they helped lift color lines from everything from the skilled trades to community-based recreational outlets. This point is not made clear by the author, leaving those who are not overly familiar with this aspect of labor history to assume that organizations such as the United Auto Workers (UAW), the Steelworkers, or the Teamsters were relatively neutral with respect to civil rights. Moreover, an opportunity is potentially lost with respect to examining the damage suffered by organized labor in the context of Red Scares throughout American history. For example, the political scientist Paul Frymer explains that because the 1935 National Labor Relations Act never contained an anti-discrimination measure that civil rights groups so desperately coveted, the possibility of using the labor movement as an instrument of civil rights advancement was not realized. Because US capitalist racist society had successfully labeled those who advocated for civil rights as foreign or subversive, it put labor leaders, such as the UAW's Walter Reuther, in a position where they were forced (or presented with an opportunity) to expel leftists from the ranks of the union and thus minimize the role they played in the quest for racial equality.

These critiques do not undermine the overall accomplishments of *Black Scare / Red Scare*. Rather, they are meant to stimulate broader discussions on the intersection of race and organized labor. *Black Scare / Red Scare* is an asset to scholars, teachers, and activists who seek a better understanding of the ways in which calls for equality have been beaten back through manipulation of political culture in service of the ruling class.

Ryan Pettengill, Collin College
DOI 10.1215/15476715-11521358

Seeking Bread and Fortune in Port Said: Labor Migration
and the Making of the Suez Canal, 1859–1906
Lucia Carminati
Oakland: University of California Press, 2023
xvi + 356 pp.; $49.95 (cloth)

In recent decades the scholarly literature on the social history of modern Egypt—
including working-class and labor history, though not necessarily in the ways those fields
were typically studied back in the 1970s and 1980s—has advanced enormously, spear-
headed by a younger generation of scholars deploying new paradigms and methodologies
and utilizing rich new sources. One landmark recent contribution is Hanan Hammad's
*Industrial Sexuality: Gender, Urbanization, and Social Transformation in Egypt* (2016), an
empirically rich and theoretically sophisticated study of life, work, and community in al-
Mahalla al-Kubra, one of Egypt's first centers of large-scale mechanized industry, from
the 1920s into the 1940s. And now, in another step forward, we have Lucia Carminati's
excellent *Seeking Bread and Fortune in Port Said.*

Port Said was an entirely new town, originally established in 1859 in a sparsely
populated region on Egypt's Mediterranean coastline as a camp for the laborers who
would build the Suez Canal. By the time the canal was officially opened a decade later it
had a population of some ten thousand and served as the main coaling station and provi-
sioning terminus for ships traveling through the waterway. To construct and then operate the canal required a large labor force, and Port Said attracted migrant workers from
across Egypt and around the Mediterranean basin. Most of those who actually dug the
canal were Egyptian peasants dragooned into forced labor by the Egyptian state in collaboration with the Suez Canal Company; but a great many others, unskilled and skilled,
migrated to this site in search of employment and, in some cases, to start a new (and
hopefully better) life far from home. As Carminati puts it, in Port Said "everybody was a
newcomer," at least in the first decades of the town's existence (4).

Drawing on a broad range of archival and other materials in multiple languages, *Seeking Bread and Fortune in Port Said* provides us with a lively and detailed narrative of the town's
growth, enriched by numerous micronarratives of the trajectories and experiences of some
of the men and women who ended up living in it. For obvious reasons, migration and mobility are at the center of this study, and Carminati convincingly shows how "the differentiated
mobility of a diversified workforce and the formation of an unequal migrant society produced
Port Said and enabled the realization of the Suez Canal project" (6). The authorities—the
company, the Egyptian government and after 1882 the British who had occupied Egypt—
sought to impose their understandings of social order and proper behavior on the inhabitants of Port Said, but they were never fully successful; Carminati shows how people often
found ways to at least partially evade social controls and pursue their own aims. At the same
time, though Port Said was not linked by railway to the rest of Egypt until 1906—hence the
end point of the book—its establishment reconfigured patterns of mobility both within
Egypt and across much larger geographies, something that the book explores very effectively.

*Seeking Bread and Fortune in Port Said* offers a rich portrait of work and life in Port
Said in its first half century. It devotes close attention to how race and gender structured

class formation, urban space, and much else in the town, and it explores what its inhabitants did in their leisure time, patterns of criminality and attempts to suppress it, social and economic interactions among its very diverse population, and much else. Along the way, labor struggles perhaps receive a bit less attention than some readers of this journal might prefer. For example, a number of scholars have cited strikes by coalheavers in the town beginning in the early 1880s as the first of their kind in modern Egypt, and they have debated whether the term *guild*, used in some contemporary accounts to denote the coalheavers' mode of organization, makes sense for what actually seems to have been a form of labor contracting. Carminati mentions these strikes but does not delve into them, nor does she tell us what her extensive research leads her to conclude about these debates.

But this is only a quibble, and there can be no doubt that the book makes important contributions to the historiography of modern Egypt, not least among them its very focus on a place like Port Said. Scholarship on Egypt has, generally speaking, been heavily Cairo-centric, with Alexandria garnering a lot of attention as well, whereas provincial cities and towns (including the cities along the canal), and the villages where the country's peasant majority lived, were too often understudied. There has been a regional bias at work as well: Egypt has what some historians have characterized as its own Southern Question, with Upper Egypt (the Sa'id) poorer than the Nile Delta in the north and its population often racialized and marginalized. Thus most of the coalheavers in Port Said were seasonally unemployed, often landless, peasants from the Sa'id, recruited and often abused by labor contractors.

These imbalances have slowly begun to change, and by illuminating the early history of Port Said, not well connected with the rest of Egypt yet a key node in regional and global circuits of transport, trade, migration, capital, and empire, Carminati has performed an important service to scholarship. *Seeking Bread and Fortune in Port Said* is a significant achievement, and it should be read not only by historians of modern Egypt and of the Suez Canal but by anyone interested in an innovative perspective on global mobilities, migration, and labor in the second half of the long nineteenth century.

Zachary Lockman, New York University
DOI 10.1215/15476715-11521414

## Illusions of Progress: Business, Poverty, and Liberalism in the American Century
Brent Cebul
Philadelphia: University of Pennsylvania Press, 2023
432 pp.; $39.95 (cloth and ebook)

*Illusions of Progress: Business, Poverty, and Liberalism in the American Century* is an ambitious book. Brent Cebul moves readers back and forth between agrarian Rome, Georgia; urban Cleveland, Ohio; and Washington, DC, where his focus shifts from local, monied elites to power brokers in the White House, Congress, and Democratic Party. Policies crafted on Capitol Hill mattered to southern boosters eager to attract industry and midwestern executives watching firms move south. But Cebul emphasizes that lawmakers were not the only ones involved in enlarging the federal government in the 1930s and helping it shape the lives of ordinary people over the next sixty years. Business leaders in cities (like Cleveland) and hamlets (like Rome) helped build a modern state that privileged free enterprise and marginalized citizens of color. This generally white male entrepreneurial cohort shaped and took advantage of liberal programs to bolster, as Cebul stresses, the supply (not the demand) side of that rudimentary equation taught in Econ 101. Their participation in construction projects and removing slums made American governance both public and private, as historians have been stressing for years. But business involvement also made them "supply-side state builders," a label Cebul uses for business boosters throughout the book (12).

That designation is almost as provocative as "supply-side liberalism" (4). Cebul chose that phrase to describe Democratic programs and policies from the New Deal through the early 1990s, when, many experts have argued, Democrat Bill Clinton presided over the New Deal's dismantlement. That descriptor likely sparks thoughts of the Reagan administration's economic policies in the 1980s, when that conservative Republican signed off on a massive tax cut, slashed social spending, and assaulted organized labor's basic right to strike. But "supply-side liberalism" was also how some pundits celebrated the Democrats eager to invest in and cooperate with executives in the 1980s to unleash the full potential of market forces. Clinton arguably became the most famous of the late twentieth century's so-called New Democrats, who made a name for themselves promoting growth, particularly in the lucrative (and nonunionized) technology sectors.

But Cebul calls Democrats "supply-side liberals" throughout the book (6). That term appeared when describing the Roosevelt administration's experiments to put people to work building public works projects (like the storied Tennessee Valley Authority), clearing slums, and turning the country into an Arsenal of Democracy. Cebul stressed that top New Dealers really sought long-term economic development, not democracy. That priority satisfied boosters (whether in small-town Rome or big-city Cleveland) regardless of their political allegiances. Thus, both southern segregationists and conservative midwestern Republicans had a role in crafting a New Deal that was great for business, which made them, in Cebul's vernacular, supply-side state builders. They took part in crafting a diffuse, public/private federal government that obscured their role in keeping the country committed to economic potency, not democracy, during and after World War II.

Cebul's argument will, in some ways, be familiar to labor historians. New Left scholars spent the 1980s stressing how hard New Dealers worked to save capitalism. Many in that cohort also highlighted that union members almost habitually campaigned and voted for Democrats after the 1935 Wagner's Act passage only to find Democrats unwilling to protect a law that had the potential to democratize eligible workplaces. Since the early 1990s, labor historians have noted that many workers in privileged sector (like manufacturing) had to use the law to make their own New Deal on and off shop floors. That research, in many ways, complemented the historical focus on American conservatism since the mid-1990s, when labor experts noted the virulent anti-unionism running throughout conservative business communities. Both small-town boosters and big-city manufacturers worked to undermine liberal programs and policies, sometimes through laws (like the 1947 Taft-Hartley Act) or movements (such as state-level right-to-work campaigns) that actively sought to undermine shop-floor democracy.

Yet *Illusions of Progress* does not offer the narrative of profits trumping democracy familiar to most labor historians. Cebul correctly stresses that a lot of New Deal policies advantaged businesses, but they also included regulations and rights that benefited consumers and some workers. Cebul does not delve into business elites' efforts to limit workplace democracy. He does note that agricultural and domestic workers were left out of the New Deal, an aside that omits the public sector employees that were an important part of the workforce in big northern cities, like Cleveland. But Cebul is more interested in the role business leaders played in constructing the modern liberal state. He offers intermittent stories of local conflicts more common in the field of urban history since the 1970s. There are, for example, powerful glimpses into the Black communities removed through slum clearance, eager to fully participate in War on Poverty programs, and frustrated with business leaders continuing to limit their participation in political life in the 1970s and after. The final chapters make clear that there would be little help from Washington, where a new generation of Democrats would double down on supporting the supply side, not democracy.

*Illusions of Progress*'s ambitious narrative subsequently raises important questions for labor historians to consider in light of the looming hundred-year anniversaries of the New Deal's still-celebrated achievements. How should scholars characterize a period of experimentation that both saved capitalism and empowered Americans to democratize some workplaces? Would it have been possible to guarantee shop-floor democracy nationwide, and would that assurance have been enough to make the kind of regional and urban economic development undertaken in Rome and Cleveland more socially democratic off, not just on, the job? In what ways can tracing the nuances of the way New Dealers sought to both promote demand and assure supply help trace the liberal origins of tax policies, business rules, and public-private partnerships that many began to attack as neoliberal by the millennium's turn? There are no easy answers to those questions, but Cebul's book will contribute to ongoing reconsiderations of the New Deal and its order.

Elizabeth Tandy Shermer, Loyola University Chicago
DOI 10.1215/15476715-11552795

## Workers of All Colors Unite: Race and the Origins of American Socialism
Lorenzo Costaguta
Urbana: University of Illinois Press, 2023
xii + 250 pp.; $110.00 (cloth), $28.00 (paper), $19.95 (ebook)

In this important and illuminating book, Lorenzo Costaguta examines nineteenth-century American socialism's evolving understandings of race. The result is a nuanced and deeply researched work about the struggles of "class-first" socialists to grapple with the complex realities of American racism. *Workers of All Colors Unite* also reframes the early history of the Socialist Labor Party (SLP) and asserts its importance as a site where "the seeds were sown for the future of the Left to grow" (16).

Costaguta uses a multilingual archive of German- and English-language sources, while avoiding the trap of dividing the history of the American left between "foreign" radicals and a "'genuinely American' (read: non-immigrant) socialist movement" (7). Although most of the chapters focus on German-speaking socialists, they are presented as telling the story not of German socialism in America but of *American* socialism. "In the period under consideration," the author rightly notes, "American socialism was thought, spoken, and written almost entirely in German" (3).

The book is primarily an intellectual history. Its core chapters scrutinize SLP members' published discussions of Chinese immigrants, African American workers, and Native Americans, respectively. These sections detail the eclectic variety of early socialist views on each group, and the ways they evolved throughout the 1870s and 1880s—sometimes in opposite directions. As Costaguta argues, most socialists' German background profoundly shaped their interpretations of the United States, and "their approaches were a mixture, a patchwork, a synthesis of ideas traveling across continents, applied to eminently American circumstances" (174). Different radicals melded Marxist internationalism with Social Darwinism, Lamarckism, scientific racialism (i.e., the belief that different biological races exist), or the anthropology of Lewis H. Morgan. Intriguingly, the author shows how some socialists who accepted "scientific" ideas of inherent racial differences, such as Adolph Douai, still argued in favor of racial egalitarianism, while others who rejected scientific racialism, such as Daniel De Leon, were nevertheless "fundamentally unable to understand race as an independent variable in shaping American working conditions" (167).

In the case of the Chinese, the SLP's position shifted from tepid support of "free" immigrants from China to support for Chinese exclusion, pressured by the success of the anti-Chinese Workingmen's Party of California in the 1870s and justified through an implicitly racialized conception of all Chinese as inherently slavish "coolies." In this case, "race remained a more important lens than class in approaching the issue of Chinese immigration to the United States" (89). As early as 1879, by contrast, the SLP officially endorsed cross-racial organizing among Black and white workers. However, as a party based almost entirely among ethnic communities in the North, the SLP's commitment to Black-white unity rarely translated into meaningful action. Instead, socialists "kept insisting that African American workers joined [*sic*] their fight for improved working and living conditions through party politics and trade union activism. In doing this, they did not realize that African Americans had problems that confrontational opposition towards employers and local politicians could not solve" (99). Less convincingly (in my opinion), Costaguta suggests that the SLP's unwillingness to form a coalition with the southern-based Greenback Labor Party in 1880 represented a missed opportunity to organize significant numbers of southern Black workers into the socialist movement—an argument that rests on several tenuous assumptions, chief among them that Black support for the nonsocialist Greenbacks would somehow translate into support for the SLP's program. Finally, socialists had little direct contact with Native Americans but viewed them with great sympathy, and in SLP members' discussions of the American frontier they inverted the categories of "savagery" and "civilization," applying the former to the behavior of white settlers and authorities. Doing so, according to the author, "led to questioning their own positionality as a 'superior' race and culture in a way that was absent in the conversations on Chinese immigration and Black labor" (131).

Only in the 1890s, with De Leon's push for ideological conformity within the party, did the SLP purge itself of scientific racialism in favor of a view "that tied historical materialism to Morgan's anthropology in a coherent if simplistic evolutionist theory that placed socialism as the inexorable future of world history" (150). Yet even so, the SLP failed to develop "a proactive racial policy that put the fight against racism at the center of its political action nor did it promote special measures to defend the equality of its members in the organization from racial prejudice" (175).

The book ends with the 1899 party split, which led to the creation of the Socialist Party of America (SPA) and "ended the period in which the SLP was a key incubator of ideas about race and ethnicity within the American socialist movement" (167). It makes a convincing case, however, that the SPA inherited from the SLP "an internationalist, class-focused, and racial-conscious socialism" that, in the 1930s, finally led both the SPA and the Communist Party to "put the fight against racism at the very center of their political action," helping to lay the foundations of the civil rights movement (5, 172).

Costaguta does leave some questions unanswered. For example, he never explains when and how (and, indeed, whether) the SLP's support for Chinese exclusion changed after 1890. He also never mentions the early socialist movement's analysis of "the Jewish Question," which, in the Gilded Age, was very much viewed by most in racial terms. And although Jewish immigrants comprised the second-largest demographic within the SLP by the 1890s, the book includes no mention of the racial analyses contained in their Yiddish-language publications—a topic touched on in studies by Gil Ribak and David S. Koffman. Such quibbles aside, *Workers of All Colors Unite* is a superb and definitive work of scholarship, and it provides insight for contemporary struggles seeking to reconcile racial justice and class solidarity within the American left and labor movement.

Kenyon Zimmer, University of Texas at Arlington
DOI 10.1215/15476715-11552808

## The Silver Women: How Black Women's Labor Made the Panama Canal
Joan Flores-Villalobos
Philadelphia: University of Pennsylvania Press, 2023
296 pp.; $39.95 (cloth and ebook)

While there are many books on the construction of the Panama Canal, Joan Flores-Villalobos is the first to focus on the experiences of Black West Indian women. *The Silver Women: How Black Women's Labor Made the Panama Canal* argues that Black women's labor was central to the construction of the canal, and she skillfully analyzes untapped sources and reads others against the grain to reveal the contours of their work and family lives. This book is an important contribution to histories of US empire, Caribbean migration, and women's history, and it will be read alongside Julie Greene's *The Canal Builders*, Kaysha Corinealdi's *Panama in Black: Afro-Caribbean World-Building in the Twentieth Century*, and Jason Colby's *The Business of Empire: United Fruit, Race, and US Expansion in Central America*.

More than a generation ago, Cynthia Enloe challenged scholars to recognize the centrality of women's work in buttressing US militarism and empire. She narrates the discovery of her own "feminist curiosity" by asking how our understanding of war might shift if we considered who did the laundry (Cynthia Enloe, Anita Lacey, and Thomas Gregory, "Twenty-Five Years of Bananas, Beaches and Bases: A Conversation with Cynthia Enloe," *Sustainability and Social Justice* 52, no. 3 [August 2016]: 537–50). Flores-Villalobos takes up this challenge. As she writes, "West Indian women took care of white American children and cleaned white American homes, physically maintaining the image of an orderly domestic sphere. In short, West Indian women's labor made the United States' imperial project possible" (3). In other words, she makes scholars look closely at who was doing the laundry in the Panama Canal Zone.

Black West Indian women navigated an economic landscape that was fairly distinct from that of their male counterparts. Most West Indian men arrived on contracts and worked on the "silver rolls" (as compared to the "gold rolls," which were almost exclusively manned by white American and European workers). In contrast, women generally entered Panama as individuals, not on contracts, so they were able to navigate and negotiate multiple economic relationships. Moreover, some worked for white American families, while others profited through their work for West Indian workers. Almost none of them were directly employed by the US government or the Canal Zone. Rather, they worked for themselves, often at the whims of their white American employers, but they also exercised a fair amount of autonomy and advocated for their rights and respect.

Flores-Villalobos begins the book with an overview of West Indian women's labor in the years after emancipation. She emphasizes that their experiences as entrepreneurs and workers pre-dated their migration to Panama. West Indian women worked as higglers (market women), domestic servants, and laundresses long before they left for the Canal Zone. In addition, she provides the social landscape whereby common law marriages and cohabitation among heterosexual couples was far more common than legal marriage practices. Both of these factors would shape West Indians' experiences in the Canal Zone and construction era. West Indian women who sought economic advancement in Panama were likely to work for themselves in a range of informal sectors, namely domestic service, laundry, and marketing, and they were unlikely to be legally married.

Given the limited sources where Black women speak for themselves, Flores-Villalobos draws on records related to criminality and sex work and looks to documents written by white women where they published fantasies of docile Black servants. She uses these sources skillfully, explaining the context of their creation, and she provides a close reading of the moments that might have ruptured the Canal Zone's facade of total control and white women's dreams of imperial nostalgia.

I was particularly impressed by her analysis of how West Indian women, both in Panama and in their home islands, petitioned for their partners' death benefits. Flores-Villalobos here dwells on the violence and constant risk of death and injury for the male canal builders. She also examines how women wielded their position as British subjects to gain the pensions from their common-law husbands. This work complements Jorge Giovannetti-Torres's scholarship on West Indians in Cuba, where he argues that they also called on their British subjecthood to gain rights and respect. Likewise, Flores-Villalobos argues that women "asserted the dignity and worth of their loved ones in the face of a bureaucracy that devalued them while also rerouting owed wages and leftover money back to family and kin who depended on them" (165). She demonstrates how West Indian women used the law and imperial bureaucracies to gain the economic security they felt owed to them.

She concludes by underscoring the importance of the Canal Zone to the broader currents of West Indian migration within the Caribbean and North America. She notes that the mothers of prominent twentieth-century intellectuals like Paule Marshall, Maida Springer Kemp, and Kenneth Clarke were all in Panama before migrating to the United States. Here we see Black West Indian women as central to the migratory and intellectual routes that stretched from Barbados to Panama to Cuba to New York City.

Flores-Villalobos concludes reiterating her central claim: "In many ways, the story told in this book is straightforward: West Indian women migrated to Panama and provided the essential labor of social reproduction that buttressed the construction of the Canal and subsequent Caribbean migrations." And she adds knowingly, "Any West Indian could tell you that" (226–27). Despite her recognition that Black women's labor was popularly acknowledged, Flores-Villalobos is the first scholar to mine the archives and document it in a scholarly text. This is no small feat. Flores-Villalobos successfully argues that women's labor, their entrepreneurship, and their economic acumen shaped a generation and, arguably, an empire.

In conclusion, Flores-Villalobos succeeds in placing West Indian women at the center of the story of the Panama Canal. She consults archives in the United States, United Kingdom, Caribbean, and Panama, finding Black women's voices and reading against the grain. These original and provocative interpretations demonstrate the centrality of West Indian women to the making of US empire and to their own communities. It turns out that who does the laundry tells us a great deal about empire, and scholars of gender, sexuality, the Caribbean, and US empire will turn to Flores-Villalobos to explain how and why.

Jana K. Lipman, Tulane University
DOI 10.1215/15476715-11521374

### Hillbilly Highway: The Transappalachian Migration and the Making of a White Working Class
Max Fraser
Princeton, NJ: Princeton University Press, 2023
viii + 336 pp.; $32.00 (cloth and ebook)

In *Hillbilly Highway*, historian Max Fraser tells the story of one of the largest population relocations in twentieth-century US history. While years of scholarship on the

Great Migration has traced the relocation of hundreds of thousands of southern African Americans to cities in the North and West and produced pathbreaking works of African American, political, urban, and labor history, relatively few historians have examined the concurrent migration of poor, rural southern whites to cities primarily in the Midwest. While much more attention has been paid to the white Okies that departed the Great Plains for the West during the Great Depression, nearly the same number of white migrants left southern Appalachia for midwestern industrial cities in the mid-twentieth century. By Fraser's estimate, at least eight million poor white southerners left rural and economically marginalized areas in the upper South for major industrial cities like Chicago, Cincinnati, and Detroit as well as smaller ones like Muncie, Indiana, and Canton, Ohio, among others. This migration was often circular: Rural whites returned to the South in much higher numbers than African Americans did. As Fraser argues, however, both those who stayed and those who returned played a little-recognized role in remaking midwestern cities, reshaping postwar politics, and forming a "class apart" from the rest of the broader white working class. Impressively researched and convincingly argued, *Hillbilly Highway* is a groundbreaking work of labor, urban, and political history.

Taking its name from the network of roads that carried white southerners between the upper South and Midwest, *Hillbilly Highway* shows how the creation of Transappalachia—a region Fraser defines both by this mobility and the unique southern character of its people—reshaped twentieth-century US history. Through six chapters, Fraser traces the impact this migration had on the region's industrial development, the maturation of the labor movement, the postwar urban crisis, and the political realignments of the 1960s and 1970s. Putting Transappalachian migrants at the center of his analysis, Fraser not only directs attention toward an overlooked population relocation but also upends a number of long-held misconceptions about the role poor southern whites played in labor, urban, and political history. For example, despite being recruited by midwestern industrialists and scorned by union leaders for their supposed docility, Fraser explains that white southerners were often more militant than stereotypes suggest. "They walked away from poorly paid jobs, confronted abusive bosses, and went out on strike with their coworkers," he argues (75). Indeed, Fraser shows that Transappalachian migrants, rather than being hostile to organized labor, were often eager supporters of the Congress of Industrial Organizations in the 1930s. He offers a similar challenge to long-established narratives about the urban crisis when he turns his attention to the so-called hillbilly ghetto of the post–World War II era. While historians typically contextualize the urban crisis as an outcome of the African American Great Migration, communities like Chicago's Uptown, Cincinnati's Over-the-Rhine, Indianapolis's Stringtown, and Muncie's Shedtown grew into "problem areas" of concentrated white poverty during the years of the Transappalachian migration. Fraser shows that this white urban poverty was not only a prominent concern for locals but also played a significant role in the formation of liberal antipoverty policy. According to Fraser, the early development of Lyndon Johnson's War on Poverty focused intently on poor southern whites in the urban Midwest and provided liberals with "a way of talking about urban poverty as a problem of culture without talking about the politically explosive issue of race" (148).

As the example of the hillbilly ghetto suggests, shared whiteness did not spare Transappalachian migrants from assumptions of difference that separated them from native-born midwesterners and the broader white working class. "Far from a monolithic category of identity," Fraser argues, "the experience of the hillbilly ghetto made clear that for some urban residents, whiteness was a much more contingent and ambiguous position during these years" (111). While Fraser acknowledges that white migrants generally prospered more than their African American counterparts, he nevertheless shows how stereotypes and prejudice against white southern rurality created a distinctive working-class experience in the urban Midwest. This examination of class formation represents one of the most crucial and revelatory contributions in Fraser's book. He deftly shows how the process of cyclical migration and urban alienation were integral parts of white working-class proletarianization in Transappalachia. The back-and-forth combined with the hostilities faced in the urban Midwest "[set] Transappalachia apart as a distinctive group in midcentury American society" (48). While Fraser's final chapter examines how Transappalachian migrants ultimately melded into a more conservative, white midwestern culture through the popularization of country music, he nevertheless complicates the evolution of white working-class conservatism by showing how "hillbilly music" was first stripped of its regional and distinctive class origins. Overall, then, Max Fraser has written a compelling and convincing account of a significant but overlooked aspect of modern American labor and working-class history that historians of the rural South, urban Midwest, and US politics will have to contend with for some time.

**Timothy J. Lombardo, University of South Alabama**
DOI 10.1215/15476715-11521294

### Ingenious Trade: Women and Work in Seventeenth-Century London
Laura Gowing
Cambridge: Cambridge University Press, 2022
x + 276 pp.; $44.99 (cloth), $29.99 (paper and ebook)

In this award-winning book, Laura Gowing tackles the world of the needle trades in seventeenth-century London, specifically the trajectory of girls and women entering the trades through the London livery companies. Apprenticeship of girls is an important pivot on which this book is built, and she readily recognizes the liminal position of girls as apprentices, not only in the livery companies but also in the context of apprenticeship. Apprenticeship was central to boys' rite of passage, and its constructs and supervision assume a masculine life cycle. Not only were girls rarely mentioned in contemporary literature, but finding them in the historical record is frequently challenging. Records are often opaque as to where, how, and why girls were trained. This is not to say that the records do not exist—they do. Until recently, finding girls was a matter of visiting separate county record offices: Guildhall in London and, for the eighteenth century, the Public Record Office at Kew. Major digitization projects have helped with this issue especially for London, which is Gowing's focus, mainly drawing on guild and tax records, including Inland Revenue Records. This still leaves many records, and many girls, out in the cold. Girls were seriously underrecorded for a variety of reasons, including the expectation that apprenticeship was for boys and that achieving freedom was not essential to girls' training. Gowing's use of complementary records, such as the livery registers and the Mayor's Court, which heard cases brought to dissolve apprenticeship contracts, illustrates the lacunae, since a comparison of the two sets of records shows that almost 80 percent of those in the court cases did not appear in the registers. This represents a significant under-registration of girls, which probably persists across records of apprenticeship.

Historians have also paid relatively little attention to girls, though study of male apprenticeship has had a resurgence with the work of Patrick Wallis and colleagues. Amy Erickson's work on early modern London and Clare Crowston's for Paris stand out, while mine deals with two English counties using the Inland Revenue Records for the eighteenth century. These latter sources, of course, were not relevant to her study. In this context, then, Gowing's holistic account of seventeenth-century London apprenticeship, looking at both apprentices and mistresses and providing a virtual life history of the needle trades, is very welcome.

An accomplished and thoughtful scholar, Gowing has used registers and court cases to understand the role and place of apprenticeship in the world of work. Apprenticeship to trades, as opposed to parish apprenticeship, for example, provided a regulated means of acquiring recognized marketable skills. Apprenticeships tended to be shorter for girls than for boys, since the learning was more important than a systematic rite of passage to the freedom of a guild. It is important to remember, however, that she is analyzing London, and county accounts may provide different pictures, though the broad conclusions do tend to mirror those of eighteenth-century scholars using county materials.

Importantly, she has examined the character of apprenticeship and apprentices. She also takes a long view to understand where apprentices fit into the world of work and the new emphasis on sociability and politeness that was emerging. As she argues, these women and their trades were fundamental to creating the fashions and styles that defined fashionable London. She also assesses the trades more widely, looking at skills, necessary requirements, and abilities to make a success, exploring the mistresses and the workshop dynamics that shaped the trades. She looks at the ways women developed strategies in trades that were formalized, organized, and regulated, ones that were literally a profession of many stripes. This study challenges the "traditional" view of women's work as "under-recognised, informal, flexible and unregulated" (8). There were status distinctions between these registered trades and the bulk of laboring women, who often color our perception of women's work, and recognition of these women is an important corrective.

She also pushes our understanding with an account that embraces physical and emotional spaces, using case studies that begin each chapter to good effect, enabling the reader to see how the trades operated in practice, and giving shape to the quantitative material that she and others have generated. For example, her chapter on discipline and resistance opens the door on the relationship between mistresses and apprentices. Notably, in contrast to Crowston's Parisian seamstresses, she argues that London female apprentices lacked a collective identity and that they did not engage in collective activities as boys did. They also were not always submissive and compliant. Her discussion of "girlhood" is important. Adolescence was an ill-formed concept, but these girls clearly were of the age group that we associate with adolescence. They were subject to the physical transitions of their age group, and apprenticeship was overtly one of several ways to discipline and control girls. It was a period of socializing as well as training them. Her exploration of the forms of resistance echoes her important work on the use of words, and how using languages of resistance were part of girls' repertoire. She also shows that they often did not want to be there and that some considered apprenticeship too subservient for them, suggesting varying social distinctions and expectations between families, mistresses, and apprentices.

Gowing also delineates the role of mistresses, and the ways that networks operated to facilitate a good profession for women married or single. She illustrates how women were important players in commerce, needle trades, and apprenticeship, while frequently building an independent persona for herself. Once again, the use of case studies makes these women visible active personalities in the world of work. With a comprehensive grasp of seventeenth-century society, social change, and the economic context, and using her skills as a reader of the uses of language, Gowing has given us a wonderful insight into the relationships and practicalities of apprenticeship and regulated recognized professional women's work.

Deborah Simonton, University of Southern Denmark
DOI 10.1215/15476715-11521430

## Futures of Socialism: "Modernisation," the Labour Party, and the British Left, 1973–1997
Colm Murphy
Cambridge: Cambridge University Press, 2023
x + 316 pp.; $110.00 (cloth), $32.99 (paper and ebook)

New Labour was the restyled British Labour Party project for electoral success and economic, social, and constitutional reforms led by Tony Blair and Gordon Brown from 1994 to 2010. Colm Murphy examines its political and intellectual origins in Labour Party and broader British left debates from 1973 to 1997. These discussions were framed, Murphy argues, by contested interpretations of "modernization."

The boundaries of Murphy's period are important. It was in 1973 that Britain joined the European Economic Community (EEC), forerunner to the European Union (EU). This was also an important year for the breakdown of the Bretton Woods system for managing international currency exchanges, which coincided with another major economic shock: the escalation of global oil prices. The left in all maturing industrial economies were now grappling with the difficulties of securing socially progressive policy outcomes at the level of individual nation-state. How could stable employment and moderate wealth redistribution be maintained in the face of inflationary pressures, lost industrial jobs through multinational capital flight, and International Monetary Fund interventions designed to "correct" public expenditure on social solidarity measures? Various progressive and social democratic parties struggled to secure election and govern effectively in Western Europe and North America in this environment. After 1974 Labour did not win a general election in the United Kingdom until 1997, when Blair as prime minister, with Brown as Chancellor of the Exchequer, took office with an agenda to match what they saw as the realities of globalization. Murphy pithily summarizes this agenda as "welfare to work, human capital, constitutional reform, the minimum wage" (183). This plan was narrower if more achievable than alternative pre-1997 modernization imaginaries, although Murphy himself avoids detailed evaluation of New Labour's record in office.

Murphy applies a modernization framework to three areas of post-1973 policy debate: economic management and challenges to the nation-state; identities of class, gender, and race; and constitutional reforms counterpoised with enabling citizens to participate in a "modern" economy. Post-Keynesian economists questioned the continued relevance of demand management and the capacity of nation-states to protect working-class jobs and living standards without supranational cooperation. Here there was a strong emphasis on the value of closer integration with the EEC and then the EU. Then there were revisionist Marxist historians and intellectuals, influenced by a "Eurocommunist" Gramscian understanding of power and its cultural as well as economic dimensions. In an important intervention, Eric Hobsbawm wrote "The Forward March of Labour Halted" in 1978. Looking back, we can see the value of this observation in Britain's conflictual sphere of industrial relations. Union activists and officials called in modernizing terms for industrial democracy, in part to arrest the phenomena of corporate disinvestment and capital flight from the United Kingdom. Proposals for worker directors on the boards of major manufacturing companies were blocked in 1977–78. Murphy arguably underestimates the significance of this major demonstration of business power.

Post-Fordist social theorists also focused on deindustrialization along with other employment-cum-labor-market changes, arguing about their implications for identities and interpretations of class. Feminists likewise invested heavily in debates about employment and identity, highlighting the divisive effects of the labor movement's preoccupation with male workers. Black and Asian activists articulated a parallel critique about the labor movement's inability to recognize and confront racial inequalities, although "modernization" language was less prominent here, given the term's historic association with Enlightenment-era colonialism and its profound racial injustices.

Murphy explores future debates in very thick detail, integrating hundreds of political and intellectual texts from myriad sources: unpublished in the collected and archived papers of public figures; published in Labour and left periodicals, plus newspapers and other print media; and from memoirs, biographies, and academic literature. No fault can be found here in Murphy's application, but I did ask myself about the added value and diminishing returns of some of these details. I also wondered about perspective and method. *Futures of Socialism* is published in Cambridge's Modern British Histories series, the goal of which "is to keep metropolitan and national histories of Britain fresh and vital in an intellectual atmosphere increasingly attuned to, and enriched by, the transnational, the international, and the comparative" (ii). Murphy's history is indeed metropolitan, focusing on elite actors who mainly viewed the world from Britain's political center in London.

Perhaps this is limiting. In discussing constitutional change, Murphy fleetingly visits the campaign for a Scottish Parliament, with devolved powers within the United

Kingdom in selected policy areas. "Up in Edinburgh," he writes, "1988–1989 witnessed the birth of the cross-party Scottish Constitutional Convention" (210). Edinburgh can be seen as "up" from London. In Scotland it is viewed as "down" from Aberdeen, "across" or "over" (the Forth) from Fife, and "through" from Glasgow. Place and perspective matter, particularly when centralized political authority is being contested. The Scottish Trades Union Congress (STUC) played a key role in the Scottish Constitutional Convention. Michael McGahey, president of the National Union of Mineworkers Scottish Area, persuaded the STUC to adopt support for a devolved Scottish Parliament in the late 1960s and early 1970s. McGahey and his union highlighted the economic insecurities in mining communities in Scotland arising from the policies of a Labour government. Devolution therefore originated in the nonmetropolitan and nonelite perspective of miners and their labor movement supporters, who looked "down" on London. The Labour government's modernizing fuel policy, substituting coal with more oil, gas, and nuclear power, arguably met a competing modernizing constitutional policy response, with trade unionists in Scotland mobilizing for greater economic security through enhanced Scottish autonomy. This, to reiterate, was two decades before the "birth" of the Scottish Constitutional Convention. Pressure from below surely influenced the other policy debates examined in *Futures of Socialism*. Future Metropolitan Histories of Britain will attain greater vitality by incorporating analysis of social movements as well as social problems.

Jim Phillips, University of Glasgow
DOI 10.1215/15476715-11521342

## Courteous Capitalism: Public Relations and the Monopoly Problem, 1900–1930
Daniel Robert
Baltimore: Johns Hopkins University Press, 2023
336 pp.; $64.95 (cloth and ebook)

This unexpectedly fascinating book is about much more than its title and argument convey. The author's main question: Why did public utilities (electricity, public transport, and telephone/telegram companies) invest so heavily in public relations and customer service? After all, they were monopolies; it was not like they could lose customers to competing firms. Robert argues that in fact there was a competing "firm" in the form of government ownership, which was a distinct political possibility in the Progressive Era. To avert the calamity of public ownership, utility executives sought to win the support of their customers by improving customer service, offering customer stock options, redesigning offices, issuing educational books and films, and otherwise rebranding themselves as good corporate citizens. By so doing, these utility executives managed to subvert the antimonopoly impulse and survive as corporate monopolies.

Each chapter provides a history of a particular ploy to dampen public ownership, as well as the effects such strategies had on workers, customers, and public opinion. Central to the book's thesis is the strategy of "courteous capitalism." The new monopolists sought to replace the attitude "The public be damned" with the new, more enlightened directive "The public be pleased" (22). And it was the clerk's job to do the pleasing. Clerks were expected to learn, internalize, and deliver this superior customer service. Here the author draws on the literature of emotional labor, associated most prominently with sociologist Arlie Hochschild. It wasn't enough to just smile: since smiling could be (and was) perceived as fake, clerks had to convey sincerity and genuine good feeling toward the customer. And how were bosses supposed to ensure that clerks were properly sincere and helpful? Here Robert details the various surveillance techniques (many still in use today), such as customer surveys, complaint desks, open floor plans, and mystery shoppers, who were essentially spies.

Selling stock to customers has its own fascinating history and historiography. Roberts argues that this practice was not just a way to give customers "public ownership" in a private enterprise but that it also helped raise money for utilities in states that restricted financing to private power companies (in order to protect municipally owned companies). These restrictions meant companies were forced to issue additional stock, which they chose to sell to customers rather than large investors. Indeed, they induced their long-suffering clerks to sell this stock to their friends, neighbors, and customers, holding monthly sales competitions and awarding pennants and kudos for top-selling teams. The author finds evidence that many employees and customers were turned off by the practice but that it persisted because customer-shareholders generally appreciated the dividends, which offset company rate hikes.

Most readers will be familiar with the ways monopolists used newspapers and public relations to improve their reputations and sow doubt about anti-monopolists and socialists. Private utilities planted apparently neutral "articles" in small-town newspapers in exchange for buying ads, a practice that, again, is still with us today. The Federal Trade Commission (FTC) and the Federal Communications Commission (FCC) investigated this practice after World War I in what was once described as "the most expensive and exhaustive investigation of private industry in American history" (190). The author exploits their extensive data and interviews to good effect. One unexpected thing we learn from these sources is that Bell System emerged from the FCC investigation with more public respect and goodwill because the hearings allowed Bell to "tell its story" (190).

In making his claims, Robert stops and assesses whether the particular ploy he is discussing actually worked. Did open offices work? Did customer stock ownership work? Were these strategies effective in achieving utility execs' political ends? So often historians assume that if business leaders deployed a strategy, the strategy "worked" as intended, so it was refreshing to have the author consider evidence of whether this was actually the case. Similarly, the author explicitly addresses counterarguments that help the reader identify his historiographical interventions. For instance, previous work identifies the rise of customer stock ownership with the Liberty Bond campaigns of World War I. Robert's evidence shows that it originated with utility companies in 1914.

The book's scope and research is truly impressive, providing fascinating information on how customers were treated before "courteous capitalism," as well as dress codes, customer complaints, and survey forms. In addition, the book provides useful minihistories of public utilities, building design, and more, throwing the reader interesting tidbits, such as how the Bell System in 1929 was the second-largest employer in the United States outside the federal government.

After describing the ploys and strategies designed to nullify the antimonopoly and public ownership movements, the author concludes that none of those strategies could have worked without courteous clerks and customer service reps. This is a significant finding in terms of business and labor history. While historians are familiar with the various strategies Progressive Era capitalists deployed to win public favor, this book reminds us how much they depended on the emotional labor of service workers.

Jennifer Delton, Skidmore College

DOI 10.1215/15476715-11552821

## The Ruined Anthracite: Historical Trauma in Coal-Mining Communities
Paul A. Shackel
Urbana: University of Illinois Press, 2023
xiv + 234 pp.; $110.00 (cloth), $30.00 (paper), $19.95 (ebook)

Deindustrialization has affected a wide swath of the nation's industrial heartland. With renewed focus on the plight of declining factory towns, especially during the 2016 presidential election, we often neglect those parts of America where industry declined many years prior. One important site for studying deindustrialization's longer-term effects is the anthracite coalfields of northeastern Pennsylvania. In an inspiring book, leading expert Paul Shackel takes readers through a deeply textured examination of how much a place's psyche can be devastated when the main source of income leaves.

An anthropologist with an extensive background in industrial archaeology, Shackel's work includes field research, especially at the Eckley Miners' Village. The author documented the everyday living conditions of mining families through the material cultural artifacts around their homes. Shackel's fieldwork also built off his prior book, *Remembering Latimer: Migration, Labor, and Race in Pennsylvania Anthracite Country* (2018). Shackel takes great advantage of a wealth of oral histories, including those collected by the Pennsylvania Historical and Museum Commission in the 1970s and 1980s. These interviews allow the residents to speak to us about their deep personal feelings of work and loss.

The author's most important contribution comes from analyzing the population's longer-term trauma. He notes, "Their ancestors faced environmental and workplace hardships and were always struggling to make do and stave off hunger" (xiii). This intervention is vitally important for studies of working-class culture. Shackel notes how this long-term trauma was "embedded in the social structures of oppression" (12). His close reading of the oral histories, newspaper accounts of mining accidents, and government studies suggest the ways structural violence was viewed in very trivial ways by mining companies. For example, he investigates xenophobic attitudes by companies toward Eastern European immigrants. Biased assumptions linking the newcomers with disease led many companies to take a cavalier attitude toward sanitation. The region saw high infant mortality rates, and few homes had indoor plumbing as late as 1920 (60). His archaeological analysis of miners' homes highlighted the common role of "wildcat sewer systems," as local communities like Lattimer tried to find ways to manage pollution and sanitation (64).

Shackel's empathetic approach, drawing from oral testimony and the built environment, is a model for wider studies of Rust Belt communities. Anthracite families found ingenious ways to survive. Miners dealt with many chronic noninfectious diseases. One common remedy was drinking a shot of whiskey or charge of beer. Although criticized by reformers, this was a cheap way to soothe coal dust in the throat and help clear it from one's lungs (116). Anthropological evidence from the early twentieth century shows evidence of miners using patent medicines, with lots of shards of balms, herbal remedies, and items from traditional healers (123–24, 128–29). Chronic stress, lackluster nutritional access, and a polluted environment impacted generations. The focus on health in all aspects is especially prescient since the COVID-19 pandemic. Shackel takes a holistic view to studying the region, with sections highlighting labor history, public memory, folk culture, and pollution. This balanced approach is something Shackel pulls off with grace and acumen.

The most intriguing section comes when Shackel investigates health and wellness. Families had to find ways of "making do," and digs in and around Eckley Village suggest a lack of protein and a heavy reliance on starchy foods (91). Oral interviewees also spoke to the lack of food access and the need to grow gardens. Archaeological evidence at Lattimer No. 1 mine, dating from 1869, confirmed these everyday conditions, and Shackel found cellar spaces with artifacts from pickled meats, sauerkraut, potatoes, and other canned foods (86–87). This "making do" culture was evident in the preponderance of Bell Mason jars, widely introduced in the 1880s (89). Other scholars, like Lou Martin in *Smokestacks in the Hills: Rural-Industrial Workers in West Virginia* (2015), have studied these self-help strategies, very evident among working-class people in rural spaces.

Shackel concludes his study by looking at the town of Hazelton. Here the book serves as a great companion to what happened in western Pennsylvania, as noted by Allen Dieterich-Ward's *Metropolitan Pittsburgh and the Fate of Industrial America* (2016). Centered at the deindustrialized core of the region, Hazelton became a hub for neoliberal economic development strategies in the 1990s through the Keystone Opportunity Zone. Initiated in 1999, the goal was to use tax incentives to relocate factories to the city. New firms provided low-wage jobs, and increasingly hired a diverse, mainly Latinx workforce. By the 2000s, the changing demographics coincided with a rising anti-immigrant politics, exemplified during a 2006 dispute over a controversial city ordinance. Shackel highlights how the decline of the United Mine Workers of America and a collective labor politics was replaced by support for conservative populism. By showing this longer historical trajectory, Shackel provides a more textured understanding of why many deindustrialized communities have shifted away from the Democratic Party. At the same time, the area witnessed renewed labor organizing by immigrant workers, especially at the Amazon fulfillment center in Hazelton. Employing over a thousand people, mostly on short 120-day contracts, these Amazon workers were on the front lines of revived labor organizing (171–73).

This book will elicit a number of emotions from the reader. Shackel's interdisciplinary focus is crucial to understanding the legacy of generational structural violence and trauma. Deindustrialized spaces, especially in rural Appalachia, have, in contemporary time, seen rising incarceration rates, low-wage economic development policies, and rising levels of opioid addiction. Shackel's book is analytically rigorous, empathetic to the suffering of ordinary people, and a damning indictment of the failures of our economic system. His ability to let the anthracite workers speak so much for themselves shows how we all need to remember the dignity and personal anguish that hard work has placed on working-class people.

**William Hal Gorby, West Virginia University**
DOI 10.1215/15476715-11521446

## Captives: How Rikers Island Took New York City Hostage
Jarrod Shanahan
London: Verso Books, 2022
448 pp.; $29.95 (cloth), $9.99 (ebook)

Jarrod Shanahan's *Captives: How Rikers Island Took New York City Hostage* begins with a dedication to Kalief Browder, who in 2010, at age sixteen, was charged with stealing a backpack and detained at Rikers Island awaiting trial. Browder maintained his innocence, refused to accept a plea deal, and was detained for more than a thousand days—mostly in solitary confinement. In 2015, Browder died by suicide at the age of twenty-two. Shanahan's dedication to Browder, and his return to Browder's story in the concluding pages of the book, highlights the book's central themes: penal institutions as a locus of concentrated state violence; the neoliberal retrenchment of welfarist policies amid growing racialized poverty; and "racially-tinged law and order politics" driving carceral expansion (244). By centering Browder at the opening and close, Shanahan illustrates how these forms of structural violence played out as individualized corporeal and psychological violence, meted out by entities endowed with upholding "public safety." But at the same time, it also highlights what is arguably the most important theme in Shanahan's text: resistance (both individual and collective) to these myriad forms of violence and the "spirit of refusal" to accept this reality as inevitable (366).

At its core, *Captives* is a historical account of how the Rikers Island jail complex became the infamous carceral behemoth it is today. While in many ways Rikers is the book's "main character," a true understanding of that character requires an elaboration of the forces that shaped New York City more broadly. As such, Shanahan details the power struggles beginning in postwar New York City, wherein larger battles between reformism and law-and-order politics "fueled by the violent contradictions at the heart of capitalist social relations" largely "play out in minutiae" of bureaucratic decisions and mundane daily life (12). Integral to Shanahan's narrative are the experiences not only of these powerful bureaucrats, politicians, and union leaders but also of those who, like Shanahan himself, were once caged on Rikers Island and in the nearby carceral facilities, such as the Women's House of Detention in Greenwich Village, that helped mold it. Shanahan's account draws on data from the archives, journalism, firsthand accounts, interviews, Department of Corrections (DOC) and other official administrative documents, and his own personal experience of incarceration on Rikers Island. While he notes that much of this history "relies on either capitalist journalism or an outright DOC perspective," Shanahan uplifts the voices of those whom Rikers and its champions attempt to silence: prisoners, Black Power activists, the poor (working and unemployed alike), and the members of the contemporary movement to permanently shutter Rikers Island (23).

One of the book's key contributions is its clear-eyed focus not only on Rikers specifically but also the jail more generally, as the space of inquiry. Often, historical examinations of penality and discussions of the political economic forces that facilitated mass incarceration are focused squarely on the prison as the carceral outcome. While prison scholarship is important and allows us to understand, in particular, national and state-level power dynamics and to discern the relationship between labor and political economy, the jail offers something different and equally important. Unlike the prison, which houses exclusively those convicted of violating criminal law, the jail also houses detainees awaiting trial or sentencing, as well as the city's undesirable "rabble." Through the vantage point of the jail, we can see how, especially in dire economic moments, the simultaneous erosion of social services and explosion of law-and-order approaches facilitates the expansion of and reliance on arrest and incarceration as the necessary (if not only) response to visible poverty and other socially undesirable behavior. When the state, which has manufactured racialized poverty, has abandoned its poor and working class, we turn to law enforcement and correctional officers to manage this population instead. When our existing jails become overcrowded with our undesirables, this process then easily justifies the construction of more, bigger, "better" jails. These then, unsurprisingly, also fill, because, as Shanahan and No New Jails NYC remind us: "If you build it, they will fill it" (23).

It is essential to note that while class plays a central role in sorting who become Rikers's decision-makers and who become its "residents," so, too, does race. Through each historical turn Shanahan documents, he carefully traces the racial dynamics that encouraged Rikers's expansion. This keen focus on race allows us to understand why the ranks of powerful police and correctional officer unions, which have vehemently pushed back against progressive reforms, were (and are) composed of working-class members: they were mostly white. Here we see that under racial capitalism, the compulsion to uphold white supremacist institutions trumps class consciousness and solidarity. However, Shanahan's keen focus on race also highlights something less grim: the work of Black and Brown activists both inside and outside Rikers. Shanahan shows how, in the face of intense structural violence, Black and Brown activists reject this subjugation and fight back through individual and collective action, even from within the belly of the carceral beast, whether Rikers or Attica or Pelican Bay.

There is much to praise about *Captives*, from its thrilling historical account to its sharp politico-economic analysis to its commitment to elevating prisoners' voices. Beyond these strengths, Shanahan's work is of vital importance in our current moment, as we face heightening intersecting crises of poverty, incarceration, overdose, and homelessness driven by the same forces that propelled Rikers's expansion: racism, neoliberalism, welfare retrenchment, and law-and-order politics. Our politicians, both in New

York City and beyond, increasingly demand the arrest and incarceration of those the state has rejected. *Captives*, however, urges us to push back against this demand. Indeed, Shanahan's work becomes a call to action and a rallying cry: rather than submit to these forces, we must resist and, like Kalief Browder, we must refuse.

**Dallas Augustine, San José State University**
DOI 10.215/15476715-11552834

# Keep up to date on new scholarship

Issue alerts are a great way to stay current on all the cutting-edge scholarship from your favorite Duke University Press journals. This free service delivers tables of contents directly to your inbox, informing you of the latest groundbreaking work as soon as it is published.

To sign up for issue alerts:

1. Visit **dukeu.press/register** and register for an account. You do not need to provide a customer number.

2. After registering, visit **dukeu.press/alerts**.

3. Go to "Latest Issue Alerts" and click on "Add Alerts."

4. Select as many publications as you would like from the pop-up window and click "Add Alerts."

**read.dukeupress.edu/journals**